COLLECTOR'S ENCYCLOPEDIA OF

DEPRESSION GLASS

THIRTEENTH EDITION

America's #1 Bestselling Glass Book!

GENE FLORENCE

COLLECTOR BOOKS

A Division of Schroeder Publishing Co., Inc.

The current values in this book should be used only as a guide. They are not intended to set prices, which vary from one section of the country to another. Auction prices as well as dealer prices vary greatly and are affected by condition as well as demand. Neither the Author nor the Publisher assumes responsibility for any losses that might be incurred as a result of consulting this guide.

On the Cover:
Top left: Cremax with castle decal, 7¾" cereal, $35.00.
Top right: Tulip candleholder, turquoise, $25.00.
Bottom: Lincoln Inn blue, 11" ruffled bowl, $100.00.

Cover design by Beth Summers
Layout by Terri Stalions

Searching For A Publisher?

We are always looking for knowledgeable people considered to be experts within their fields. If you feel that there is a real need for a book on your collectible subject and have a large comprehensive collection, contact us.

Additional copies of this book may be ordered from:

Collector Books
P.O. Box 3009
Paducah, KY 42002-3009

or

Gene Florence
P.O. Box 22186   P.O.Box 64
Lexington, KY 40522   or   Astatula, FL 34705

@ $19.95. Add $2.00 for postage and handling.

ACKNOWLEDGMENTS

I treasure all the data dealers, readers, and collectors have provided me through their writing, calling, and talking to me at various shows around the country! Thanks for carrying those newly discovered pieces to shows so that I can corroborate them and for sending measurements and photographs supporting new findings! A picture being worth a thousand words has never been more true than in authenticating a new piece. (If you have trouble photographing glass, take it outside in natural light, place the glass on a neutral surface {concrete works}, and ignore the camera's flash attachment. A bright, cloudy day is preferred.) Please enclose a **SASE** (self-addressed stamped envelope) that is **large enough** to send back your pictures, if you wish them returned!

There have been **33 previously uncataloged pieces added to the listings** since the twelfth edition**!** Those of you who feel that nothing new is ever found should look closely at your favorite pattern or check out the *Very Rare Glassware of the Depression Years* series of books. Similarly, there have been four deletions from the book of pieces that have never been found that were listed in catalogs or had mysteriously appeared in my price listings.

Over 30 measurements have been added or corrected in this book. These corrections have occurred due to original catalog misinformation, entry mistakes, or errors in measurement in the past. Realize, too, that the size of the **same patterned** plate or tumbler **can** vary from each moulded creation, especially if the pattern was made for a long time. American Sweetheart plates deviate nearly every time you measure one. Be sure to read about measurements on page 4.

I have enjoyed the shows that Depression glass clubs and private show promoters have invited me to attend. I have received inestimable information and knowledge from them, and hopefully, contributed to them.

An incontestable acknowledgment is always due family. Cathy, my wife, has worked many long hours as chief editor, critic, and proofreader and spends days trying to make sure you understand what I wanted to say. This time she has battled bronchitis for nearly two months while helping me on this book. Marc, my son, has taken over shipping book orders and operating my web page (http://www.geneflorence.com) while attending electronics school! No, I do not have time to surf the net myself! These books take more of my time than I care to admit or you will ever imagine! Chad, my eldest, and now married, is still available to help load and unload boxes for shows and photography sessions when the old man needs help!

It is painful to compose acknowledgments for a book without remembering Grannie Bear who spent hours organizing and helping price previous books. For those who have not heard, my mom, Grannie Bear, died suddenly in July 1993. Her assistance was important! Dad has since remarried and divorced.

Thanks, too, to Cathy's folks, Charles and Sibyl, who helped sort and pack glass for photography. Thanks to Charles for all the shelves built to hold glass. (He told a customer at a show that he had built me more shelves for glass than there was in the entire show. I don't think he was believed!) Both Charles and Sibyl have helped us at recent glass shows when we have suffered some health or accident problems. I believe they like Florida in January and February. I'm grateful to all the family who tried to keep everything under control at home while we traveled.

Glass and information for this book were furnished by Earl and Beverly Hines, Dick and Pat Spencer, Sam and Becky Collings, Dan Tucker and Lorrie Kitchen, Calvin and Gwen Key, Matt and Angela Koester, Bill and Millie Downey, Joe and Florence Solito, and numerous readers from across the U.S.A., Puerto Rico, Canada, England, New Zealand, and Australia!

Photographs for this book were created by Richard Walker of New York and Charles R. Lynch of Collector Books. They both provided multiple photographs during one six day session plus five more sessions of photographing glass. Glass arranging, unpacking, sorting, carting, and repacking was accomplished by Jane White, Zibby Walker, Dick and Pat Spencer, and Cathy Florence. Van loading and unloading was facilitated by Billy Schroeder and some of Collector Books' shipping crew.

In addition, Jane White and many of the crew mentioned previously helped on other photography shoots over the two year period since the twelfth edition. There is no way anyone would believe what we do to get you these photographs short of being there. Thanks to the special people in the Editorial Department at Collector Books: Lisa Stroup, Della Maze, Laurie Swick, and Terri Stalions who transferred all my e-mail into a book!

This thirteenth book was written in Florida. Sitting here, writing and watching cruising alligators and boats of people fishing, beats anything outside my Kentucky office this time of the year, especially shoveling snow! Fishing from my dock has been poor, but I would not be doing **any** of that in Kentucky. Maybe it will improve when I have time to actually get in my boat instead of looking at it hanging in the sling!

I do my best; but there is no way I could do this without you! As we go to press with this edition, **thank you** for making this America's #1 bestselling glass book! Do teach your friends about Depression glass! In the grand scheme of things, it still appears that only a lucky few of us comprehend its value. I am astonished nearly every day by letters from people who have just heard about Depression glass — or just discovered they practically "gave away" some family pieces at a sale! Education is the key!

FOREWORD

Depression glass as defined in this book is the colored glassware made essentially during the Depression years in the colors of amber, blue, black, crystal, green, pink, red, yellow, and white. There are other colors and some glass made before, as well as after, this time; but primarily, **the glass within this book was made from the 1920s through 1940**. This book is especially concerned with the economically made dinnerware turned out by machine in bulk and sold through smaller stores or given away as promotional or premium items for other products of that time. Depression glass was often packed in cereal boxes, flour sacks, or given as gifts at the local movie theaters, gasoline stations, and grocery stores. However, collectors have also been seeking later made patterns encompassing the time from the 1940s through the 1960s and that has led to a companion book, *Collectible Glassware from the 40s, 50s, 60s...*, which is now in its fourth edition. To correctly date glassware from that later period, it was necessary to **move some patterns previously exclusive to this book** into the era encompassed by the 50s book. All patterns manufactured **after 1940** are now in that book covering those years after the Depression era.

Writing books from January through May leaves little time to answer the 100 or more letters that arrive each week. Last year, I wrote five books and did not finish until mid June. The first week of August a gas hose "attacked" me, breaking my right elbow and wrist (which was not discovered until two weeks later). That lost an additional six or seven weeks of answering mail since I am right-handed. Realize, too, I do have other things in life to accomplish besides answering questions that often do not concern the patterns in my books.

In fact, to grouse a bit, I get an inordinate amount of mail asking questions about everything **except** patterns in the book — which I try to point out is the criteria for a letter along with the infamous SASE — which stands for SELF ADDRESSED, STAMPED ENVELOPE for those who ignore that! I have some research knowledge of the patterns in the books I write, not every piece of glass on the face of the earth! We won't even discuss the *described glass*, violins, china wares, glass bottles, wooden furniture, iron dinner bells, and the hand drawings by unlikely artists, as well the blurred, out of focus glass pictures where the letter starts out — "I know you cannot see, but..." or "it's exactly like except...!" On the other side of that irritating, time consuming coin was a wonderfully creative, self-addressed postcard included in a letter with three possible answers to the person's question listed! All I had to do was put a check on the correct answer and drop it in the mail. I loved it!

There have been changes in collecting Depression glass since my first book was released in 1972. Prices have soared; seemingly plentiful patterns have been assembled into myriad collections and removed from the market. Smaller Depression patterns and previously ignored crystal and satinized wares have attracted buyers; "Rainbow" (many colors) of patterns are being assembled (as sets) rather than the monocolored collecting of old. Truly, **anything** that is Depression glass, whether it is a known pattern or not, suddenly has added value and collectibility. Collectors have become more knowledgeable and sophisticated in their collecting. Glass is now sold on the Internet which few people knew about when I wrote this page in the book two years ago! Many enthusiasts are enhancing their collections of "A to W" (Adam to Windsor) with patterns of handmade glassware made during the same time. This broadening interest of collectors prompted me to research and write eight more books in the field of Depression glass, one on ELEGANT glassware of the time, one on the glass KITCHENWARE items of the Depression, and five others on the VERY RARE glassware of the Depression era, not to mention the latest on STEMWARE IDENTIFICATION which one dealer told me had already saved him many hours of searching through his own library of books!

Information for this book comes through years of research, experience, via fellow dealers, collectors, and over 1,240,000 miles of travel pursuant to glassware. However, some of the most fascinating information has come from readers, like you, who shared catalogs, magazines, photographs of glass, and their specific information with me! These contributions to the growing body of knowledge are valued by everyone, but me in particular!

PRICING

All prices in this book are retail prices for MINT CONDITION glassware. This book is intended to be only a GUIDE to prices as there are some regional price differences that cannot reasonably be dealt with herein!

You may expect dealers to pay from 30% to 50% less than the prices quoted. Glass that is in less than mint condition, i.e., chipped, cracked, scratched, or poorly molded, will bring only a **small percentage** of the price of glass that is in mint condition.

Prices have become fairly well standardized due to national advertising by dealers, Depression glass shows that are held from coast to coast, and now the Internet. I have my own web page operated for books and glass (http://www.geneflorence.com). Several nationally known dealers have assisted in revising prices for this book. However, **there are still some regional differences in prices due partly to glass being more readily available in some areas than in others.** Companies distributed certain pieces in some areas that they did not in others. Generally speaking, however, prices are about the same among dealers from coast to coast.

Prices **tend to increase dramatically** on rare items and, in general, they have increased as a whole due to more and more collectors entering the field and people becoming more aware of the worth of Depression glass. However, I receive letters **regularly** from new enthusiasts who have just "discovered" Depression glass!

One of the more important aspects of this book is the attempt made to illustrate as well as realistically price those items that are in demand. The desire is to give you the most accurate guide to collectible patterns of Depression glass available.

MEASUREMENTS

To illustrate why there are discrepancies in measurements, I offer the following sample from just two years of Hocking's catalog references:

Year	Item	Ounces	Item	Ounces	Item	Ounces
1935	Pitcher	37, 58, 80	Flat Tumbler	5, 9, 13½	Footed Tumbler	10, 13
1935	Pitcher	37, 60, 80	Flat Tumbler	5, 9, 10, 15	Footed Tumbler	10, 13
1936	Pitcher	37, 65, 90	Flat Tumbler	5, 9, 13½	Footed Tumbler	10, 15
1935	Pitcher	37, 60, 90	Flat Tumbler	5, 9, 13½	Footed Tumbler	10, 15

All measurements in this book are exact as to some manufacturer's listing **or** to actual measurement. You may expect variance of up to ½" or 1 – 5 ounces. This may be due to mould variations or changes by the manufacturer as well as rounding off measurements for catalog listings.

CONTENTS

ADAM JEANNETTE GLASS COMPANY, 1932–1934

Colors: Pink, green, crystal, some yellow, and Delphite blue. *(See Reproduction Section.)*

Adam is yet again the inaugural and alphabetically placed pattern for this thirteenth book! For years, there was enough Adam being found to keep the prices realistic on everything except rarely seen items. Now, even previously common pieces are vanishing into collections.

Fewer pieces of Adam are being seen at shows and not many are being advertised in the *Daze* or listed on the Internet. Will wonders never cease? Now, there are many ads for glassware on the "net." My son, Marc, even set me up a web page to promote my books and glass. I can be found at http://www.geneflorence.com if you come looking for me in cyberspace. Actually, you'll first find Marc who has more time (and skill) to play online than I.

Pink Adam is less costly than green Adam; green is less abundant, so prices are generally higher. Yet, prices for green have remained steadfast for years. A little increase has been seen in prices for butter dishes, candy jars, candlesticks, and shakers. If you start collecting green Adam, buy those pieces first — if you can find them for sale! There have been fewer collectors starting to collect Adam in green the last few years, probably because it is becoming so elusive in the market place.

With more collectors buying pink Adam, those prices are increasing faster than for green. Ordinarily, prices of pink have had a way to go to catch up to green; but several items, such as tumblers and serving pieces, are now selling for as much as green! The pink vase is the most evasive piece of Adam unless you include the Adam/Sierra butter dish. Watch out for pink vases that tilt or appear lopsided! Many collectors are unwilling to pay a lofty price for these less than perfect vases.

The Adam/Sierra butter dish has **both** pattern designs on the **top.** Adam is found on the outside of the top and Sierra is found on the inside of this lid. These tops have been found on **both** Adam and Sierra butter bottoms; those respective butter bottoms contain only **one** pattern. Several times I have seen an Adam butter top on a Sierra bottom or a Sierra top on an Adam bottom priced as the rare butter. Sorry! That is not it. You can see one of these pictured in the *Very Rare Glassware of the Depression Years —Fifth Series.* I have only seen one of these for sale in the last five years and the price listed below is the actual selling price of that one! I assume it would market for more now.

Sugar and candy lids are interchangeable, something Jeannette Glass did to save money, which is a blessing for collectors today. Sugar and candy lids are customarily more troublesome to find than the bottoms in many Depression glass patterns.

Inner rim roughness is a major problem on most Adam pieces. That is especially true of cereal bowls. Damage to these came from both using and stacking them over the years. You should not expect to pay mint condition prices, if you are willing to accept **less than perfect** glass. If it comes time to resell, you will be happier with the prices obtained for mint glassware. Prices in this book are for mint (like new) condition glass. Admittedly, some damaged glass can be nicely repaired by competent artisans, but not all glass grinders and repairers are proficient! Ask to see samples of their work before you turn your glass over to them.

Adam lamps are scarce. In the Floral pattern on page 81, you can see a pink lamp that is designed the same way Adam lamps were. A sherbet was frosted to hide the wiring and a notch was cut into the top edge of the sherbet to accommodate a switch. A metal cover was fitted to the top of the frosted sherbet through which a tall bulb was connected to the switch that fit the notch. The prices listed are for working lamps. That **bulb assembly** is hard to find. The notched, frosted sherbets are available and could even be made today without much difficulty!

The Adam butter dish is the **only** piece that has been reproduced! **Do not use** the information given in the Reproduction Section in the back of the book *for any other pieces* in the pattern. This goes for all reproductions I have listed in the back. Only apply the telltale clues to the **piece** I describe. Transferring information to some other item in the pattern will not work.

	Pink	Green		Pink	Green
Ash tray, 4½"	30.00	25.00	**Cup	24.00	23.00
Bowl, 4¾" dessert	20.00	20.00	Lamp	275.00	300.00
Bowl, 5¾" cereal	42.00	42.00	Pitcher, 8", 32 oz.	40.00	45.00
Bowl, 7¾"	26.00	27.00	Pitcher, 32 oz. round base	47.50	
Bowl, 9", no cover	40.00	42.50	Plate, 6" sherbet	9.00	10.00
Bowl, cover, 9"	25.00	42.50	***Plate, 7¾" square salad	15.00	15.00
Bowl, 9" covered	65.00	85.00	Plate, 9" square dinner	33.00	30.00
Bowl, 10" oval	30.00	32.00	Plate, 9" grill	20.00	22.00
Butter dish bottom	25.00	65.00	Platter, 11¾"	30.00	32.00
Butter dish top	55.00	260.00	Relish dish, 8" divided	20.00	25.00
Butter dish & cover	80.00	375.00	Salt & pepper, 4" ftd.	80.00	110.00
Butter dish combination			****Saucer, 6" square	6.00	6.00
with Sierra Pattern	1,250.00		Sherbet, 3"	30.00	35.00
Cake plate, 10" ftd.	25.00	27.50	Sugar	17.50	20.00
*Candlesticks, 4" pr.	87.50	95.00	Sugar/candy cover	25.00	40.00
Candy jar & cover, 2½"	90.00	100.00	Tumbler, 4½"	30.00	28.00
Coaster, 3¼"	22.00	20.00	Tumbler, 5½" iced tea	60.00	57.50
Creamer	20.00	22.00	Vase, 7½"	325.00	60.00

* Delphite $225.00   ** Yellow $100.00   *** Round pink $60.00; yellow $100.00   **** Round pink $75.00; yellow $85.00

AMERICAN PIONEER LIBERTY WORKS, 1931–1934

Colors: Pink, green, amber, and crystal.

American Pioneer design incorporates plain fields of glass, narrow ridges, and bumpy hobs, a mixing of design types not unlike the peoples represented by its name. The overall look is one of quiet refinement.

Green American Pioneer is the most desired color, but you should be aware of three distinct shades available. Color variances do not seem to restrain collectors of American Pioneer as much as they do collectors of other patterns. So few green pieces are found that collectors are happy to attain any additional item no matter the hue. No newly found items have been reported to me this time.

Fewer enthusiasts search for crystal or amber American Pioneer, but collectors of amber have informed me that only basic luncheon pieces are being found. To date, only one set of amber covered pitchers (urns) has ever surfaced! Liners for urns are regular 6" and 8" plates. That should make it easier to find those liners except for the 6" **pink** plate for the small urn, which is also rare.

The dresser set is the most valuable commodity in this pattern. Only a couple have been located in pink and just a few more in green. An occasional odd piece to these sets turns up, but putting the complete dresser set together is rather difficult. Dresser sets have recently become even more difficult for Depression glass collectors to possess due, in part, to the many perfume and cologne bottle collectors also searching for them! Often items in a Depression glass pattern become more valuable because collectors from other fields of collecting are latching on to that particular item. It makes for an animated rivalry and some feeling of frustration when you are out there looking for such an item!

There are two styles of American Pioneer cups being found. Some cups have more rim flair than others which makes one style have a 4" diameter (2¼" tall) the other a 3⅜" diameter (2⅜" tall). Saucers are the same for these cups.

Amber cocktails have been reported in two sizes. No cocktails have been reported in any other color. One holds 3 oz. and stands 3¹³⁄₁₆" high while the other holds 3½ oz. and stands 3¹⁵⁄₁₆" tall.

You will have difficulty in matching lids for covered bowls. I have been told that there are three different covered bowl sizes instead of the two I have listed. If you find a different size from those listed, please let me know the measurements. The same goes for any additional items in American Pioneer not listed. I do appreciate the information you share with me; and I make a concentrated effort to pass that information along to collectors.

Candy jar lids are interchangeable in American Pioneer even though the jars are shaped differently. The 1½ pound candy is pictured with the lid in the top row of page 9. The pound candy is on the left, but is shown topless. This interchangeable lid represented a factory cost-cutting measure during this economically depressed time.

	Crystal, Pink	Green		Crystal, Pink	Green
* Bowl, 5" handled	20.00	20.00	Lamp, 5½" round, ball		
Bowl, 8¾" covered	95.00	125.00	shape (amber $80.00)	75.00	
Bowl, 9" handled	22.00	27.50	Lamp, 8½" tall	100.00	110.00
Bowl, 9¼" covered	95.00	135.00	Mayonnaise, 4¼"	57.50	90.00
Bowl, 10¾" console	55.00	65.00	Pilsner, 5¾", 11 oz.	125.00	125.00
Candlesticks, 6½" pr.	70.00	90.00	** Pitcher, 5" covered urn	150.00	210.00
Candy jar and cover, 1 lb	85.00	100.00	*** Pitcher, 7" covered urn	175.00	225.00
Candy jar and cover, 1½ lb.	95.00	125.00	Plate, 6"	12.50	15.00
Cheese and cracker set (in-			* Plate, 6" handled	12.50	15.00
dented platter and comport)	55.00	65.00	* Plate, 8"	10.00	12.00
Coaster, 3½"	30.00	30.00	* Plate, 11½" handled	18.00	20.00
Creamer, 2¾"	25.00	20.00	* Saucer	4.00	5.00
* Creamer, 3½"	20.00	22.00	Sherbet, 3½"	16.00	20.00
* Cup	10.00	12.00	Sherbet, 4¾"	32.50	37.50
Dresser set (2 cologne, powder			Sugar, 2¾"	20.00	22.00
jar, on indented 7½" tray)	395.00	345.00	* Sugar, 3½"	20.00	22.00
Goblet, 3¹³⁄₁₆", 3 oz., cocktail (amber)	40.00		Tumbler, 5 oz. juice	30.00	35.00
Goblet, 3¹⁵⁄₁₆", 3½ oz., cocktail (amber)	40.00		Tumbler, 4", 8 oz.	30.00	50.00
Goblet, 4", 3 oz. wine	40.00	50.00	Tumbler, 5", 12 oz.	40.00	50.00
Goblet, 6", 8 oz. water	45.00	50.00	Vase, 7", 4 styles	85.00	100.00
Ice bucket, 6"	50.00	60.00	Vase, 9", round		235.00
Lamp, 1¾", w/metal pole 9½"		60.00	Whiskey, 2¼", 2 oz.	50.00	90.00

   * Amber — Double the price of pink unless noted
   ** Amber $275.00
   *** Amber $325.00

Please refer to Foreword for pricing information

AMERICAN SWEETHEART MacBETH-EVANS GLASS COMPANY, 1930–1936

Colors: Pink, Monax, red, blue; some Cremax and color trimmed Monax.

Blue American Sweetheart continues to bewitch more collectors than red.

The photograph of blue American Sweetheart below replaces those photos of red previously shown. Although this setting is not as elaborately illustrated as was Pat Spencer's red display, it does show the unusual blue American Sweetheart which is getting extremely hard to come by these days. One tid-bit consists of 8" and 12" plates while the other shows the 8" and 15". One of the reasons that I do not list many tid-bits in this book is that they are being newly made. A few may have been made at the factory, but others were recently assembled. I was at a flea market in north central Ohio last fall where a seller was set up with nine different patterned tid-bits priced from $30.00 to $50.00. His $50.00 Dogwood tid-bit I have seen advertised from $45.00 to $195.00. Which would you buy? In American Sweetheart I list the ones with 15½" plates, since it would be quite a costly gamble (on breaking one of those) to make up a tid-bit. Most original tid-bits in common colors sell in the $50.00 range for two tiers and $75.00 for three. Rarer colors, of course, bring more!

That 15½" plate pictured in the center was bought as "Cambridge" (priced $115.00 firm) in a Florida antique mall not long ago. Don't you love people who **label** glassware, but have no idea what it really is?

Those 18" console bowls have taken a jump in price. Amazingly, there were three console bowls at the Cambridge Glass Convention last year! Two blue ones and a red shared the spotlight with all that Cambridge glass.

Several years ago, I saw a **plain** (no pattern) red 18" console bowl in a Columbus, Ohio, antique show. That bowl was water stained. Last year, I spotted another at a show, but that dealer evidently thought that **pattern** was not a necessity to sell his bowl. It was priced a mere brow raising $800.00! Perhaps you could spot a plain blue one, also.

Red and blue American Sweetheart sets were originally sold in fifteen piece groups consisting of four each cups, saucers, and 8" plates with a creamer, sugar, and 12" salver. Additional pieces in these colors were **very limited** in distribution. Observe the latest price increases on the larger pieces in these colors on page 12.

If you are a new collector trying to learn terminology, notice that Cremax is a beige-like **color** made by MacBeth-Evans Glass Company in several patterns. (See the overturned bowl on the bottom right of page 13.) Monax is the white made by MacBeth-Evans. The Monax with the grayish-blue/**black edge** pictured on the bottom of page 12 is called "Smoke" by collectors. Much of regular Monax American Sweetheart has a bluish cast to its edges. To be the rarely found "Smoke" color however, it will always have a black trim at the edge. (See photo.)

I have tried to show a variety of other color-trimmed and decorated pieces of Monax on top of page 13. You will sometimes find pieces trimmed in pink, green, yellow, black, or 22K gold. Gold was often used as a glass "trim" then. Unfortunately, today there is no premium for gold trim; in fact, many dealers have difficulty selling it because it is worn. The gold (only) can be removed by using a pencil eraser on it. Do not use a scouring pad since you will damage the glass! I only point this out because badly worn gold-trimmed items will not sell, but plain Monax will.

AMERICAN SWEETHEART (Cont.)

	Red	Blue	Cremax	Smoke & Other Trims
Bowl, 6" cereal			10.00	37.50
Bowl, 9" round berry			40.00	195.00
Bowl, 9½" soup				125.00
Bowl, 18" console	925.00	1,100.00		
Creamer, ftd.	125.00	145.00		95.00
Cup	85.00	125.00		85.00
Lamp shade			450.00	
Lamp (floor with brass base)			695.00	
Plate, 6" bread and butter				20.00
Plate, 8" salad	85.00	97.50		30.00
Plate, 9" luncheon				40.00
Plate, 9¾" dinner				95.00
Plate, 12" salver	150.00	210.00		110.00
Plate, 15½" server	300.00	395.00		
Platter, 13" oval				195.00
Saucer	20.00	25.00		15.00
Sherbet, 4¼" ftd. (design inside or outside)				75.00
Sugar, open ftd.	125.00	145.00		95.00
Tid-bit, 2 tier, 8" & 12"	225.00	295.00		
Tid-bit, 3 tier, 8", 12" & 15½"	595.00	695.00		

Please refer to Foreword for pricing information

AMERICAN SWEETHEART (Cont.)

Prices for American Sweetheart pink and Monax continue to increase, but harder to find pieces have made some drastic adjustments. The prices for the small pink pitcher, small berry bowl, and shakers have again risen considerably. In Monax (white color), shakers and the sugar lid have made price increases. Collectors sometime avoid buying the higher priced pieces for years; and suddenly, everyone collecting the pattern decides now is the time to splurge. The only problem with that is that there are not enough pieces to go around; so prices rise because of the surge in demand. Advanced collectors, needing one or two pieces to complete a set, decide to pay "whatever it takes." Some dealer is willing to raise the price to the "whatever it takes" level. Word gets out that a piece sold for "X" dollars, and the next piece is priced the same or higher. The price is now established at the next level! Many times it has taken a year or more for other collectors to adjust their thinking and purse strings to that price level!

Prices on flat and cream soup bowls, and serving pieces have had only minor upward price adjustments. For rookie collectors, a cream soup is a two-handled bowl that was used for consommé or creamed soups. A pink cream soup can be seen on the left of the bottom picture. Soups of either style were not sold in basic sets which means that today, there are fewer of these encountered. At least there is no sugar lid in pink to find; so collectors of pink only have to lose sleep over finding the pitchers!

There are two sizes of pink pitchers and three sizes of tumblers. Some collectors buy only the water tumbler since the juice and iced tea tumblers are troublesome to find. Please remember that there are pitchers **shaped** like American Sweetheart that do not have the moulded design of American Sweetheart. You can see one of these on the left in the bottom photograph on page 15. It is **not** American Sweetheart (or Dogwood, which has to have the silk screened Dogwood design), but is the blank made by MacBeth-Evans to go with the plain, no design tumblers they made. The **design has to be moulded** into the pitcher for it to truly be American Sweetheart as is shown on the right of that photo. Plain pitchers without pattern sell in the $30.00–35.00 range and plain tumblers $8.00–10.00 each. I have just received photos of a boxed set of American Sweetheart that had plain Dogwood shaped tumblers in the box and the MacBeth-Evans square ash trays that were packed with most boxed sets of MacBeth-Evans at that time. Unfortunately, today those plain tumblers are not considered to be American Sweetheart; so the boxed sets suffer greatly in price because of this. Some collectors are content to use these plain tumblers with their MacBeth-Evans sets however; and since they came boxed with sets, why not?

Demand for American Sweetheart pattern continues even with the short supply of many pieces. Novice collectors are delighted with the numerous colors and that American Sweetheart has not been reproduced. There is also an abundant supply of basic pieces in Monax (white color) such as cups, saucers, plates, sugars, and creamers that can still be found at moderate prices. Monax plates were widely distributed, and can be found in almost all parts of the country, making them an excellent starting point for new collectors. Please know that today locating rare pieces of Monax and pink American Sweetheart presents a formidable task to collectors who have already procured all the basics.

Sherbets came in two sizes. The sherbet on the plate is ½" smaller in diameter than the larger one pictured behind it in the bottom photograph. The smaller, 3¾", is more difficult to find than the larger; but many collectors seek only one size, making price parity closer than rarity indicates. Rarity does not always set price. Demand does! A rarely found item that no one wants will remain reasonably priced because no one is buying it! Many dealers have been taught that lesson over the years!

Sets of pink or Monax can still be collected with patience. Monax would be less expensive, but there were fewer pieces made in that color. Collect what you truly like. Eventually, you will be able to accumulate a set even if it is only a small one!

	Pink	Monax		Pink	Monax
Bowl, 3¾" flat berry	65.00		Plate, 15½" server		210.00
Bowl, 4½" cream soup	75.00	110.00	Platter, 13" oval	55.00	65.00
Bowl, 6" cereal	17.00	16.00	Pitcher, 7½", 60 oz.	825.00	
Bowl, 9" round berry	50.00	65.00	Pitcher, 8", 80 oz.	650.00	
Bowl, 9½" flat soup	70.00	80.00	Salt and pepper, ftd.	500.00	400.00
Bowl, 11" oval vegetable	65.00	80.00	Saucer	4.00	2.00
Bowl, 18" console		450.00	Sherbet, 3¾" ftd.	23.00	
Creamer, ftd.	13.00	10.00	Sherbet, 4¼" ftd.		
Cup	18.00	10.00	(design inside or outside)	20.00	22.00
Lamp shade		450.00	Sherbet in metal holder		
Plate, 6" or 6½" bread & butter	5.00	6.00	(crystal only)	3.50	
Plate, 8" salad	11.00	9.00	Sugar, open, ftd.	12.00	8.00
Plate, 9" luncheon		12.00	* Sugar lid		395.00
Plate, 9¾" dinner	40.00	25.00	Tid-bit, 2 tier, 8" & 12"	60.00	60.00
Plate, 10¼" dinner		25.00	Tid-bit, 3 tier, 8", 12" & 15½"		295.00
Plate, 11" chop plate		18.00	Tumbler, 3½", 5 oz.	95.00	
Plate, 12" salver	20.00	18.00	Tumbler, 4¼", 9 oz.	80.00	
			Tumbler, 4¾", 10 oz.	110.00	

*Three styles of knobs.

Please refer to Foreword for pricing information

AUNT POLLY U.S. GLASS COMPANY, Late 1920s

Colors: Blue, green, and iridescent.

Thanks for all the compliments of the shelf photographs! Many patterns do not lend themselves as well to this style of photo as does Aunt Polly. Space (or rather lack thereof) is the major problem with shelf shots. A two page minimum is required for any pattern depicted this way!

That two-handled candy on the far right of row 2 has increased in price by fifty percent since the last book! Nothing else in Aunt Polly has made such a jump! Desirability of Aunt Polly is somewhat affected by its lack of cups or saucers. Prices would soar if any were ever found. That quandary exists for most U.S. Glass patterns including Strawberry, Cherryberry, and Swirl.

In the nineteen years since I discovered that U.S. Glass was the manufacturer of Aunt Polly (and her sister patterns mentioned above) not one additional piece of blue has surfaced! A covered candy is shown in green next to the sugar in row 4. This candy dish has never been found in blue. That candy lid is compatible with the sugar lid, giving sugar and creamer collectors an extra venue for finding lids in green and iridescent. This is an expensive candy dish because perfect lids are difficult to find today!

Note the two variations of blue creamers shown in row 2. One has a more pronounced lip than the other. These lips were formed by hand using a wooden tool; that no doubt accounts for these irregularities. It is also the reason that ounce measurements are so difficult to list. The same piece can vary several ounces due to the shape of the lip. This is also noticeable in water pitchers whose lips were formed the same way!

There is an Aunt Polly look-alike shown in two colors. The blue tumbler next to the plate in the top row and the Vaseline colored tumbler in the row 5 are moulded differently from the normally found tumblers. The paneled lines are wider and there is no design in the bottom. The ground bottoms on these items may indicate prototypes that were redesigned, because the Vaseline (Canary) colored tumbler is a typical U.S. Glass color of the late 1920s. Vaseline is a collectors' name for the glowing, yellow-green shown by that tumbler. Most companies had their name for this color, be it Canary or yellow. A petroleum jelly product (made in early 1930s) lent the glass this commonly mentioned name.

This pattern tends to have mould imperfections such as rough seams and pieces of extra glass. If you are inflexible about mint condition glass, I recommend you look for another pattern.

The Aunt Polly oval vegetable, sugar lid, shakers, and butter dish have always created problems for collectors searching for these items. Acquiring only the blue butter top or bottom can create a headache. I'll explain. Ironically, butter bottoms in green or iridescent are plentiful since all the U.S. Glass butter bottoms are interchangeable. The starred bottom design also fits Cherryberry, Strawberry, and U.S. Swirl as well as Aunt Polly tops. That is the reason that the **butter top** prices are so much more than the bottoms in green and iridescent. However, there is **no blue color** in the other U.S. Glass patterns mentioned; so there have always been fewer butter bottoms to be discovered in blue!

Blue is still **the** most collected color of Aunt Polly pattern, but a few collectors of iridized and green persevere. The dilemma in collecting green relates to the disparate shades. Green is found from almost yellow in appearance to the vivid green you see in the photograph on the next page. Only recently have I perceived distinct color variations in the blue. Be aware of that especially when shopping for a sugar lid. I speak from experience!

	Green, Iridescent	Blue
Bowl, 4¾" berry	8.00	17.50
Bowl, 4¾", 2" high	15.00	
Bowl, 5½" one handle	14.00	22.00
Bowl, 7¼" oval, handled pickle	15.00	40.00
Bowl, 7⅞" large berry	20.00	45.00
Bowl, 8⅜" oval	45.00	110.00
Butter dish and cover	235.00	210.00
Butter dish bottom	100.00	90.00
Butter dish top	135.00	120.00
Candy, cover, 2-handled	75.00	
Candy, ftd., 2-handled	25.00	45.00
Creamer	30.00	50.00
Pitcher, 8" 48 oz.		175.00
Plate, 6" sherbet	6.00	14.00
Plate, 8" luncheon		20.00
Salt and pepper		225.00
Sherbet	10.00	14.00
Sugar	25.00	30.00
Sugar cover	60.00	160.00
Tumbler, 3⅝", 8 oz.		30.00
Vase, 6½" ftd.	30.00	50.00

Please refer to Foreword for pricing information

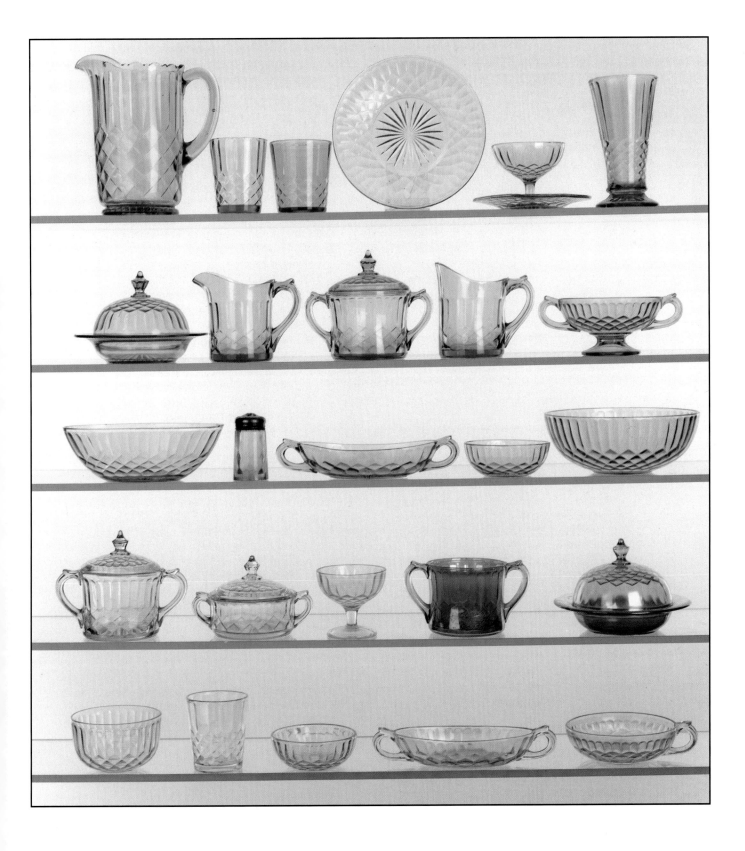

"AURORA" HAZEL ATLAS GLASS COMPANY, Late 1930s

Colors: Cobalt blue, pink, green, and crystal.

"Aurora" used to be a pattern I recommended as economical, but any more I could hardly call small bowls selling at $55.00 each economical! That little 4½" deep bowl has flown out of sight, but creamers and tumblers are also disappearing from dealers' inventories. Actually, even with the price of the little bowl now being $55.00, an eight place setting would not involve negotiating an equity loan against the house as some other cobalt blue sets will; so, if you like cobalt blue, here is a smaller pattern to check out!

Several readers have suggested that patterns with a tall creamer and no sugar should have the creamer listed as a milk pitcher. A reader reported that the creamers were given away as premiums for buying a breakfast cereal in her home town in Iowa. She remembers boxed displays on the counter from which the proprietor handed you one with your purchase. Her grandmother had over a dozen of the creamers in her attic!

Several pieces have also been found in pink, and these command a price similar to the blue due to scarcity. You will probably not be able to put a complete set together in pink since the small bowl, creamer, and tumbler have, so far, never been seen in that color. A Canadian reader felt pink was more likely to be found there than in the States.

Both green and crystal cereal bowls, cups, and saucers have been found. Canadian readers report finding green "Aurora" cereal bowls. So far, only collectors of cup and saucers have been very excited over this news.

	Cobalt, Pink			Cobalt, Pink
Bowl, 4½" deep	55.00		Plate, 6½"	12.00
* Bowl, 5⅜" cereal	17.50		*** Saucer	6.00
Creamer, 4½"	25.00		Tumbler, 4¾", 10 oz.	25.00
** Cup	15.00			

*Green $7.00 or crystal $5.00   **Green $7.50   ***Green $2.50

"AVOCADO," NO. 601 INDIANA GLASS COMPANY, 1923–1933

Colors: Pink, green, crystal, and white. *(See Reproduction Section.)*

All sixteen pieces of **green** "Avocado" manufactured (plus one crystal bowl) are shown! "Avocado" remains expensive, but little is being found.

Prices for green pitchers continue to escalate; but prices for tumblers have slowed, possibly because so few are being seen that they haven't had a chance to climb! Crystal pitchers have been found, but I have heard of no crystal tumblers. Several sets of milk glass pitchers and tumblers have surfaced. These are snagged by both pitcher and "Avocado" collectors. These white items were a part of Indiana's experimenting with that color in the mid-1950s. You may also find a few Pyramid and Sandwich pieces in white.

Prices for crystal are not advancing as are those for colors. So far, there are only a few collectors for it. The deep bowl is the piece most often seen.

Reproduced green items are much darker than the original green shown here. Any color not in the listing in this book is a Tiara reproduction. For example, if you spot any pieces in yellow, they are of **recent** vintage! It's a pretty 1980s yellow!

Reproduced pink items have an orange cast to the color, but this does vary. Buyers beware! Prices for pink have finally recovered from those reproduced pitchers and tumblers introduced in 1974; but it is doubtful they will ever again catch the prices of green!

	Crystal	Pink	Green		Crystal	Pink	Green
Bowl, 5¼" 2-handled	10.00	25.00	33.00	* Pitcher, 64 oz.	350.00	800.00	1,075.00
Bowl, 6" ftd. relish	9.00	25.00	25.00	*** Plate, 6⅜" sherbet	5.00	14.00	16.00
Bowl, 7" 1 handle preserve	8.00	20.00	25.00	** Plate, 8¼" luncheon	7.00	17.00	20.00
Bowl, 7½" salad	12.00	35.00	55.00	Plate, 10¼" 2-handled cake	14.00	35.00	55.00
Bowl, 8" 2-handled oval	11.00	22.00	27.50	Saucer, 6⅜"		22.00	24.00
Bowl, 9½", 3¼" deep	22.00	110.00	135.00	*** Sherbet		50.00	55.00
*** Creamer, ftd.	12.00	30.00	35.00	*** Sugar, ftd.	12.00	32.00	35.00
Cup, ftd., 2 styles		30.00	37.50	* Tumbler	35.00	165.00	265.00

* Caution on pink. The orange-pink is new!
* White: Pitcher $400.00; Tumbler $35.00.
** Apple design $10.00. Amber has been newly made.
*** Remade in dark shade of green.

Please refer to Foreword for pricing information

BEADED BLOCK IMPERIAL GLASS COMPANY, 1927–1930s

Colors: Pink, green, crystal, ice blue, Canary, iridescent, amber, red, opalescent, and milk white.

Something has inspired more interest in Imperial's Beaded Block than I have ever seen before. It makes me realize that not buying that collection of 1,200 plus pieces about six years ago might have been a mistake. Unfortunately, over half the pieces were plates and at the time it seemed like a bad idea. Today, maybe not!

The abundance of colors found in Beaded Block is matched by few other patterns in this book. It is the primary Depression pattern that is labeled by unenlightened antique dealers as carnival, Vaseline, or pattern glass. I just saw five crystal Beaded Block bowls labeled Sandwich glass at the Webster flea market last Monday. They had $35.00 price tags.

Imperial originally made Beaded Block in the late 1920s and early 1930s. I say "originally" because Imperial had a reissue of pink and iridized pink in the late 1970s and early 1980s. These pieces are easily spotted since they are marked IG in the bottom. When I visited the factory in 1981, I was told that the white was made in the early 1950s and the IG mark (for Imperial Glass) was first used about that time. Only a few marked pieces are found, but they include the white covered pear pictured below. If you have an extra top, I know where you can find the elusive bottom now that I have a completed one! This two-part candy in the shape of a large pear is found only occasionally. These have been found in yellow, green, and even amber, a color I have seen more than any other. They seem to occur more frequently on the West Coast. You can see a green one in the top photo. I have seen these candy jars priced from $35.00 to $650.00. I do know that the green pictured here and the yellow shown in *Very Rare Glassware of the Depression Years, Fourth Series* sold for $250.00 each.

You can see a crystal, non-footed vase pictured in the *Very Rare Glassware of the Depression Years, Fifth Series* which is the only one of those I have had reported to me.

Square Beaded Block plates continue to be found, but few round plates have surfaced. Most round plates must have been transformed into bowls. The edges of plates were rolled up to make a bowl. That makes for size variances in this pattern and a major headache for collectors. **The sizes listed here were all obtained from actual measurements of the pieces and not those listed in catalogs.** The 2-handled jelly which most companies called a cream soup measures from 4¾" to 5". Be sure to read the section on measurements at the bottom of page 4! Company listings were often approximations as I have discovered after nearly thirty years of research.

Several more pink Beaded Block pitchers have turned up! I have had reports of eight white pitchers now, but only four pink ones! Green pitchers are being found in such quantities that the price has adjusted downward!

Only the 4½" Beaded Block lily bowl has appeared in red. It seems to be on every collectors wish list!

The 6" vases shown in cobalt and pink are really not Beaded Block. They have no beading and no scalloped edge as do all the other pieces except candy bottoms. Imperial called these tall pieces "footed jellies." These were attained at groceries with a product inside. One found with the original label read "Good Taste Mustard Seed, 3½ oz., Frank Tea & Spice Co., Cin., O." Remember, these are "go-with" pieces and not truly Beaded Block.

Most collectors buy any color Beaded Block they can find!

	Crystal*, Pink, Green, Amber	Other Colors
Bowl, 4⅞"-5" 2-handled jelly	10.00	20.00
** Bowl, 4½" round lily	12.00	24.00
Bowl, 5½" square	12.00	24.00
Bowl, 5½" 1 handle	12.00	24.00
Bowl, 6" deep round	15.00	30.00
Bowl, 6¼" round	14.00	28.00
Bowl, 6½" round	14.00	28.00
Bowl, 6½" 2-handled pickle	17.00	35.00
Bowl, 6¾" round, unflared	14.00	25.00
Bowl, 7¼" round, flared	14.00	25.00
Bowl, 7½" round, fluted edges	22.00	35.00
Bowl, 7½" round, plain edge	20.00	30.00
Bowl, 8¼" celery	18.00	30.00
Creamer	18.00	30.00
*** Pitcher, 5¼", pint jug	85.00	
Plate, 7¾" square	10.00	12.00
Plate, 8¾" round	22.00	30.00
Stemmed jelly, 4½"	12.00	25.00
Stemmed jelly, 4½", flared top	14.00	27.00
Sugar	16.00	30.00
Vase, 6" bouquet	14.00	30.00

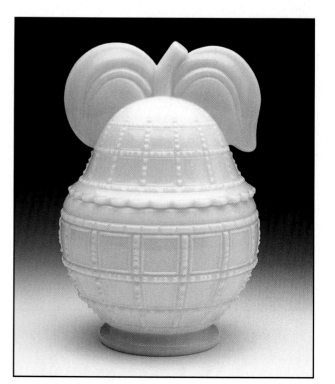

* All pieces 25% to 40% lower.
** Red $150.00
*** White $175.00, pink $160.00

BLOCK OPTIC, "BLOCK" HOCKING GLASS COMPANY, 1929–1933

Colors: Green, pink, yellow, crystal, and some amber and blue.

When I mentioned in the last book that the newly discovered Block Optic 2" tall, 11¾" diameter, rolled-edge console bowl was pictured for the first time, I did not know it had been selected to be used on the cover! The interesting thing is that I have received over a dozen letters asking what was the pattern of the green bowl on the cover! Item descriptions of cover pieces are usually found on the copyright pages of most Collector Books titles, so look there first.

Collectors (who thought they had completed sets) are now searching for a Block Optic console bowl, grill plates, and 3½" short wines. That short wine was finally found in green, but you will have to check the *Very Rare Glassware of the Depression Years, Fourth Series* to see it. (Note that the true Block Optic grill plate in the bottom picture on page 25 has the same rings and designed center as does the dinner plate.) Some collectors have unknowingly bought Hazel Atlas grill plates instead of Anchor Hocking plates. The Hazel Atlas plates are plain centered, non-ringed grill plates; so be aware of that when shopping!

You can see a pink, center-handled sandwich server pictured at the bottom of page 24. This is missing from many collections, but not all collectors want one in their sets.

The 4¼" diameter bowl with a height of 1½" is the one shown in the center of the lower photograph on page 25. This bowl is difficult to find and appears to be made thicker than most Block Optic. The 7" salad bowl pictured to the right of that bowl took a big leap in price! The price listing is not a mistake now! Originally, it was supposed to be listed at $50.00 but was printed $150.00. Now they are selling for $165.00. Several have sold at the price listed; but some collectors are swearing to do without it.

A reader in California sent some interesting information about the green butter dish top. In the nearly 30 years I have been buying Depression glass, I have seen 15 to 20 green Block butter tops for every bottom. I had assumed that the heavy top had destroyed many of the bottoms since it is somewhat difficult to grasp. However, it seems that the tops were also sold as a butter holder in those old ice boxes. This top slid into a metal holder eliminating the need for a glass bottom! They must have sold very well in that capacity!

Block Optic has always been a pattern selected by many new collectors of Depression glass since it was broadly dispersed and a piece or two seems to have resided in everyone's family. When new collectors used to ask me to recommend a green or pink pattern, I would mention Block Optic because it was inexpensively priced and a novice could not only find it easily but could also afford to buy it. Today, the cost is no longer so inexpensive as it once was! Of course, groceries and gas are not either! As far as collectibility goes, Block continues to be high on the list of collector demand. There is still an abundant supply of almost all fundamental pieces; and infrequently found items are not completely "sky high" as has happened in some other Depression patterns.

Be aware that there are at least five styles of cups and that there are **four *shapes* of creamer and sugars.** Several exacting collectors state that there are even more varieties than these four. Let me know what you find!

There are variations in handles and slight differences in style to make **a total of five *styles* of creamers and sugars** that can be collected in Block Optic. There are four basic **shapes** but five **styles.** In yellow, only the fancy handled, rounded type has been found. There are three styles of pink creamer/sugar sets, flat bottomed and two styles of cone-shaped pairs. One of those cone styles has a base that is plain whereas the other has a rayed base. (This is true of many of Hocking's patterns. Some tumblers or stems also show variations of plain and ribbed bases.) In green creamers/sugars, there are two cone-shaped styles with one of these having pointed handles, the flat bottomed variety, and the rounded style with plain handles evidenced by the frosted pair in the bottom photo. I have never seen a green, fancy handled set. Let me know if you have such a pair!

Regarding the frosted green cup, saucer, creamer, and sugar shown in the lower picture of page 25, Hocking, as well as other companies, satinized (frosted by using camphoric acid) many of their dinnerware lines. Evidently, these were special orders or promotions since many were hand decorated with flowers or fruit. For years, collectors shied away from these pieces; but lately, I've begun to notice more collectors buying satinized wares. Frosted items in Block Optic are beginning to command the price of their unfrosted counterparts. Even though these pieces are more scarce, lack of a strong demand has kept the price in line. That is one of the lessons beginners need to learn as soon as possible about collectibles. Rarity does not always determine price! **Demand** is a far more potent determining factor of price!

A tumble-up set has been found that explains how they were marketed. A stopper in a bottle was marked "Bareé Fragrant Bath Salts Paris, New York."

Some green Block is found with a black foot or stem. As far as I can determine, that black is fired-on and cannot be removed! These, too, used to be ignored. Recently, we've had two different requests from collectors searching for these black-trimmed items!

Note the Deco decorated pink candy on the bottom of page 23. I have seen more than one of these in my travels; thus, these candies may also have been a special order or promotional item at one time. No more pink 3½" short wines have surfaced; and many of the stems in this pattern have encountered large price increases in the last few years. New collectors and the dearth of stems available have contributed to this. Be aware that many pink stems are very light in color and do not match the normally found pink ones very well. Not only are stems scarce now, but when have you seen any serving pieces in pink?

There is enough crystal Block Optic being found that you could put a basic set together if you were inclined to do so. You will have to tell dealers you are searching for crystal since many stock only colored Block Optic at shows. Presently only the crystal butter dish has a premium value. Other crystal pieces sell for a little less than prices of green. Don't totally dismiss it. Crystal Block Optic could set a lovely table!

BLOCK OPTIC, "BLOCK" (Cont.)

	Green	Yellow	Pink
Bowl, 4¼" diam., 1⅜" tall	8.50		11.00
Bowl, 4½" diam., 1½" tall	27.50		30.00
Bowl, 5¼" cereal	15.00		28.00
Bowl, 7¼" salad	165.00		
Bowl, 8½" large berry	25.00		35.00
* Bowl, 11¾" rolled-edge console	60.00		65.00
** Butter dish and cover, 3" x 5"	50.00		
Butter dish bottom	30.00		
Butter dish top	20.00		
*** Candlesticks, 1¾" pr.	100.00		75.00
Candy jar & cover, 2¼" tall	55.00	65.00	55.00
Candy jar & cover, 6¼" tall	60.00		135.00
Comport, 4" wide mayonnaise	35.00		70.00
Creamer, 3 styles: cone shaped, round, rayed-foot & flat (5 kinds)	13.00	13.00	13.00
Cup, four styles	7.00	8.00	7.00
Goblet, 3½" short wine	450.00		450.00
Goblet, 4" cocktail	37.00		37.00
Goblet, 4½" wine	37.00		37.00
Goblet, 5¾", 9 oz.	25.00		30.00
Goblet, 7¼", 9 oz. thin		38.00	
Ice bucket	42.00		75.00
Ice tub or butter tub, open	60.00		95.00
Mug	33.00		
Pitcher, 7⅝", 54 oz., bulbous	70.00		125.00
Pitcher, 8½", 54 oz.	60.00		50.00
Pitcher, 8", 80 oz.	90.00		90.00
Plate, 6" sherbet	3.00	3.00	3.00
Plate, 8" luncheon	5.00	5.00	5.00
Plate, 9" dinner	23.00	45.00	35.00
Plate, 9" grill	30.00	40.00	30.00

	Green	Yellow	Pink
Plate, 10¼" sandwich	25.00		25.00
Plate, 12¾"	30.00	30.00	
Salt and pepper, ftd.	35.00	85.00	80.00
Salt and pepper, squatty	100.00		
Sandwich server, center handle	75.00		75.00
Saucer, 5¾", with cup ring	10.00		8.00
Saucer, 6⅛", with cup ring	10.00		8.00
Sherbet, non-stemmed (cone)	4.00		
Sherbet, 3¼", 5½ oz.	6.00	10.00	7.50
Sherbet, 4¾", 6 oz.	17.00	17.00	17.00
Sugar, 3 styles: as creamer	12.50	12.50	12.50
Tumbler, 3 oz., 2⅝"	22.00		25.00
Tumbler, 5 oz., 3½", flat	22.00		25.00
Tumbler, 9½ oz. flat, 3¹³⁄₁₆" flat	15.00		15.00
Tumbler, 10 or 11 oz., 5" flat	22.00		18.00
Tumbler, 12 oz., 4⅞" flat	25.00		25.00
Tumbler, 15 oz., flat, 5¼"	42.00		38.00
Tumbler, 3 oz., 3¼", ftd.	28.00		28.00
Tumbler, 9 oz. ftd.	18.00	22.00	15.00
Tumbler, 6", 10 oz. ftd.	30.00		32.00
Tumble-up night set	65.00		
Tumbler, 3" only	50.00		
Bottle only	15.00		
Vase, 5¾" blown	295.00		
Whiskey, 1⅝", 1 oz.	38.00		43.00
Whiskey, 2¼", 2 oz.	30.00		30.00

* Amber $55.00

** Green clambroth $225.00, blue $495.00, crystal $125.00

*** Amber $60.00

Please refer to Foreword for pricing information

"BOWKNOT" MANUFACTURER UNKNOWN, Probably late 1920s

Color: Green.

"Bowknot" is a diminutive pattern containing only seven pieces that has captivated the interest of some tenacious collectors! This has caused price hikes on several items that were already scarce! "Bowknot" remains a mystery pattern as to its manufacturer or the exact dates it was made. Should you ever run across any documentation (magazine or catalog ads) please send it to me!

The crucial thing to look for in "Bowknot" is inner rim roughness on bowls and sherbets. Add to that a cup with no saucer and two different style tumblers with no pitcher and you have a real conundrum. That cup has driven collectors mad for years trying to discover why there is only a cup with no saucer.

You can view that rarely seen cereal bowl standing up behind the cup. I had a troublesome time finding one without damage! The price has vaulted on perfect pieces. Many dealers who set up at glass shows do not carry some of the smaller patterns such as "Bowknot." After all, it takes up the same space to display popular cups such as Mayfair, as it does "Bowknot" cups. Space is valuable, so it is usually not used for "Bowknot." However, I find "Bowknot" pieces among the first to leave the table in my show booths! Ask dealers if they have any elsewhere!

I still receive letters from amateur collectors who feel that they have found the first "Bowknot" creamer and sugar. Fostoria patterns "June" and "Romance" have a bow; but neither of these patterns were made in green. If you find a **green** "Bowknot" creamer or sugar or any green piece not listed in this pattern, give me a call or send a picture!

	Green		Green
Bowl, 4½" berry	16.00	Sherbet, low ftd.	17.50
Bowl, 5½" cereal	22.50	Tumbler, 5", 10 oz.	22.50
Cup	8.00	Tumbler, 5", 10 oz. ftd.	22.50
Plate, 7" salad	12.00		

Please refer to Foreword for pricing information

CAMEO, "BALLERINA," or "DANCING GIRL" HOCKING GLASS COMPANY, 1930–1934

Colors: Green, yellow, pink, and crystal w/platinum rim. (*See Reproduction Section.*)

The Cameo pattern, as we have come to recognize it, was manufactured by Hocking Glass Company in the early 1930s; evidently the pattern was incorporated from a Monongah Glass Company design named "Springtime." Monongah was bought by Hocking and many of their patterns were altered or continued by Hocking. To see the Springtime pattern as it existed before being machine mass produced as Cameo pattern, I have shown a crystal cocktail on the bottom of this page. Monongah's glass was plate etched and is of exceptional quality when compared to our renown Cameo. By the way, there are collectors now seeking "Springtime" — so latch onto any you find. There's a market for it, too!

The rarely seen Cameo centered-handled sandwich server (shown below) has presently disappeared from the market place. All known ones are in collections and it has been several years since one has been found outside those accumulations. That doesn't mean you couldn't stumble upon one at the next garage sale down the street! I sincerely doubt all of them have been found that are out there!

I receive more letters and calls about Cameo saucers than any other piece of Cameo. **The real Cameo saucer has an indented cup ring.** Hocking made very few of these indented saucers. They ordinarily made a dual purpose saucer/sherbet plate for their patterns. If you will look on the bottom of page 29, the difference can be seen in front. The saucer on the left has a **distinct indented** ring (1¾" center). Now that I have put the measurements in for green, I am receiving calls about yellow saucers. I assume that any yellow, cup ring saucers **(which have never yet been seen)** would have the **same center measurement** as the green ones! I have had two calls this month from excited readers who thought they had found elusive yellow Cameo ringed saucers. Alas, not yet; but I wish someone would.

Speaking of yellow Cameo, I should mention that the butter dish and milk pitcher are extremely elusive. Yellow Cameo cups, saucer/sherbet plates, footed tumblers, grill, and dinner plates were heavily promoted by Hocking. Boxed sets of these items are still being "discovered." These five pieces are quite bountiful today! In fact, until recently, they were difficult to sell. Prices on commonly found yellow pieces have begun to rise, albeit, slowly. It's an exceptionally charming yellow pattern; so if you find it attractive, right now may be the time to acquire a set!

Green Cameo remains one of the most desirable Depression glass patterns. There is a satisfactory quantity of easily found items, enough to obtain a fundamental set. Many collectors cannot afford every piece made. They do not try to find all stems and every tumbler; instead they purchase only one or two sizes of tumblers and stems. You can still build a large set of green Cameo without investing a large amount of money as long as you stay away from buying the rarer pieces. In many other patterns, it is nearly impossible to assemble a large set by avoiding rare items.

Cameo has two styles of grill plates. (A grill plate is a sectioned or divided plate that keeps the food separated. They were used mostly in restaurants and "grills" of that day; hence the name.) Both styles are shown in yellow on the top of page 29. One has tab handles and one does not. Both styles are common in yellow. In green, however, the grill with the tab or closed handles is harder to find. It is pictured at the bottom of page 29. The 10½" rare, rimmed dinner or flat cake plate is just like the heavy edged (no tabs) grill plate only without the dividers! The regular dinner plate has a large center as opposed to the small centered sandwich plate. The less expensive sandwich plate is often priced as the more expensive dinner plate; so be sure to avoid buying into that trap!

The darker green bottles with Cameo design are marked underneath "Whitehouse Vinegar." These originally came from the grocery with vinegar — and a cork. Glass stoppers, however, are found atop water bottles. These stoppers do not have a Cameo pattern on them, but are plain, paneled stoppers with hollow centers.

All the **miniature** pieces in Cameo are **new**! No smaller Cameo (children's) dishes were ever made during the Depression era. See the Reproduction Section in the back of the book for information on this. A new importer is making a sometimes weakly patterned shaker in pink, cobalt blue, and a darker shade of green than the original color. If new shaker tops are the first thing you notice — beware!

CAMEO, "BALLERINA," or "DANCING GIRL" (Cont.)

	Green	Yellow	Pink	Crystal, Plat		Green	Yellow	Pink	Crystal, Plat
Bowl, 4¼" sauce				6.00	Jam jar, 2" and cover	175.00			160.00
Bowl, 4¾" cream soup	130.00				Pitcher, 5¾", 20 oz.				
Bowl, 5½" cereal	32.00	32.00	150.00	6.50	syrup or milk	225.00	2,000.00		
Bowl, 7¼" salad	57.50				Pitcher, 6", 36 oz. juice	60.00			
Bowl, 8¼" large berry	37.50		175.00		Pitcher, 8½", 56 oz. water	60.00		1,500.00	500.00
Bowl, 9" rimmed soup	65.00		135.00		Plate, 6" sherbet	4.00	2.50	90.00	2.00
Bowl, 10" oval vegetable	30.00	42.00			Plate, 7" salad				3.50
Bowl, 11", 3-legged					Plate, 8" luncheon	10.00	11.00	33.00	4.00
console	75.00	95.00	55.00		Plate, 8½" square	42.00	250.00		
Butter dish and cover	225.00	1,500.00			Plate, 9½" dinner	19.00	9.00	85.00	
Butter dish bottom	135.00	500.00			Plate, 10" sandwich	13.00		42.00	
Butter dish top	90.00	1,000.00			** Plate, 10½" rimmed dinner	100.00		175.00	
Cake plate, 10", 3 legs	22.00				Plate, 10½" grill	9.00	6.00	50.00	
Cake plate, 10½" flat	100.00		175.00		Plate, 10½" grill				
Candlesticks, 4" pr.	100.00				with closed handles	70.00	6.00		
Candy jar, 4" low					Plate, 10½" with closed				
and cover	85.00	95.00	495.00		handles	12.00	12.00		
Candy jar, 6½" tall					Platter, 12", closed handles	20.00	40.00		
and cover	165.00				Relish, 7½" ftd., 3 part	33.00			160.00
Cocktail shaker (metal					* Salt and pepper, ftd. pr.	70.00		850.00	
lid) appears in crystal only				750.00	Sandwich server,				
Comport, 5" wide					center handle	5,500.00			
mayonnaise	30.00		195.00		Saucer with cup ring	185.00			
Cookie jar and cover	52.00				Saucer, 6" (sherbet plate)	4.00	2.50	90.00	
Creamer, 3¼"	23.00	20.00			Sherbet, 3⅛" molded	15.00	40.00	75.00	
Creamer, 4¼"	28.00		125.00		Sherbet, 3⅛" blown	17.00		75.00	
Cup, 2 styles	14.00	7.50	85.00	5.50	Sherbet, 4⅞"	35.00	45.00	100.00	
Decanter, 10"					Sugar, 3¼"	21.00	18.00		
with stopper	175.00			225.00	Sugar, 4¼"	27.50		125.00	
Decanter, 10"					Tumbler, 3¾", 5 oz. juice	30.00		90.00	
with stopper, frosted					Tumbler, 4", 9 oz. water	26.00		80.00	9.00
(stopper represents ⅓					Tumbler, 4¾", 10 oz. flat	30.00		95.00	
value of decanter)	35.00				Tumbler, 5", 11 oz. flat	30.00	60.00	95.00	
Domino tray, 7"					Tumbler, 5¼", 15 oz.	70.00		135.00	
with 3" indentation	140.00				Tumbler, 3 oz. ftd. juice	60.00		135.00	
Domino tray, 7"					Tumbler, 5", 9 oz. ftd.	25.00	16.00	115.00	
with no indentation			250.00	125.00	Tumbler, 5¾", 11 oz. ftd.	65.00		135.00	
Goblet, 3½" wine	850.00		900.00		Tumbler, 6⅜", 15 oz. ftd.	495.00			
Goblet, 4" wine	75.00		225.00		Vase, 5¾"	225.00			
Goblet, 6" water	50.00		175.00		Vase, 8"	37.50			
Ice bowl or open butter,					Water bottle (dark green)				
3" tall x 5½" wide	175.00		700.00	265.00	Whitehouse vinegar	17.50			

* Beware Reproductions
** Same as flat cake plate

Please refer to Foreword for pricing information

CHERRYBERRY U.S. GLASS COMPANY, Early 1930s

Colors: Pink, green, crystal; some iridized.

Cherryberry "picking" began with collectors gathering Strawberry. Small notice of this pattern existed, except for those who were searching for Strawberry and were perpetually running into cherries instead of strawberries. Now, Cherryberry has become a viable Depression glass pattern with a few carnival glass supporters attacking our ranks to secure the iridescent pitchers, tumblers, and butter dishes, which are the most prized pieces in both collectible areas. Not only do collectors of Cherryberry and carnival glass appreciate these, but also, collectors of butters and pitchers hunt them.

Crystal is the rarest "color"; yet, there are few collectors buying it.

The color inconstancies of green in the photograph are not caused by the printing or photography. This represents an additional problem in Cherryberry. The green can be found from a very yellow hue to a blue one. There is not as much color variance with the pink, but there are some pieces that are distinctly lighter than others. Some collectors worry about matching color hues; if you are one of these, this may not be the pattern for you.

This is another of the U.S. Glass patterns that has no cup or saucer and has a plain butter base. If all these U.S. Glass patterns are "sister" patterns, then Strawberry and Cherryberry are twins. You can only tell them apart by careful scrutiny of the fruits.

	Crystal, Iridescent	Pink, Green		Crystal, Iridescent	Pink, Green
Bowl, 4" berry	6.50	8.50	Olive dish, 5" one-handled	9.00	18.00
Bowl, 6¼", 2" deep	40.00	85.00	Pickle dish, 8¼" oval	9.00	18.00
Bowl, 6½" deep salad	16.00	22.00	Pitcher, 7¾"	160.00	175.00
Bowl, 7½" deep berry	17.00	25.00	Plate, 6" sherbet	6.00	10.00
Butter dish and cover	145.00	175.00	Plate, 7½" salad	8.00	18.00
Butter dish bottom	77.50	100.00	Sherbet	6.50	10.00
Butter dish top	67.50	75.00	Sugar, small open	12.00	20.00
Comport, 5¾"	16.00	25.00	Sugar, large	15.00	25.00
Creamer, small	12.00	20.00	Sugar cover	30.00	60.00
Creamer, 4⅝" large	15.00	40.00	Tumbler, 3⅝", 9 oz.	20.00	35.00

CHERRY BLOSSOM JEANNETTE GLASS COMPANY, 1930–1939

Colors: Pink, green, Delphite (opaque blue), crystal, Jade-ite (opaque green), and red. *(See Reproduction Section.)*

In the early '70s, collecting Cherry Blossom Depression glass was all the rage. Then, in 1973 reproductions occurred and scared people away. For a while, dealers were rejecting the acquisition of Cherry Blossom because it was not selling due to the reproductions in the market place. Well, time and education regarding discrepancies between old and new have now made collecting Cherry Blossom a conceivable choice again! If you are a beginner turn to the Reproduction section in the back of the book for your instruction on Cherry Blossom repros. (See page 230 – 231.) Almost all pieces in Cherry Blossom have increased in price since the last book, but prices on basic dinnerware pieces have really pulled this pattern past the doldrums. It is a pretty pattern — and it's nice to see collectors turning to it once more!

Again, prices have inflated past pre-repro days except for the pink shakers that still have a long way to go. The problem with shakers is not only the large number of reproductions made, but that many collectors are willing to buy these duplicates to have a pair of shakers for their sets. I continue to get many calls and letters on pink Cherry shakers. The stories I've heard told at auctions and estate sales boggles the mind! Ask yourself, why would anyone offer you something worth $1,000.00 for only a few hundred…or less? **Only two pairs of original pink Cherry Blossom shakers were ever documented**; so the possibility of your finding another old pair, particularly at a bargain price is on par with winning the lottery. I've learned never to say "never," however. People **are** still discovering unusual Depression glass even now — if not daily, then at least monthly.

The 9" platter is the hardest piece to find (after the genuine shakers). I have only seen **one** green 9" platter! (Measure this platter **outside edge to outside edge**.) Even with this explanation I have had three new collectors call for verification if I really mean that. **I do!** The 11" platter measures only 9" from the **inside** rims and that is the common piece that people so want to be the rare 9" platter. Again, the rare 9" platter is only 9" long from outside to outside rim!

Inner rims of Cherry Blossom pieces have a proclivity for chips, nicks, or those famous "chigger bites" that some auctioneers like to term them. Most chips I have seen referred to as "chigger bites" look much larger to me! Inner rim roughness was caused as much from stacking as from utilization. You can safely store dishes with proper sized paper plates between them. This is particularly true at glass shows where stacks of plates are often mauled over and over. I have often wondered why a customer looks at every plate only to announce that he is glad he already has those for his set!

Pieces of Cherry Blossom that are harder to acquire include the aforementioned 9" platter, mugs, flat iced teas, soup and cereal bowls, and the 10" green grill plate. That plate has never even been found in pink!

Crystal Cherry Blossom appears at times. Normally, it is the two-handled bowl that sells in the $18.00 range. It is scarce, but there is not enough crystal found to be collectible as a set. A few red pieces have been found, but the reproduction red wiped out most collectors' desire for these.

The letters AOP in listings and advertisements stand for "all over pattern" on the footed tumblers and rounded pitcher. The footed large tumblers and the AOP pitcher come in two styles. One style has a scalloped or indented foot while the other is merely round with no indentations. The letters PAT stands for "pattern at the top" illustrated by the flat bottomed tumblers and pitchers.

There are some known experimental pieces of Cherry such as a pink cookie jar, some pink five-part relish dishes, orange with green trim slag bowls, and amber children's pieces. You can see most of these pieces in *Very Rare Glassware of the Depression Era* books. Pricing on experimental items is difficult to determine; but keep your eye out for any of these pieces, and do not pass them up if the price is right — for you! There is always some market demand for rare items of Depression glassware.

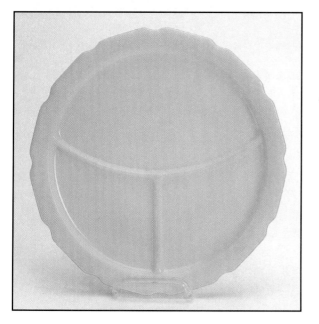

CHERRY BLOSSOM (Cont.)

	Pink	Green	Delphite
Bowl, 4¾" berry	16.00	18.00	15.00
Bowl, 5¾" cereal	45.00	47.50	
Bowl, 7¾" flat soup	85.00	80.00	
* Bowl, 8½" round berry	48.00	48.00	50.00
Bowl, 9" oval vegetable	40.00	40.00	50.00
Bowl, 9" 2-handled	45.00	65.00	25.00
** Bowl, 10½", 3 leg fruit	95.00	90.00	
Butter dish and cover	75.00	100.00	
Butter dish bottom	15.00	25.00	
Butter dish top	60.00	75.00	
Cake plate (3 legs) 10¼"	30.00	35.00	
Coaster	14.00	13.00	
Creamer	20.00	20.00	20.00
Cup	20.00	21.00	18.00
Mug, 7 oz.	265.00	195.00	
*** Pitcher, 6¾" AOP, 36 oz. scalloped or round bottom	58.00	58.00	80.00
Pitcher, 8" PAT, 42 oz. flat	55.00	55.00	
Pitcher, 8" PAT, 36 oz. footed	55.00	55.00	
Plate, 6" sherbet	8.00	8.00	10.00
Plate, 7" salad	20.00	22.00	
**** Plate, 9" dinner	24.00	25.00	20.00
***** Plate, 9" grill	30.00	30.00	

	Pink	Green	Delphite
Plate, 10" grill		95.00	
Platter, 9" oval	850.00	995.00	
Platter, 11" oval	40.00	45.00	45.00
Platter, 13" and 13" divided	70.00	70.00	
Salt and pepper (scalloped bottom)	1,250.00	995.00	
Saucer	5.00	5.00	5.00
Sherbet	17.50	20.00	16.00
Sugar	14.50	17.50	18.00
Sugar cover	18.00	20.00	
Tray, 10½" sandwich	30.00	30.00	22.00
Tumbler, 3¾", 4 oz. footed AOP	17.00	20.00	22.00
Tumbler, 4½", 9 oz. round foot AOP	35.00	35.00	22.00
Tumbler, 4½", 8 oz. scalloped foot AOP	35.00	35.00	22.00
Tumbler, 3½", 4 oz. flat PAT	20.00	30.00	
Tumbler, 4¼", 9 oz. flat PAT	18.00	24.00	
Tumbler, 5", 12 oz. flat PAT	60.00	75.00	

   * Yellow – $395.00

  ** Jade-ite – $325.00

 *** Jade-ite – $325.00

 **** Translucent green – $225.00

***** Jade-ite – $85.00

CHERRY BLOSSOM — CHILD'S JUNIOR DINNER SET

	Pink	Delphite
Creamer	47.50	50.00
Sugar	47.50	50.00
Plate, 6"	12.50	13.00 (design on bottom)
Cup	37.50	40.00
Saucer	6.50	7.25
14 Piece set	325.00	350.00

Original box sells for $35.00 extra with pink sets.

Please refer to Foreword for pricing information

CHINEX CLASSIC MacBETH-EVANS DIVISION OF CORNING GLASS WORKS, Late 1930s–Early 1940s

Colors: Ivory, ivory w/decal decoration.

Chinex devotees are still attempting to match all those different floral adornments. It is difficult enough to find Chinex; but to find the piece you need only to have it decorated with a decal other than the one you need is annoying. The blue and pink edge trimmed pieces with a red flower in the center are not being found regularly, nor is the brown castle scene. My personal preference leans to the blue trimmed castle decal decoration. I have found a butter bottom as you can see in the bottom photo. What I do not know is whether the top has a castle decal or just a blue trim. I suspect that it will have the castle decal, since the butter top shown in the top picture has a floral design on it. A reader was kind enough to hook me up with that Chinex floral top. Thanks! Unfortunately, I have not been able to find the bottom for that one either. The floral decal on that top is like those pieces on the left of the photograph. If you have either one of these butter pieces to match mine, please let me know!

More Chinex is uncovered in the Pittsburgh area than any other part of the country. Of course, MacBeth-Evans was just down the road and that has a great deal to do with this! I have found most of the items shown either in that area or from dealers who shop there. This pattern grows on you if you give it a chance. You will have limited competition in searching for Chinex Classic; that might be a determining factor for some new collectors!

The plainer, undecorated ivory pieces are still awaiting collectors' notice. Undecorated Chinex works wonderfully in the microwave according to several collectors. I must admit that I have never tried it; so remember to test it first by putting it in for a **short** time (a few seconds) and checking for hot spots just as you would any other dish not designed **specifically** for microwave usage. After removing the piece from the microwave, be sure to place it on a place mat or some surface that is not cold. A sudden temperature change may crack it. I speak from experience on Fire-King Ovenware that we used to use. Do not try this with decorated pieces of Chinex —just the unadorned!

Castle decal items are the most fascinating to collectors; darker blue trims seem to be more popular than the lighter blue or brown.

Remember, butter bottoms look like Cremax pattern instead of Chinex. The butter tops have the scroll-like design that distinguishes Chinex, but this scroll design is missing from the butter bottoms. The bottom has a plain "pie crust" edge. The floral or castle designs will be inside the base of the butter, and apparently on the outside of the top. I cannot seem to put one together for absolute confirmation!

	Browntone or Plain Ivory	Decal Decorated	Castle Decal
Bowl, 5¾" cereal	5.50	8.00	15.00
Bowl, 6¾" salad	12.00	20.00	40.00
Bowl, 7" vegetable	14.00	25.00	40.00
Bowl, 7¾" soup	12.50	22.00	40.00
Bowl, 9" vegetable	11.00	25.00	40.00
Bowl, 11"	17.00	35.00	45.00
Butter dish	55.00	75.00	150.00
Butter dish bottom	12.50	27.50	50.00
Butter dish top	42.50	47.50	100.00
Creamer	5.50	10.00	18.00
Cup	4.50	6.50	15.00
Plate, 6¼" sherbet	2.50	3.50	7.50
Plate, 9¾" dinner	4.50	8.50	20.00
Plate, 11½" sandwich or cake	7.50	13.50	25.00
Saucer	2.00	4.00	6.00
Sherbet, low ftd.	7.00	11.00	25.00

CIRCLE HOCKING GLASS COMPANY, 1930s

Colors: Green, pink, and crystal.

Sets in Circle can be attained over time if you stick to green, but it will take more than good fortune to gather a pink set. Let me know if you have somehow accomplished that endeavor.

Two styles of cups add to the idiosyncrasies of Circle. The flat bottomed style fits a saucer/sherbet plate while the rounded cup takes an indented saucer. Both styles are pictured in the foreground. I have not found an indented saucer for my rounded pink cup. There have **never** been reports of tumblers, pitchers, or bowls in pink. I presume only a pink luncheon set was made, but two styles of cups makes one wonder what else might be obtainable.

Both the green bowls pictured, 9⅜" and 5¼", have ground bottoms. At Hocking, ground bottoms usually indicated early production pieces. The 5" flared bowl is shown on the right front of the photograph. Observe how it is clearly a darker shade of green when contrasted with the other pieces.

I received a letter from an individual who says she owns three 9½" Circle dinner plates! The green dinner would have a larger surface area in the center of the plate than the 10" sandwich plate pictured in the back. I haven't seen one yet — but she has made me look harder at Circle plates!

You will find green colored stems with crystal tops more frequently than you will find plain green stems; however, few collectors currently desire the crystal topped items. I, personally, like the two-toned variations better. In Elegant glassware, two-toned stems are often more desirable!

Circle is noticed by collectors of kitchenware (especially reamer collectors). That 80 oz. Circle pitcher with a reamer top is highly favored! A quandary with the pitcher and reamer is that color inconsistencies on these pitchers make it difficult to find a reamer separately that correctly matches the green hue of the pitcher. The pitcher shown here is more yellow when contrasted with the other green pieces.

	Green, Pink		Green, Pink
Bowl, 4½"	8.00	Plate, 6" sherbet/saucer	1.50
Bowl, 5¼"	10.00	Plate, 8¼" luncheon	4.00
Bowl, 5" flared, 1¾" deep	14.00	Plate, 9½"	12.00
Bowl, 8"	18.00	Plate, 10" sandwich	14.00
Bowl, 9⅜"	20.00	Saucer w/cup ring	2.50
Creamer	9.00	Sherbet, 3⅛"	4.00
Cup (2 styles)	5.00	Sherbet, 4¾"	6.00
Decanter, handled	50.00	Sugar	7.00
Goblet, 4½" wine	12.50	Tumbler, 3½", 4 oz. juice	8.00
Goblet, 8 oz. water	11.00	Tumbler, 4", 8 oz. water	9.00
Pitcher, 60 oz.	35.00	Tumbler, 5", 10 oz. tea	16.00
Pitcher, 80 oz.	30.00	Tumbler, 15 oz. flat	22.00

CLOVERLEAF HAZEL ATLAS GLASS COMPANY, 1930 – 1936

Colors: Pink, green, yellow, crystal, and black.

Cloverleaf pattern is recognized by even the non-collecting public when arrangements are displayed at shows. Those shamrocks are symbols of luck which is what you need in finding some of the rarer pieces in this pattern. In holiday displays I usually see green used to commemorate St. Patrick's Day and black for Halloween!

There seem to be balanced numbers of collectors for yellow, black, and green. Very few are turning to pink or crystal since they are limited to only a luncheon set. Besides the traditional luncheon pieces in pink, a flared, 10 oz. tumbler exists! That pink tumbler was quite sparsely distributed and has not been found in crystal at all.

All Cloverleaf colors are selling well with green leading the way. In green, the 8" bowl and tumblers are selling briskly. All the bowls, as well as grill plates and tumblers are becoming more difficult to round up. In yellow, the candy dish, shakers, and bowls no longer seem to be available at any price. Latch on to them if you get a chance — even if you do not collect them! There'll be someone who does!

Black Cloverleaf prices have slowed somewhat with the small ash trays being ignored while the larger ones are still selling — albeit slowly. Mentioning that smoking accessories were selling slowly convinced one reader that he was going to start a collection of them — which may be a prudent move! The black sherbet plate and saucer are the same size. The saucer has no Cloverleaf design in the center, but the sherbet plate does! These sherbet plates still turn up in stacks of saucers occasionally; so keep your eyes open!

Some black Cloverleaf pieces in the photograph on page 39 are gold decorated, probably for a special promotion. I have included a creamer and sugar on the bottom of page 38 in hopes the Cloverleaf pattern will show better.

I have been advised by dealers to point out that the Cloverleaf pattern comes on both the inside and outside of the pieces. That does not seem to make a difference in value or collectibility. In order for the black to show the pattern, moulds had to be designed with the pattern on the visible side of pieces. On transparent pieces, the pattern could be on the bottom or the inside and it would still show. In black, the pattern on the bottom of a plate makes it look like a plain black plate. Over the years, transparent pieces also were made using the moulds designed for the black; so, you now find these pieces with designs on both sides.

CLOVERLEAF (Cont.)

	Pink	Green	Yellow	Black
Ash tray, 4", match holder in center				65.00
Ash tray, 5¾", match holder in center				85.00
Bowl, 4" dessert	15.00	22.00	27.50	
Bowl, 5" cereal		30.00	35.00	
Bowl, 7" deep salad		45.00	55.00	
Bowl, 8"		60.00		
Candy dish and cover		55.00	110.00	
Creamer, 3⅝" ftd.		10.00	18.00	20.00
Cup	7.00	9.00	11.00	20.00
Plate, 6" sherbet		5.00	8.00	40.00
Plate, 8" luncheon	7.00	8.00	14.00	15.00
Plate, 10¼" grill		22.00	25.00	
Salt and pepper, pr.		35.00	110.00	95.00
Saucer	3.00	3.00	4.00	6.00
Sherbet, 3" ftd.	6.00	8.00	12.00	22.00
Sugar, 3⅝" ftd.		10.00	18.00	20.00
Tumbler, 4", 9 oz. flat		55.00		
Tumbler, 3¾", 10 oz. flat flared	22.00	40.00		
Tumbler, 5¾", 10 oz. ftd.		25.00	35.00	

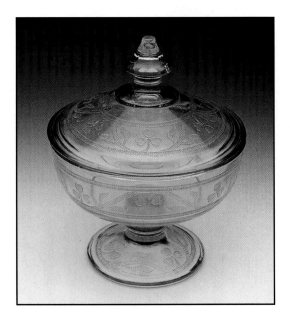

COLONIAL, "KNIFE AND FORK" HOCKING GLASS COMPANY, 1934–1936

Colors: Pink, green, crystal, and opaque white.

Green Colonial has again begun to sell! For a couple years, after my buying trips, Cathy would say, "Why are you still buying that (green Colonial)?" Collectors were turning to buying pink and crystal instead of the more expensive green. There are more green pieces obtainable since there are no stems found in pink. The problem in collecting colors (other than green) is limited availability. Green Colonial may have been more strongly promoted while Hocking pushed their more popular pink pattern Mayfair. My inventory of green Colonial has almost sold out at the last few shows. Color preference in collecting has been cyclical for the nearly 30 years that I have been watching Depression glass. Green is again preferred!

Prices for crystal stems have risen! For years, these sold for about half the price of green because there were few collectors of crystal Colonial. There is a scarcity of crystal stemware, yet not enough collectors have discovered this. I mentioned a 5" high stem that fit between the wine and the claret in the last book, but no new information has been forthcoming. The edge was rolled inward. It may have been a claret with the top rim treated differently. If you find one, please send ounce capacities.

Only footed tumblers are found in pink; do not mistake them for stems. All three sizes of green footed tumblers are shown in the bottom photograph on page 42. You should be able to distinguish the **footed tumblers** in the bottom photo from **the stems** pictured in the top photo. That has always been somewhat of a problem for beginning collectors; and yes! there are scores of these enthusiastic neophytes writing me now!

In the top photo on page 42 is the first **beaded top** green Colonial pitcher to appear. The pink one was bought at an auction in the Cincinnati area in 1975. I bought the green one about 30 miles north of there almost 20 years later. Surely there were more than two made. Keep your eyes open for others!

Soup bowls (both cream and regular), cereals, mint shakers, and dinner plates are still difficult to obtain in all colors of Colonial. Cereal bowls may be the most difficult cereals to obtain in all of Depression glass. Fortunately, they are not yet the most expensive; but time could change that!

Colonial mugs occasionally surface but few have been found lately. A couple of months ago I received photos of a great looking **mug** collection! A green Colonial mug was recently found in the northern Kentucky area at a very reasonable price — $5.00! Bargains are still around! It just takes work and a little luck to find these deals. I find a few occasionally in my travels. Of course, I put a minimum of 40,000 miles on my vehicles every year, too! Also, I visited over 450 different antique malls last year — many, several times!

The 11 oz. Colonial tumbler measures 2¾" across the top while the 12 oz. measures exactly 3". These two tumblers are frequently confused. It is easier to measure across the top than to measure the contents if you are out shopping! The spooner stands 5½" tall while the sugar without a lid is only 4½" high. That inch makes a big difference in price. You can occasionally find a spooner for the price of the sugar if you recognize the difference.

The cheese dish lid is only ¼" shorter than the butter top, not the ½" previously thought. The butter top is 4" tall and the cheese top is only 3¾" tall. The cheese dish consists of a wooden board with an indented groove on which the lid rests. The cheese top has a more flattened look when you have the two tops together. So far, the cheese has only been found in green; but the pink butter is already nearly impossible to find without looking for a cheese dish!

	Pink	Green	Crystal		Pink	Green	Crystal
Bowl, 3¾" berry	50.00			Salt and pepper, pr.	140.00	150.00	60.00
Bowl, 4½" berry	16.00	18.00	10.00	Saucer/sherbet plate (white 3.00)	6.00	8.00	4.00
Bowl, 5½" cereal	60.00	90.00	33.00	Sherbet, 3"	25.00		
Bowl, 4½" cream soup	70.00	70.00	65.00	Sherbet, 3⅜"	12.00	15.00	7.00
Bowl, 7" low soup	65.00	65.00	27.50	Spoon holder or celery, 5½"	130.00	125.00	75.00
Bowl, 9" large berry	27.50	33.00	25.00	Stem, 3¾", 1 oz. cordial		27.00	20.00
Bowl, 10" oval vegetable	35.00	38.00	22.00	Stem, 4", 3 oz. cocktail		25.00	16.00
Butter dish and cover	650.00	55.00	40.00	Stem, 4½", 2½ oz. wine		25.00	16.00
Butter dish bottom	450.00	32.50	25.00	Stem, 5¼", 4 oz. claret		25.00	18.00
Butter dish top	200.00	22.50	15.00	Stem, 5¾", 8½ oz. water		30.00	22.00
Cheese dish		225.00		Sugar, 4½"	25.00	15.00	10.00
Cream/milk pitcher, 5", 16 oz.	60.00	25.00	20.00	Sugar cover	60.00	22.00	15.00
Cup (white 7.00)	12.00	12.00	8.00	Tumbler, 3", 5 oz. juice	20.00	25.00	15.00
Mug, 4½", 12 oz.	500.00	800.00		** Tumbler, 4", 9 oz. water	20.00	20.00	15.00
+ Pitcher, 7", 54 oz.	50.00	55.00	30.00	Tumbler, 5⅛" high, 11 oz.,	35.00	42.00	22.00
*+ Pitcher, 7¾", 68 oz.	65.00	75.00	35.00	Tumbler, 12 oz. iced tea	50.00	50.00	24.00
Plate, 6" sherbet	6.00	8.00	4.00	Tumbler, 15 oz. lemonade	65.00	75.00	45.00
Plate, 8½" luncheon	9.00	9.00	4.50	Tumbler, 3¼", 3 oz. ftd.	17.00	25.00	13.00
Plate, 10" dinner	55.00	65.00	30.00	Tumbler, 4", 5 oz. ftd.	32.00	42.00	22.00
Plate, 10" grill	25.00	25.00	15.00	*** Tumbler, 5¼", 10 oz. ftd.	47.00	47.00	27.50
Platter, 12" oval	32.00	22.00	15.00	Whiskey, 2½", 1½ oz.	12.00	15.00	11.00

*Beaded top $1,100.00   **Royal ruby $110.00   ***Royal ruby $160.00   +With or without ice lip

COLONIAL

COLONIAL BLOCK HAZEL ATLAS GLASS COMPANY, Early 1930s

Colors: Green, crystal, black, pink, and rare in cobalt blue; white in 1950s.

Amazingly, a newly discovered piece of Colonial Block has been found. It is a footed juice tumbler that stands 5¼" tall and holds five ounces. So far, these have only been seen in green; but there are pink goblets, so anything is possible. You can check out one of these rare tumblers in *Very Rare Glassware of the Depression Years — Fifth Series.*

I have conversed with several collectors who are trying to put together a set of pink Colonial Block, and they are having a time! Several report that they have never seen a pink pitcher; so, enjoy the one shown! Sets of green are easier to assemble, but **not very easy**. Both 4" and 7" bowls, butter tub, sherbets, and the pitcher are the pieces most often lacking in collections. You may now add to that the newly listed juice tumbler!

That goblet by the green pitcher is Colonial Block and not Block Optic as it is often mislabeled. Many Block Optic collectors use these goblets with their sets since they are inexpensive compared to those of Block Optic. The heavier Colonial Block goblets are certainly more durable when compared to the thinner Block Optic. More green sherbets have been found recently! How a piece like that can go undiscovered for years is astounding!

Many pieces of Colonial Block are marked HA, but not all. The **H** is atop the **A** which confuses some inexperienced collectors who assume that this is the symbol for Anchor Hocking. The anchor is a symbol used by Anchor Hocking and that was not used until after the 1930s.

U.S. Glass made a pitcher similar to Colonial Block. There is little difference in them except most Hazel Atlas pitchers are marked. Collectors today are not as rigid in their collecting standards as they once were. Many collectors will buy either pitcher to go with their set. That is why items that are similar to a pattern, but not actually a part of it, are referred to as "go-with" or "look-alike" pieces. Usually, these items are more reasonably priced.

The cobalt blue Colonial Block creamer is shown in my *Very Rare Glassware of the Depression Years, Second Series.* So far, no sugar bowl has been forthcoming. It's a shame more cobalt blue was not made!

A few black and frosted green Colonial Block powder jars are being found. We photographed a black powder jar, but this picture was chosen instead. To my knowledge the white creamer, sugar, and lid are the only white pieces to surface.

	Pink, Green	White		Pink, Green	White
Bowl, 4"	6.50		Creamer	12.00	7.00
Bowl, 7"	20.00		Goblet	12.50	
Butter dish	45.00		Pitcher	45.00	
Butter dish bottom	12.50		*Powder jar with lid	17.50	
Butter dish top	32.50		Sherbet	10.00	
Butter tub	45.00		Sugar	10.00	5.50
Candy jar w/cover	40.00		Sugar lid	12.00	4.50
			Tumbler, 5¼", 5 oz., ftd.	25.00	

*Black $22.50

COLONIAL FLUTED, "ROPE" FEDERAL GLASS COMPANY, 1928–1933

Colors: Green and crystal.

Colonial Fluted was a functional pattern that was widely used; you will find many pieces with heavy wear marks. Knives scratch the surface of most glassware and this pattern displays that well. Today, you need to choose your menus carefully, if you serve on your collection. I would not recommend a thick grilled steak!

The "F" in a shield found at center of many Colonial Fluted pieces is the trademark used by the Federal Glass Company. Not all pieces are marked.

Colonial Fluted is usually a starter set for beginning collectors; some find it an ideal bridge set. In fact, much of the original advertising for this pattern was for bridge parties. Crystal is seldom collected, except for decaled pieces with hearts, spades, diamonds, and clubs. Cathy felt that we ought to own some of these pieces; so she bought some last year for us to have for future books. (I had left them as the price was not what I considered reasonable. I usually like to be able to break even on pieces I buy to photograph, and I do not apologize for hoping to make a little profit when I finally sell them!)

Colonial Fluted is normally priced moderately enough to use. Most guests recognize this old glass as antique and treat it very gently.

There is no dinner plate in Colonial Fluted pattern. There is a dinner-sized plate made by Federal that goes very well with this, having the roping around the outside of the plate, but not the fluting. It is shown in the back of the photograph along with the grill plate that also goes well with the pattern. It has no roping either. Both of these pieces can expand the number of items in your set without looking out of place. Being made by Federal, they match color wise.

Colonial Fluted can be blended with other sets, too, which is a present trend with collectors.

	Green		Green
Bowl, 4" berry	7.50	Plate, 6" sherbet	2.50
Bowl, 6" cereal	10.00	Plate, 8" luncheon	5.00
Bowl, 6½", deep (2½") salad	25.00	Saucer	2.00
Bowl, 7½" large berry	20.00	Sherbet	6.00
Creamer	6.50	Sugar	5.00
Cup	5.00	Sugar cover	16.00

Please refer to Foreword for pricing information

COLUMBIA FEDERAL GLASS COMPANY, 1938–1942

Colors: Crystal, some pink.

Two sizes of Columbia tumblers have now been confirmed, the 2⅞", 4 ounce juice and 9 ounce water. Both are pictured. However, a problem has recently occurred with "like" tumblers. Notice the two juice tumblers pictured in front. The one on the right is marked "France" on the bottom; so devotees of this glass need to be aware of this before paying big bucks for foreign-made glassware. I have had periodic reports of other sizes and have also had other tumblers shown to me at Depression glass shows. So far, these have all turned out to be Duncan and Miller Hobnail and not Columbia. You can find Columbia water tumblers with advertisements for dairy products printed on them. Cottage cheese seems to have been the most popular product contained therein.

The snack tray is shown standing up in the back left. Many collectors have not known what to look for since it is an unusual piece and shaped differently from most Columbia. The pictures in recent editions have shown the tray so well that collectors are finding these to the point that supply is over running demand right now. These snack plates were found with Columbia cups in a boxed set over 20 years ago in northern Ohio. The box was labeled "Snack Sets" by Federal Glass Company. No mention was made of Columbia on the box. Snack trays are also being found with Federal cups **other than Columbia**. I have been told that they turn up regularly in Colorado. As a matter of record, I have pictured a bowl and snack set that are designed like the Columbia snack tray. These are being found in original boxes labeled "Homestead." You decide if you want to use them with your set. They were manufactured by Federal.

You will find examples of Columbia butter dishes with various flashed colors and floral decal decorations. Some were even satinized (frosted) and others were flashed with color after the satinized finish was applied. Federal must have fervently promoted these since there are so many found today! It is the only butter dish in this book that has not increased in price at least 25 percent in the last 10 years.

Pink Columbia sells extremely well for a pattern that has only four pieces! Prices continue to increase on crystal bowls, tumblers, and all pink items.

Satinized, pastel-banded, and floral-decaled luncheon sets have been found. Even though these sets can be considered rare, they are difficult to sell, unless you find a complete set.

	Crystal	Pink		Crystal	Pink
Bowl, 5" cereal	18.00		Cup	8.50	25.00
Bowl, 8" low soup	22.00		Plate, 6" bread & butter	3.50	15.00
Bowl, 8½" salad	20.00		Plate, 9½" luncheon	10.00	35.00
Bowl, 10½" ruffled edge	20.00		Plate, 11" chop	12.00	
Butter dish and cover	20.00		Saucer	3.50	10.00
Ruby flashed	(22.00)		Snack plate	30.00	
Other flashed	(21.00)		Tumbler, 2⅞", 4 oz., juice	25.00	
Butter dish bottom	7.50		Tumbler, 9 oz., water	30.00	
Butter dish top	12.50				

CORONATION, "BANDED RIB," "SAXON" HOCKING GLASS COMPANY, 1936–1940

Colors: Pink, green, crystal, and Royal Ruby.

Coronation's claim to fame for years were the tumblers that were continually confused with the rarely found Old Colony ("Lace Edge") tumblers. Look at the **fine ribs above the middle** of the Coronation tumbler. These ribs are missing on an Old Colony footed tumbler. Look in the store display photograph on page 153 or on the bottom of that page to see the differences. Many collectors buy Coronation tumblers and use them with Old Colony since they cost a third as much. Both are the same shape and color and both were made by Hocking. Just don't confuse the two since there is quite a price disparity! The price of Coronation tumblers has risen 50 percent in the last two years, and that may be attributable to Old Colony collectors instead of Coronation buyers. Of course, if you see Old Colony tumblers priced as Coronation, you had better make that purchase!

Coronation pitchers are rarely seen, but you can view one on the next page! That is the one piece missing from most collections of Coronation. Years ago, these were bought by collectors of pitchers and tumblers. Few were bought by Coronation collectors because they were relatively expensive. Now, avid Coronation collectors are willing to pay the price, but few pitchers are being found to satisfy that market.

Notice that the handles on Royal Ruby Coronation bowls are open; handles on the pink are closed, and handles on the green are nonexistent. If you should find another style of handle on a different color, please let me know.

Since I mentioned closed handles on the pink, I should qualify that with — if they have handles. Two newly discovered bowls in pink have been without handles! They measure 4¼" and 8" like the previously discovered green ones. The smaller pink berry is shown with the green one in the foreground of the top photo. I felt the larger bowl was priced more than I wanted to pay (for a photo), so it is not shown yet!

It has been fifteen years since I first verified the existence of green Coronation. The green pieces at the bottom of page 47 are from Anchor Hocking's morgue and the ones in the top picture are a couple of pieces I have found while "out and about." The larger green tumbler in the lower photograph is 5⁷⁄₁₆" tall and holds 14¼ oz. This tumbler has never been seen outside the morgue except for in my picture. For new readers the lower photo was taken at Anchor-Hocking in their morgue. The morgue was so named since it contained examples of past (dead production) patterns made by the company. Unfortunately, this was not well kept. Many examples "walked" or were thrown out or given away over the years. It is now under lock! Who knew Depression glass was going to be so significant? Even movie producers are increasingly concerned to show correct dishes in their period movies! A dealer reported a wonderful sale of Depression ware for such a production.

Amateur dealers still stick big prices on those commonly found red, handled, Coronation berry bowls. They have always been plentiful and some years ago a large accumulation was discovered in an old warehouse. They are hard to sell; yet, I regularly see them priced for two to three times their worth. They are usually marked "rare" or "old" or "pigeon blood." That "pigeon blood" terminology comes from old time collectors who used that term to describe dark red glass (not made from the blood of dead birds). One dealer assured me that his Royal Ruby goblets were rare "old pigeon blood" pieces, and very valuable! He thought so — since they were priced at $30.00 each!

Royal Ruby Coronation cups were sold on crystal saucers. Those crystal saucer/sherbet plates and cups are the only common crystal pieces found in Coronation. Other crystal pieces are beginning to turn up, but there is little demand for these at present. No Royal Ruby Coronation saucer/sherbet plates have ever been seen. I would not go so far as to say that red saucers do not exist. If I have learned anything in the last 25 years, it is never to say some piece of glass was never made. Royal Ruby is the name of the **red glass that was made by Hocking** and only their red glassware can be called Royal Ruby.

	Pink	Royal Ruby	Green
Bowl, 4¼" berry, handled	4.50	7.00	
Bowl, 4¼", no handles	75.00		45.00
Bowl, 6½" nappy, handled	6.00	12.00	
Bowl, 8" large berry, handled	8.50	15.00	
Bowl, 8", no handles	150.00		175.00
Cup	5.50	6.50	
Pitcher, 7¾", 68 oz.	550.00		
Plate, 6", sherbet	2.00		
Plate, 8½" luncheon	4.50	10.00	45.00
* Saucer (same as 6" plate)	2.00		
Sherbet	5.00		75.00
Tumbler, 5", 10 oz. ftd.	30.00		175.00

* Crystal $.50

Please refer to Foreword for pricing information

CREMAX MacBETH-EVANS DIVISION OF CORNING GLASS WORKS, Late 1930s–Early 1940s

Colors: Cremax, Cremax with fired-on colored trim or decals.

Canadian readers have thanked me for adding the blue Cremax to the book. I have been informed by readers that, as I surmised last time, the lighter "robin egg" blue was distributed by Corning almost exclusively in Canada. Most of the pieces I have found have been in northern states. Notice the distinctly different hues of blue as well as the two shapes. The Delphite colored blue has the same shapes as what we are familiar with, but the "robin egg" blue has a flat sugar and creamer and a slightly smaller cup. At this time, price both shades of blue about the same as the pieces with decals. You might have a difficult time assembling a set of the light blue unless you live near the Canadian border or cultivate dealers who do a lot of traveling in northern states! Barring this, there is always the Internet!

The green castle decal is the most difficult decal to find. The one piece pictured in the top photo on page 49 is the only piece I have ever found! Besides collectors seeking the red floral decorated Cremax (bottom page 49), there is not much activity in this pattern. Like Chinex, the undecorated ware should be **usable** in the microwave; but be sure to test it before putting it in for a long time. A Cremax set could be collected without imposing a complete drain on the checkbook.

I found an 11½" Cremax sandwich plate decorated with the same red floral design as is found on Petalware (page 170). If you have pieces with this red floral design or additional decorations, let me know about those and I will pass the information to collectors.

Cremax demitasse sets are being found in sets of eight. Some have been on a wire rack. The usual make-up of these sets has been two sets each of four colors: pink, yellow, blue, and green. I have finally obtained three of these to show you.

Persistently the bottom to the butter dish in Chinex is believed to be Cremax. The scalloped edges of the butter bottom are just like the edges on Cremax plates; however, the only tops to the butter ever found have the Chinex **scroll-like pattern**. If you find only the bottom of a butter, it is a Chinex bottom! There have been no Cremax butters found — so far!

Another dilemma surrounds the pattern name Cremax. The beige-like **color** made by MacBeth-Evans is also called Cremax. Be aware that two glass companies used the name, one for a color, one for a pattern!

	Cremax	*Blue, Decal Decorated		Cremax	*Blue, Decal Decorated
Bowl, 5¾" cereal	3.50	7.50	Plate, 6¼" bread and butter	2.00	4.00
Bowl, 7¾" soup	7.00	20.00	Plate, 9¾" dinner	4.50	10.00
Bowl, 9" vegetable	8.00	15.00	Plate, 11½" sandwich	5.50	12.00
Creamer	4.50	8.00	Saucer	2.00	3.50
Cup	4.00	5.00	Saucer, demitasse	5.00	10.00
Cup, demitasse	15.00	25.00	Sugar, open	4.50	8.00

*Add 50% for castle decal

"CROW'S FOOT," PADEN CITY GLASS COMPANY, LINE 412 & LINE 890, 1930s

Colors: Ritz blue, Ruby red, amber, amethyst, black, pink, crystal, white, and yellow.

Pricing "Crow's Foot" for this book has been an experience. New collectors are causing inflation in this pattern and there is no Greenspan to slow it down! "Crow's Foot" is the most commonly used blank for Paden City etchings. The squared shape is Line #412, and the round is Line #890. Collectors formerly searching for Orchid or Peacock & Rose etched patterns are setting their eyes on "Crow's Foot" blanks to satisfy their collecting needs.

A red "Crow's Foot" punch bowl has been found. There are similar punch bowls without the telltale "Crow's Foot" pattern on them. Similar is not enough! If I had a dollar for every time I have heard, "It's just like that, except..." over the years, I would not have to write any more books! No exceptions! Perhaps a blue punch set could surface; so keep your eyes peeled! Tumblers remain evasive with Ruby red tumblers creating special problems for collectors wishing a brilliant red color. Many "Crow's Foot" pieces tend to run to amberina (especially tumblers), instead of true red. Some collectors will do without before they add a piece showing yellow color. Amberina is a collector's term for the yellowish tint in pieces that were supposed to be red. It was originally a not thoroughly heated glass mistake and not a color that glass manufacturers tried to make! However, there are now other collectors who seek this amberina colored ware!

	Red	Black/ Blue	Other Colors
Bowl, 4⅞", square	25.00	30.00	12.50
Bowl, 8¾" sq.	50.00	55.00	25.00
Bowl, 6"	30.00	35.00	15.00
Bowl, 6½", rd., 2½" high, 3½" base	45.00	50.00	22.50
Bowl, 8½", square, 2-hdld.	50.00	60.00	27.50
Bowl, 10", ftd.	75.00	75.00	32.50
Bowl, 10", square, 2-hdld.	65.00	75.00	32.50
Bowl, 11", oval	35.00	42.50	17.50
Bowl, 11", square	60.00	70.00	30.00
Bowl, 11", square, rolled edge	65.00	75.00	32.50
Bowl, 11½", 3 ftd., round console	85.00	100.00	42.50
Bowl, 11½", console	75.00	85.00	37.50
Bowl, cream soup, ftd./flat	20.00	22.50	10.00
Bowl, Nasturtium, 3 ftd.	185.00	210.00	90.00
Bowl, whipped cream, 3 ftd.	55.00	65.00	27.50
Cake plate, sq., low pedestal ft.	85.00	95.00	42.50
Candle, round base, tall	75.00	85.00	37.50
Candle, square, mushroom	37.50	42.50	20.00
Candlestick, 5¾"	25.00	30.00	12.50
Candy w/cover, 6½", 3 part (2 styles)	65.00	75.00	25.00
Candy, 3 ftd., rd., 6⅛" wide, 3¼" high	150.00	185.00	75.00
Cheese stand, 5"	25.00	30.00	12.50
Comport, 3¼" tall, 6¼" wide	27.50	32.50	15.00
Comport 4¾" tall, 7⅜" wide	50.00	60.00	35.00
Comport, 6⅝" tall, 7" wide	60.00	75.00	30.00
Creamer, flat	12.50	15.00	6.50
Creamer, ftd.	12.50	15.00	6.50
Cup, ftd. or flat	10.00	12.50	5.00
Gravy boat, flat	85.00	100.00	40.00
Gravy boat, pedestal	135.00	150.00	65.00
Mayonnaise, 3 ftd.	45.00	55.00	22.50
Plate, 5¾"	2.25	3.50	1.25
Plate, 8", round	9.00	11.00	4.50

	Red	Black/ Blue	Other Colors
Plate, 8½", square	7.00	9.00	3.50
Plate, 9¼", round, small dinner	35.00	40.00	15.00
Plate, 9½", rd., 2-hdld.	65.00	75.00	32.50
Plate, 10⅜", rd., 2-hdld.	50.00	60.00	25.00
Plate, 10⅜", sq., 2-hdld.	40.00	50.00	20.00
Plate, 10½", dinner	90.00	100.00	40.00
Plate, 11", cracker	45.00	50.00	22.50
Platter, 12"	27.50	32.50	15.00
Relish, 11", 3 pt.	85.00	100.00	45.00
Sandwich server, rd., center-hdld.	65.00	75.00	32.50
Sandwich server, sq., center-hdld.	45.00	50.00	17.50
Saucer, 6", round	2.50	3.00	1.00
Saucer, 6", square	3.00	3.50	1.50
Sugar, flat	11.00	13.50	5.50
Sugar, ftd.	11.00	13.50	5.50
Tumbler, 4¼"	75.00	85.00	37.50
Vase, 4⅝" tall, 4⅛" wide	60.00	70.00	40.00
Vase, 10¼", cupped	95.00	100.00	45.00
Vase, 10¼", flared	85.00	95.00	32.50
Vase, 11¾", flared	135.00	175.00	65.00

CUBE, "CUBIST" JEANNETTE GLASS COMPANY, 1929–1933

Colors: Pink, green, crystal, amber, white, Ultra Marine, canary yellow, and blue.

Cube is a pattern design that captures the eye of non-collectors. It is frequently confused with Fostoria's American by novice collectors, especially the crystal Cube 3⁹⁄₁₆" creamer and 3" sugar on the 7½" round tray. Very little Cube was made in crystal and very little Fostoria American was made in green. Too, the only original pink Fostoria American was really a lavender/pink; so those colors should be no problem. Cube is less vibrant and more wavy in appearance when compared to the brighter, clearer quality of Fostoria's American pattern. If you find a Cube-like pitcher shaped differently than the ones pictured on page 53, you probably are the victim of Indiana's Whitehall pattern that is in current production. I've been getting a lot of letters about these pitchers! Other pieces of Cube-like pink Whitehall and a darker shade of green are also being made. Cube tumblers are flat as pictured. If you see footed tumblers in color, they are also Whitehall.

Prices for pink Cube pitchers and tumblers are steadily rising. Nearly all collectors are looking for four, six, or eight tumblers; as a result, it usually takes longer to find all these tumblers than the pitcher. Be sure to check the pointed sides of the tumblers and pitchers since they chipped on the sides long before the heavy rims did!

Green Cube is more troublesome to find than the pink, but there are more collectors for pink. The only difficulty in collecting pink (after finding it), is locating it in the right hue. Pink Cube varies from a light pink to an orange-pink. This illustrates how difficult it was for glass factories in the Depression to consistently mass produce **quality** glassware. As glass tanks got hotter, the pink color got lighter. The orange shade of pink is almost as troublesome to sell as it is difficult to match. However, I did notice a collector buying an orange-pink Cube pitcher at a market recently. I overheard her tell the dealer she didn't much care for the color — but at least she'd have a pitcher, now. This again illustrates to me that as supplies dwindle, off colors are becoming more palatable than they once were! There are also two distinct shades of green. For now, the darker shade of green is not as desirable as the ordinarily found green. Both colors of Cube create problems when ordering by mail if you want your colors to match. That is one reason it is preferable to attend Depression glass shows and see what you are buying! You might even be willing to pay a little more for that convenience!

The Cube powder jar is three footed and shown to the left of the lower photo. A few experimental colors have turned up in these. Canary yellow and blue are two colors that have appeared in recent years. Occasionally, these jars are found with celluloid or plastic lids. Powder jars were not made with those lids at the factory. These may have been replacements when tops were broken. Another possibility is that powder bottoms were bought from Jeannette and non-glass lids were made up elsewhere to fit the bottoms. In any case, prices below are for intact, original glass lids. The powder jars with other types of lids sell for half or less. As with most items having lids, it was the top that was most often destroyed, leaving behind far too many bottoms. In any instance, a celluloid lid is better than no lid at all!

	Pink	Green
Bowl, 4½" dessert	6.50	7.00
* Bowl, 4½" deep	8.00	
** Bowl, 6½" salad	10.00	15.00
Butter dish and cover	65.00	65.00
Butter dish bottom	20.00	20.00
Butter dish top	45.00	45.00
Candy jar and cover, 6½"	30.00	33.00
Coaster, 3¼"	7.00	7.50
*** Creamer, 2⅝"	2.00	
Creamer, 3⁹⁄₁₆"	6.00	9.00
Cup	7.50	9.00
Pitcher, 8¾", 45 oz.	210.00	235.00
Plate, 6" sherbet	3.50	4.00
Plate, 8" luncheon	6.50	7.00
Powder jar and cover, 3 legs	27.50	27.50
Salt and pepper, pr.	35.00	35.00
Saucer	2.50	2.50
Sherbet, ftd.	7.00	7.50
*** Sugar, 2⅝"	2.00	
Sugar, 3"	7.00	8.00
Sugar/candy cover	15.00	15.00
Tray for 3⁹⁄₁₆" creamer and sugar, 7½" (crystal only)	4.00	
Tumbler, 4", 9 oz.	67.50	72.50

* Ultra Marine – $35.00
** Ultra Marine – $70.00
*** Amber or white – $3.00; crystal $1.00

Please refer to Foreword for pricing information

"CUPID" PADEN CITY GLASS COMPANY, 1930s

Colors: Pink, green, light blue, peacock blue, black, canary yellow, amber, and crystal.

In Paden City glassware "Cupid" is again leading the way on price increases! I mentioned that "Crows Foot" prices have increased because collectors were not finding much etched Paden City glassware. Well, those who have found "Cupid" etched pieces have been paying up to double the prices from the last book! Other etchings are up an average of 20 to 30 percent. All that scouring every nook and cranny to find any piece of "Cupid" must have worked because I have seen more "Cupid" pieces for sale in the last year than at any time in the past. People have been known to buy **one** piece of this pattern just to own an appealing piece of glass. You can be a collector with only a few pieces that you like!

There are several new pieces of "Cupid" to report. A bottom to a tumble up has been found; alas, there was no tumbler with it. I tried to buy it to picture, but it was not for sale! A 10" vase, like the ones commonly found in Peacock & Rose, was brought into a show for me to look at, but it was not for sale either. Pink and green casseroles have been found in Washington, Texas, and Florida. I previously have pictured one in black with a silver overlaid pattern.

Blue "Cupid" pieces found include a 10½" plate, mayonnaise, and a 6¼" comport. It surely would be nice to find a liner and spoon for that mayo! Got one?

Samovars are rarely found, but are fetching "big bucks" when they are! I might point out that to be a **"Cupid"** samovar, the "Cupid" pattern has to be etched on it. I bought one through the mail that was "just like the blue one in the book." However, when it arrived there was a Cambridge etch on it and not a cupid in sight. When I called, the dealer just did not understand that the "Cupid" etch had to be on the piece for it to be "Cupid." Never **assume** anything!

Prices are the toughest part of writing this book. Even with all the help from other dealers around the country, prices will never please everyone. If you own a piece, you want it to be highly priced; however, if you are wanting to buy the same piece and do not own it, you want the price to be low! **Keep in mind that one sale at a high price does not mean that everyone would be willing to pay that price.** That is especially true of rare glass. Ultimately, only **you** can determine whether a piece of glass is worth that price to you. The dealer sets an asking price, and you have to decide if you will pay that price. No one can tell you what to pay!

New discoveries in Paden City glassware are the norm rather than unusual! Most pieces were shown in catalogs with no etchings; and until a piece shows up with a Paden City etching, there is no way to know if it exists in that pattern.

Those center-handled pieces were called sandwich trays and the odd, center-handled bowls of Paden City were called candy trays.

A cobalt vase with silver overlay was brought to me in Miami a few years ago. It was the wrong color and shape to be "Cupid," yet it had the design! I looked at the bottom and saw the words "Made in Germany" there. The collector was shocked when I showed him since he had never noticed those words. Hold on! This is not the only piece. Cathy and I have found two other vases since then. One is yet a different shaped cobalt vase and the other is a stately lavender. They both have silver overlays of the exact "Cupid" pattern found on the Paden City pieces. Also, someone in Arizona notified me of finding one of these German cobalt vases. How this happened is beyond me, but with Europe's doors opening wider, we may see some other mysteries unveiled in the future. If anyone knows anything more about these pieces, I would enjoy hearing from you.

	Green/Pink		Green/Pink
Bowl, 8½" oval-ftd.	250.00	Ice bucket, 6"	295.00
Bowl, 9¼" ftd. fruit	275.00	Ice tub, 4¾"	295.00
Bowl, 9¼" center-handled	225.00	*** Lamp, silver overlay	425.00
Bowl, 10¼", fruit	200.00	**** Mayonnaise, 6" diameter,	
Bowl, 10½", rolled edge	195.00	fits on 8" plate, spoon, 3 pc.	195.00
Bowl, 11" console	195.00	***** Plate, 10½"	150.00
Cake plate, 11¾"	195.00	Samovar	850.00
Cake stand, 2" high, ftd.	195.00	Sugar, flat	150.00
Candlestick, 5" wide, pr.	225.00	Sugar, 4¼" ftd.	135.00
Candy w/lid, ftd., 5¼" high	395.00	Sugar, 5" ftd.	135.00
Candy w/lid, 3 part	275.00	Tray, 10¾" center-handled	185.00
* Casserole, covered	350.00	Tray, 10⅞" oval-ftd.	225.00
** Comport, 6¼"	185.00	Vase, 8¼" elliptical	595.00
Creamer, flat	150.00	Vase, fan-shaped	425.00
Creamer, 4½" ftd.	135.00	Vase, 10"	300.00
Creamer, 5" ftd.	135.00		

* black (silver overlay) $500.00   ** blue – $225.00   *** possibly German   **** blue – $295.00   ***** blue – $225.00

Please refer to Foreword for pricing information

DELLA ROBBIA #1058 WESTMORELAND GLASS COMPANY, Late 1920s – 1940s

Colors: Crystal w/applied lustre colors, milk glass.

I received several dozen letters from collectors thanking me for including Della Robbia in my eleventh edition. There were many collectors of Della Robbia who had no idea what pieces were made. Its popularity has extended to new collectors and supplies of many pieces are beginning to be sorely depleted. My listing is only a beginning from catalog information that I own. Hopefully, you will let me know of additional pieces or of other catalog information to which you may have access.

You will find Della Robbia in crystal, milk glass, and crystal with applied lustre colors. Notice that the fruits on each piece are apples, pears, and grapes. A similar pattern has bananas in the design; do not confuse the patterns.

Note that Della Robbia is Pattern #1058. On page 62 at the bottom of the catalog reprint are candlesticks and a console bowl in Pattern #1067. They are not priced in my listings and neither is the Zodiac plate on page 63 because they are not Della Robbia!

There are two distinct color variations in the fruit decorations. All apples are red; pears, yellow; and grapes, purple; but the intensity of the colors applied is distinct. Look at the pictures on page 59 and compare them to the pieces at the bottom of page 58. The darker colored fruits on page 59 are the variation that is most in demand. The dilemma with this darker color is that the applied lustre scuffs very easily. Presumably, there is no difference in these color varieties, but most collectors prefer not to mix the two.

The dinner plates in pristine condition will cause you sleepless nights as you search for them. All serving pieces need to be carefully examined for wear. Remember the prices below are for mint condition pieces and not ones that are worn or scuffed.

The punch set on page 58 is rarely seen; but if you ever tried to cart around an 18" plate, you will understand why you see so few of these for sale at shows.

For the listings, I should discuss some terminology of Westmoreland. Cupped means turned in from the outside as opposed to belled which is turned out from the inside. The flanged pieces have an edge that is parallel to the base of the piece.

The sweetmeat is the comport shown to the right rear of the bottom photograph on page 59. In the same picture is the 14" footed salver or cake plate. The indentation in the center must have made for interesting cakes. I guess they had bundt pans before I was aware of them! The two-part candy with the ruffled bottom is the one shown on the left in that shot. Its catalog description is "candy jar, scalloped edge, w/cover."

The moulds of a Della Robbia pitcher and tumbler were used to make some carnival colored water sets. These were made for Levay just as were pieces of red English Hobnail. In any case, they were made in light blue and amethyst carnival and maybe another color. If you have more information than this, share it please!

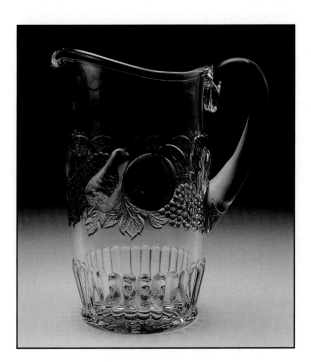

DELLA ROBBIA (Cont.)

Basket, 9"	195.00	Plate, 6", finger liner	10.00
Basket, 12"	295.00	Plate, 6⅛", bread & butter	10.00
Bowl, 4½", nappy	27.50	Plate, 7¼", salad	22.00
Bowl, 5", finger	35.00	Plate, 9", luncheon	35.00
Bowl, 6", nappy, bell	35.00	Plate, 10½", dinner	100.00
Bowl, 6½", one hdld. nappy	35.00	Plate, 14", torte	95.00
Bowl, 7½", nappy	42.00	Plate, 18"	185.00
Bowl, 8", bell nappy	50.00	Plate, 18", upturned edge, punch bowl liner	185.00
Bowl, 8", bell, hdld.	65.00	Platter, 14", oval	165.00
Bowl, 8", heart, hdld.	125.00	Punch bowl set, 15 pc.	650.00
Bowl, 9", nappy	75.00	Salt and pepper, pr.	55.00
Bowl, 12", ftd.	125.00	Salver, 14", ftd., cake	135.00
Bowl, 13", rolled edge	125.00	Saucer	10.00
Bowl, 14", oval, flange	195.00	Stem, 3 oz., wine	25.00
Bowl, 14", punch	250.00	Stem, 3¼ oz., cocktail	22.00
Bowl, 15", bell	200.00	Stem, 5 oz., 4¾", sherbet, high foot	20.00
Candle, 4"	35.00	Stem, 5 oz., sherbet, low foot	18.00
Candle, 4", 2-lite	85.00	Stem, 6 oz., champagne	22.00
Candy jar w/cover, scalloped edge	85.00	Stem, 8 oz., 6", water	30.00
Candy, round, flat, chocolate	80.00	Sugar, ftd.	15.00
Comport, 6½", 3⅝" high, mint, ftd.	30.00	Tumbler, 5 oz., ginger ale	25.00
Comport, 8", sweetmeat, bell	110.00	Tumbler, 8 oz., ftd.	30.00
Comport, 12", ftd., bell	125.00	Tumbler, 8 oz., water	25.00
Comport, 13", flanged	125.00	Tumbler 11 oz., iced tea, ftd.	32.00
Creamer, ftd.	16.00	Tumbler 12 oz., iced tea, bell	35.00
Cup, coffee	18.00	Tumbler 12 oz., iced tea, bell, ftd.	35.00
Cup, punch	15.00	Tumbler 12 oz., 5³⁄₁₆", iced tea, straight	40.00
Pitcher, 32 oz.	225.00		

DELLA ROBBIA

Westmoreland's Handmade,
Hand=Decorated Crystal

WESTMORELAND GLASS COMPANY
GRAPEVILLE, PENNSYLVANIA

Handmade Glassware
of Quality
SINCE 1889

"Della Robbia" in deep Lustre Colors

1058/9"
Plate

1058
Candy Jar

1058
Sherbet

1058
Ice Tea

1058
Goblet

1058
Mint

1058
Nappy, Heart

1058
Sugar/Cream

757
Basket

1058
Candle

1058
Bowl, Bell

1058
Candle

1058/14"
Plate

1067
Candle

1067
Bowl

1067
Candle

1067
Plate

"Della Robbia" Pattern in Crystal with Applied Lustre Colors.

"Della Robbia"

"Zodiac"
Plate

TOP ROW: 1058/9″/L126. Plate, Luncheon.
1058/7½″/L126. Plate, Salad.
1058/8 oz./L126. Goblet.
1058/11 oz./L126. Ice Tea, Footed.
1058/8 oz./L126. Tumbler, Footed.
1058/L126/3¼ oz. Cocktail.
1058/L126. Sherbet, Low Foot.

SECOND ROW: 1058/L126. Sugar and Cream

Set, Individual. "Della Robbia."
1058/L126. Salt, with Chrome Top.
1058/L126. Pepper, with Chrome Top.
1058/L126. Cup and Saucer.
1058/8 oz./L126. Tumbler.
1058/6½″/L126. Nappy, Cupped, Handled.

THIRD ROW: 1058/6½″/L126. Mint, Footed.
1058/4″/L126. Candlestick.

1058/12″/L126. Bowl, Bell.
1058/½ lb./L126. Candy Jar and Cover.
1058/4½″/L126. Nappy, Round.

BOTTOM ROW: 1058/14″/L126. Plate, Torte.
1058/8″/L126. Nappy, Heart Shape, Handled.
25/15″/L126. Plate, "Zodiac." Pictures the twelve signs of the Zodiac. An attractive serving piece for sandwiches or canapes.

DIAMOND QUILTED, "FLAT DIAMOND" IMPERIAL GLASS COMPANY, Late 1920s–Early 1930s

Colors: Pink, blue, green, crystal, black; some red and amber.

Large sets of Diamond Quilted can only be collected in pink or green. Not all pieces are found in the other colors. Red and amber Diamond Quilted are rarely found. There are few collectors of either color, but red and amber colors are elusive in case you find a piece or two. Blue and black colored pieces can be found with searching, but it will take a long time to accumulate a luncheon set of either color unless you get lucky enough to find a complete set.

Unfortunately, Diamond Quilted has no dinner-sized plate. Lack of a dinner plate stops a few collectors from further pursuit who plan on entertaining with their collection! I have always said that you should collect what you like. With some creativity, you can enjoy a less than perfect sized pattern. One very svelte young individual told me 1930s small size luncheon plates were a "plus" in her mind. "The plate fills up faster; and you need less food!"

There is a Hazel Atlas quilted diamond pitcher and tumbler set made in pink, green, cobalt blue, and a light blue similar to the blue shown here that is often confused with Imperial's Diamond Quilted. The quilting on Hazel Atlas pieces ends in a **straight line** around the top of each piece. Notice **Imperial's** Diamond Quilted pattern ends **unevenly** in points. You may also notice that the diamond designs on Hazel Atlas pieces are flat as opposed to those Imperial ones that are curved. While we are discussing what is and what isn't, I failed to mention that the two blue baskets pictured in both the eleventh and twelfth editions of *Collector's Encyclopedia of Depression Glass* were both made by Fenton!

Punch bowls are the creme de la creme of this pattern. Two collectors told me that they started collecting Diamond Quilted only after spotting a punch bowl for the first time.

Flat black pieces have the design on the bottom. Thus, the design on the plate can only be seen if it is turned over. Other black items have the pattern on the inside.

The candle shown in the catalog ad at the bottom of the page is sometimes confused with Windsor Diamond. Console sets at 65¢ and a dozen candy dishes in assorted colors for $6.95 would be quite a bargain today! No, I do not have any for sale at that price. This ad is from a 1930s catalog. I mention that since I get about 10 letters every year from people trying to order glass from these old catalog ads placed throughout the book! They even send their Visa or MasterCard number and ask that I send several sets. Nobody ever orders just **one** set. It has to be multiples! One individual said she understood if I had to add postal charges to the order. Considering the ad states the six sets weigh thirty pounds, she was being generous! One lady wrote three times! I am still not sure she ever understood that these were 67-year-old advertisement prices!

	Pink, Green	Blue, Black		Pink, Green	Blue, Black
Bowl, 4¾" cream soup	10.00	20.00	Pitcher, 64 oz.	50.00	
Bowl, 5" cereal	7.50	15.00	Plate, 6" sherbet	4.00	5.00
Bowl, 5½" one handle	7.50	18.00	Plate, 7" salad	6.00	9.00
Bowl, 7" crimped edge	9.00	18.00	Plate, 8" luncheon	6.00	12.00
Bowl, 10½", rolled edge console	20.00	60.00	Punch bowl and stand	450.00	
Cake salver, tall 10" diameter	60.00		Plate, 14" sandwich	15.00	
Candlesticks (2 styles), pr.	25.00	50.00	Sandwich server, center handle	25.00	50.00
Candy jar and cover, ftd.	65.00		Saucer	3.00	5.00
Compote, 6" tall, 7¼" wide	45.00		Sherbet	5.00	14.00
Compote and cover, 11½"	95.00		Sugar	8.00	17.50
Creamer	8.00	17.50	Tumbler, 9 oz. water	9.00	
Cup	9.50	17.50	Tumbler, 12 oz. iced tea	9.00	
Goblet, 1 oz. cordial	12.00		Tumbler, 6 oz. ftd.	8.50	
Goblet, 2 oz. wine	12.00		Tumbler, 9 oz. ftd.	12.50	
Goblet, 3 oz. wine	12.00		Tumbler, 12 oz. ftd.	15.00	
Goblet, 6", 9 oz. champagne	11.00		Vase, fan, dolphin handles	55.00	75.00
Ice bucket	55.00	85.00	Whiskey, 1½ oz.	8.00	
Mayonnaise set: ladle, plate, comport	36.00	56.00			

Covered Bowl—6⅜ in. diam., deep round shape with 3 artistic feet, dome cover, fine quality brilliant finish **pot glass**, allover block diamond design, transparent Rose Marie and emerald green.
1 C5603—Asstd. ½ doz. in carton, 20 lbs.
Doz $6.95

1 C989—3 piece set, 2 transparent colors (rose and green), good quality, 10½ in. rolled rim bowl, TWO 3½ in. wide base candlesticks. Asstd. 6 sets in case, 30 lbs. .... SET (3 pcs) 65¢

DIANA FEDERAL GLASS COMPANY, 1937–1941

Colors: Pink, amber, and crystal.

Pink Diana has sustained a few price increases of late, and that could be an indicator that other colors are soon to adopt that trend. Those price advances are not as exorbitant as they were five or six years ago when many new collectors started this pattern about the same time! Diana is one of the **used-to-be less expensive** patterns! A bevy of collectors all searching for the same pattern will often dry up precious supplies very quickly. Diana is not as available as it once was and collectors have been paying more to finish sets that they started!

Pink Diana is still **the** color to collect. Some amber and a little crystal sell occasionally, but it is pink that is snatched up as soon as a piece is spotted. Collectors of crystal Diana have found out what collectors of other colors noticed years ago. There are a small number of tumblers available! Tumblers, demitasse sets, candy dishes, shakers, sherbets, and even platters are seldom found in any Diana colors. There are fewer demitasse sets being marketed than in the past. These sets in crystal are more plentiful, as are the sprayed-on cranberry pink or red sets. Flashed red demitasses are selling for $10.00 to $12.00 each. Pink demitasse cup and saucer sets are found occasionally, but you will have to search long and hard for an entire pink set of six on a rack!

The prices listed below are **actual selling** prices of Diana and **not advertised prices.** There is a **major difference** between an advertised price for an item and the price actually being accepted by both buyer and seller. Rarely have I heard of something selling for more than advertised, but often I have heard of less! Today, dealers coast to coast are sharing information on prices realized on glassware. That's been a tremendous equalizer and help to me as I work to keep pricing current in these books! I attend as many Depression glass shows as possible and spend many hours checking prices and talking to dealers about what is and what is not selling — and for what price!

I have now added the price for the amber 9" salad bowl that was inadvertently left out of earlier editions even though it was pictured. Sorry! Thanks for pointing it out!

Frosted or satinized pieces of Diana that have shown up in crystal or pink have a few admirers. Some crystal frosted pieces have been trimmed in colors, predominantly red. A set of frosted items with different colored trims is not as strange looking as you might imagine! However, completing any of these specialty sets is a major dilemma!

New collectors often confuse Diana with other swirled patterns such as Swirl and Twisted Optic. The centers of Diana pieces are swirled where the centers of other patterns are plain. That elusive and somewhat odd Diana sherbet is shown in amber and in pink. The spirals on this sherbet are often mistaken for Spiral by Hocking and it causes debate as to authenticity; but it is shown in an original advertisement for Diana. As with many other patterns, pieces advertised along with a pattern are often accepted as that pattern. An excellent example is the Moderntone tumbler.

I have seen pictures of one collector's "rainbow" Diana collection — a mixture of the colors. It was charming as she'd arranged it! Creativity is always a plus!

	Crystal	Pink	Amber
* Ash tray, 3½"	2.50	3.50	
Bowl, 5" cereal	6.00	10.00	12.00
Bowl, 5½" cream soup	8.00	25.00	17.50
Bowl, 9" salad	10.00	20.00	20.00
Bowl, 11" console fruit	12.00	40.00	20.00
Bowl, 12" scalloped edge	12.00	30.00	20.00
Candy jar and cover, round	16.00	45.00	40.00
Coaster, 3½"	2.50	7.00	10.00
Creamer, oval	5.00	12.00	9.00
Cup	3.00	18.00	7.00
Cup, 2 oz. demitasse and 4½" saucer set	13.00	45.00	
Plate, 6" bread & butter	1.50	4.00	2.00
Plate, 9½"	5.00	16.00	9.00
Plate, 11¾" sandwich	8.00	25.00	10.00
Platter, 12" oval	9.00	30.00	13.00
Salt and pepper, pr.	25.00	75.00	100.00
Saucer	1.50	5.00	2.00
Sherbet	3.00	12.00	10.00
Sugar, open oval	5.00	12.00	8.00
Tumbler, 4⅛", 9 oz.	25.00	45.00	27.50
Junior set: 6 demitasse cups & saucers with round rack	100.00	300.00	

* Green $3.00

DOGWOOD, "APPLE BLOSSOM," "WILD ROSE" MacBETH-EVANS GLASS COMPANY, 1929–1932

Colors: Pink, green, some crystal, Monax, Cremax, and yellow.

Dogwood reigns as one of the more popular Depression patterns! Pink is the color most collected; and that is good because green is being found infrequently. I mentioned that I had not found a pink Dogwood large bowl or platter in almost five years in the last book. Within a few months of that writing I found a large bowl and not one, but two platters! It has taken two years to find homes for those platters at the current quadrupled price!

One of the reasons that the large fruit bowls are so difficult to find is that these were sold to someone who frosted the bowls, drilled a hole in the center, and made ceiling globes out of them. These globes sell in the $125.00 range. There is a growing trend among collectors to own Depression glass shades. It's a shame so many bowls were made into shades, but at least they can still be put to use!

There is an adequate supply of pitchers and most sizes of tumblers in both colors, but price may be an obstacle! Only the pink juice tumbler is rarely found, but the price has escalated, and few collectors buy more than one!

There are tumblers that have the same shape as the Dogwood tumblers, but are missing the Dogwood silk screening. These are **not** Dogwood without the design! There are pitchers shaped like Dogwood that do not have the silk screen design of Dogwood. These are **not** Dogwood either! They are merely the blanks made by MacBeth-Evans to go with the plain, no design tumblers that they made and sold separately with various sets of their pink patterns! The pattern (Dogwood) has to be silk screened onto the pitcher for it to be considered Dogwood and to command those prices shown below. Many collectors have bought these blanks to use with their sets, however; and that's perfectly fine. It is also easier on the pocketbook to replace a $8.00 or $10.00 tumbler than one that costs $50.00! However, I've gotten letters from unknowing collectors who've been duped into paying high (Dogwood) prices for these plain tumblers. Don't!

Few pieces of yellow are being found, but there is not much demand for it either. It is a rare color in Dogwood!

Cremax (beige) and Monax (white) are rare colors of Dogwood that unfortunately do not excite many collectors. See a description and photo of these MacBeth-Evans colors under American Sweetheart. The Monax salver (12" plate) is considered hard to find; but, over the years, it has turned out to be more of a novelty with collectors than a highly desired piece. In fact, you can buy them today for less than you could 15 years ago. I used to sell them in the $25.00 range, but have recently had a couple that are not selling at $20.00!

There is a rolled edge cereal bowl being found that is entirely different from the regular cereal. The flattened edge turns outward making it not as tall nor would it hold as much as the normally found cereal. These are being priced in a wide range but will sell for $5.00 to $10.00 more than the regular cereal. How rare these are is debatable. Most collectors never gave them much thought until a few dealers started pricing them higher than the usual cereal.

The pink sugar and creamer illustrate the thick, footed style Dogwood while the green creamer and sugar show the thin, flat style. Pink is found in both styles, but green is only found in the thin variety. Thin creamers were made by adding a spout to thin cups and some of these have a very undefined spout. They look more like lopsided cups. Even though there are thick and thin pink cups, the saucers for both styles are the same. Green cups are only found in thin style.

Pink grill plates come in two styles. Some have the Dogwood pattern all over the plate as the pink one does, and others have the pattern only around the rim of the plate as on the green one pictured. Sherbets, grill plates (rim pattern only), and the large fruit bowls are difficult to accumulate in green Dogwood.

Dogwood sherbets come in two styles. Some have a Dogwood blossom etched on the bottom; some do not. Please be sure to specify which style you are trying to match if ordering. It really makes no difference in price since they are only from different moulds.

Very Rare Glassware of the Depression Years, Second Series has a picture of the only known Dogwood coaster!

	Pink	Green	Monax Cremax		Pink	Green	Monax Cremax
* Bowl, 5½" cereal	32.00	35.00	5.00	Plate, 9¼" dinner	37.50		
Bowl, 8½" berry	60.00	120.00	40.00	Plate, 10½" grill AOP or			
Bowl, 10¼" fruit	525.00	275.00	110.00	border design only	25.00	25.00	
Cake plate, 11" heavy				Plate, 12" salver	30.00		15.00
solid foot	1,000.00			Platter, 12" oval (rare)	650.00		
Cake plate, 13" heavy				Saucer	6.00	6.50	20.00
solid foot	125.00	115.00	195.00	Sherbet, low footed	37.50	110.00	
Coaster, 3¼"	550.00			Sugar, 2½" thin, flat	18.00	45.00	
Creamer, 2½" thin, flat	20.00	47.50		Sugar, 3¼" thick, footed	18.00		
Creamer, 3¼" thick, footed	22.00			Tumbler, 3½", 5 oz.			
Cup, thick	18.00		40.00	decorated	275.00		
Cup, thin	16.00	40.00		Tumbler, 4", 10 oz. decorated	40.00	95.00	
Pitcher, 8", 80 oz. decorated	225.00	500.00		Tumbler, 4¾", 11 oz.			
Pitcher, 8", 80 oz. (American				decorated	45.00	100.00	
Sweetheart Style)	595.00			Tumbler, 5", 12 oz. decorated	65.00	115.00	
Plate, 6" bread and butter	8.00	9.00	21.00	Tumbler, moulded band	22.00		
* Plate, 8" luncheon	7.00	8.00					

* Yellow – $65.00

Please refer to Foreword for pricing information

DORIC JEANNETTE GLASS COMPANY, 1935–1938

Colors: Pink, green, some Delphite, Ultra Marine, and yellow.

Green Doric prices on scarce items continue to increase! Many collectors are searching for more cereal bowls, footed tumblers or cream soups. Those pieces in pink are not common either, but they can all be found with persistent searching except for that cream soup that has never been detected in pink. Cream soups, or consommés as some companies called them, are always **two-handled**. Cereal bowls have no handles. The green, 48 ounce pitcher, with or without the ice lip, is a nemesis for nearly everyone. There have been only a couple found in the last five years.

In spite of the fact that green Doric collecting is a task, it probably will not quickly consume your checking account since you may require years to finish a set. I have had three collectors tell me recently that they do not care how difficult the pattern is to find because it's the "chase" that interests and entertains them as much as the glass itself! "But when you find a piece," one said, "there's **nothing** like that feeling!" (I think this is called a glass "high"!) Although prices for green continue to dominate Doric, some prices in pink are escalating!

Doric collectors should know that there are mould seams on many pieces, especially footed tumblers and cereals. This discourages collectors who are looking for flawlessness. There are collectors who have never seen cereal bowls or footed tumblers! I, personally, would not let a little roughness stop me from owning these pieces if I saw them for sale! Perfection is worthwhile in glass collecting, but it can be carried to extremes. Magnifying glasses are usually confined to coin and stamp collecting; however, I have begun to see this instrument used in our collecting world! A black (ultraviolet) light will show repairs on any glassware that is fluorescent. Pink or blue glass does not "glow," but green and yellow glass does very well!

Since moving to Florida, I have noticed more green Doric than any place I have traveled. One difficulty in buying glass in Florida, however, is cloudy (or "sick") glass. Evidently, well water created mineral deposits that react with the glass. You could make a fortune if you could figure out a way to easily remove these deposits. I know I have heard of everything from Tidy Bowl to Efferdent! As far as I know, this cloudiness cannot be removed short of polishing it out over a period of time. Do not become duped into buying cloudy glass unless it is very inexpensive or you have that magic cure! A reader sent me some concoction that was supposed to remove cloudiness. It had all leaked from the taped container and only succeeded in removing color from our new kitchen counter top where I set the box! It also wiped out the return address and became such a household sore subject that I never pursued it further!

The yellow Doric pitcher in the bottom photo is still the only one known! Large, footed Doric pitchers come with or without an ice lip as shown in the pink. Candy and sugar lids in this pattern are **not interchangeable**. The candy lid is taller and more domed.

I still get letters about Delphite (opaque blue) pieces. The sherbet and cloverleaf candy are commonly found in Delphite. All other Delphite pieces are rare in Doric. The price is still reasonable for so rare a color. Only the pitcher creates much of a pricing stir. There is demand for it!

An iridized, three-part candy was made in the 1970s and sold for 79 cents in our local dish barn. All other colors of the three-part candy are old. You will sometimes find this candy in a piece of hammered aluminum!

The top shown on the pink shaker is the original nickel plated top; the one on the green is a newly made aluminum top. Original tops are favored when available; but there is a choice (new tops) to having no tops at all.

	Pink	Green	Delphite		Pink	Green	Delphite
Bowl, 4½" berry	9.00	10.00	45.00	Plate, 6" sherbet	4.00	5.00	
Bowl, 5" cream soup		395.00		Plate, 7" salad	19.00	22.00	
Bowl, 5½" cereal	65.00	75.00		Plate, 9" dinner			
Bowl, 8¼" large berry	28.00	30.00	125.00	(serrated 150.00)	16.00	19.00	
Bowl, 9" 2-handled	18.00	20.00		Plate, 9" grill	20.00	24.00	
Bowl, 9" oval vegetable	35.00	40.00		Platter, 12" oval	25.00	28.00	
Butter dish and cover	70.00	85.00		Relish tray, 4" x 4"	10.00	10.00	
Butter dish bottom	25.00	32.50		Relish tray, 4" x 8"	12.00	18.00	
Butter dish top	45.00	52.50		Salt and pepper, pr.	35.00	37.50	
Cake plate, 10", 3 legs	22.50	22.50		Saucer	3.50	4.50	
Candy dish and				Sherbet, footed	14.00	16.00	7.00
cover, 8"	37.50	40.00		Sugar	12.00	12.50	
*Candy dish, 3-part	10.00	10.00	12.00	Sugar cover	14.00	25.00	
Coaster, 3"	18.00	18.00		Tray, 10" handled	15.00	18.00	
Creamer, 4"	12.00	14.00		Tray, 8" x 8" serving	22.00	25.00	
Cup	9.00	10.00		Tumbler, 4½", 9 oz.	65.00	100.00	
Pitcher, 5½", 32 oz. flat	37.50	42.50	1,100.00	Tumbler, 4", 10 oz.			
Pitcher, 7½", 48 oz.				footed	65.00	90.00	
footed (yellow at $2,000.00)	650.00	995.00		Tumbler, 5", 12 oz.,			
				footed	80.00	125.00	

*Candy in metal holder – $40.00. Iridescent made recently. Ultra Marine $20.00.

Please refer to Foreword for pricing information

DORIC AND PANSY JEANNETTE GLASS COMPANY, 1937–1938

Colors: Ultra Marine; some crystal and pink.

Ultra Marine Doric and Pansy continues to filter into America from English and Canadian suppliers. Until a few years ago, I had only ever owned six or seven butter dishes in this pattern. Recently, I've bought nine or ten in a two year period! No wonder we always thought Doric and Pansy was rare. It is in the continental United States, but evidently not so outside these boundaries! The price on the butter dish is holding firm, but you can not attend a glass show without seeing one or two butter dishes for sale! (I had a very good contact for Depression glass in England, but lost it when I did not choose to buy overpriced Fostoria American. There is a book circulating among English dealers with retail prices that no one can approach here. Many of the pieces listed are evidently English made but represented as Fostoria American.)

Even though sugars and creamers are also being found along with those butter dishes, their price has not been as adversely affected since they were not so highly priced as the butters. Tumblers and large and small berry bowls are not being found in the accumulations abroad. There are two tumblers pictured on the right. The customarily found tumbler is shaped like the flat Doric tumbler and is shown in front of the rarely found one. Only two of the 4¼", 10 ounce tumblers have been seen. Strangely, there have been no reports of pink Doric and Pansy found abroad. There have also been no reported discoveries of the children's sets in England or Canada — just things needed for serving "tea." So, yes, we know how these Doric and Pansy items were marketed!

Lookout for weak patterned shakers. These should fetch less (20 or 25 percent) than the price listed. If the only way you can tell that the shaker is Doric and Pansy comes from color and shape instead of pattern, then leave it alone unless it is very inexpensive!. Weak pattern and cloudiness occur with the shakers coming from England, also. Remember, cloudy shakers are not worth mint prices! Cloudiness is caused by a chemical reaction between the glass and its contents. As a matter of fact, I have bought enough shakers full of salt and pepper over the years to state that pepper causes as much cloudiness as salt! Usually, the cloudy salt container will wash out, but not the pepper!

Another problem facing collectors of Ultra Marine Doric and Pansy is color deviation. Many pieces have a distinct green cast instead of blue. Few collectors presently buy the green shade of Ultra Marine. Unless you are able to buy an entire lot of the greener shade, you may have trouble trying to resell it. A matching group is easier to sell than a few pieces. Nevertheless, there is a positive side to this greener shade. Usually, you can purchase it at a lower price, and who is to know how it may be valued in the future.

Only berry and children's sets have been found in pink. Only a luncheon set in crystal can be amassed. Sugar and creamer sets in crystal are usually bought by collectors of sugar and creamers rather than Doric and Pansy collectors. Someday, these crystal pieces may turn out to be very desirable!

	Green, Teal	Pink, Crystal		Green, Teal	Pink, Crystal
Bowl, 4½" berry	20.00	10.00	Plate, 7" salad	38.00	
Bowl, 8" large berry	80.00	25.00	Plate, 9" dinner	35.00	12.00
Bowl, 9" handled	35.00	17.50	Salt and pepper, pr.	400.00	
Butter dish and cover	450.00		Saucer	5.00	4.00
Butter dish bottom	70.00		Sugar, open	110.00	75.00
Butter dish top	380.00		Tray, 10" handled	30.00	
Cup	16.00	10.00	Tumbler, 4½", 9 oz.	110.00	
Creamer	115.00	75.00	Tumbler, 4¼", 10 oz.	500.00	
Plate, 6" sherbet	10.00	7.50			

DORIC AND PANSY
"PRETTY POLLY PARTY DISHES"

	Teal	Pink		Teal	Pink
Cup	45.00	35.00	Creamer	45.00	35.00
Saucer	8.00	7.00	Sugar	45.00	35.0
Plate	10.00	8.00	14-Piece set	345.00	275.00

Please refer to Foreword for pricing information

ENGLISH HOBNAIL WESTMORELAND GLASS COMPANY, 1920s–1940s

Colors: Pink, turquoise/ice blue, cobalt blue, green, black, and red.

English Hobnail encompasses both eras of my glassware books. To present some practical sequence, I have placed crystal and amber into the *Collectible Glassware of the 40s, 50s, 60s...* and am including the balance of the colors in this book. It is taking several editions to straighten out each piece that exists in the colors. In the *Collectible Glassware of the 40s, 50s, 60s...* there are numerous pages of catalog listings from the later years of Westmoreland's production (when only amber and crystal were being regularly manufactured). Refer to that book for a company identification guide.

For now, I am compiling two price groupings. Pink and green will make up one column and turquoise/ice blue will make up the other. A piece in **cobalt blue will bring 25 to 30 percent more** than the turquoise blue price listed. Very little cobalt English Hobnail is being found. Turquoise blue, therefore, has more collectors than the cobalt because so many more pieces can be found in that shade of blue and you can see it more in the market.

Bear in mind that some pieces of turquoise were produced in the late 1970s. The later-made production seems to be of poorer quality and deeper color when compared to the older pieces. Note the ruffled comport on the bottom of page 77. This is an example of the later blue. Collectors use the term ice blue and turquoise blue interchangeably; so do not become mystified on that issue. A large collection of turquoise English Hobnail was placed on the market a few years ago. En masse, it was exquisite and captivated the crowd at the show!

Amazingly, a new color, black, has been discovered in English Hobnail. You can see four pieces on the bottom of page 75. Note the flat, pink shaker in the same photograph. This is also a recent discovery. I had a report of a flat shaker in turquoise, but I did not see it. You never know what may turn up even in patterns that have been collected for years!

A set of English Hobnail can be gathered in pink or green with time and perseverance. English Hobnail is another pattern that has color inconsistencies. Pink is the easiest color to find, but there are two distinct shades of pink. There are three different greens, from a light, yellow-green to a deep, dark green. Some collectors mix shades of color, but others cannot endure mixing them. That only becomes a dilemma when you have searched for ages for a specific piece; and then find it, in the wrong hue. Many collectors are beginning to soften their stances on mixing various shades of the same pattern! Indeed, a growing number of them are doing so deliberately — and referring to them as their "rainbow collections."

For new collectors, here is how to distinguish English Hobnail from Miss America. The centers of English Hobnail pieces have rays of varying distances. Notice the upright pieces in the photographs for this six-point star effect. In Miss America, shown on page 128, the center rays all end equidistant from the center. The hobs on English Hobnail are more rounded and feel smoother to the touch; goblets flare and the hobs go directly into a plain rim area. Miss America's hobs are sharper to touch and the goblets do not flare at the rim. All goblets and tumblers of Miss America have three sets of rings above the hobs before entering a plain glass rim. If you have a candy jar that measures more or less than 11½" including the cover, then it is most likely English Hobnail. The Miss America candy jar measures 11½".

	Pink/Green	Turquoise/ *Ice Blue		Pink/Green	Turquoise/ *Ice Blue
Ash tray, 3"	20.00		Bowl, 6½", grapefruit	22.00	
Ash tray, 4½"		22.50	Bowl, 6½", round nappy	20.00	
Ash tray, 4½", sq.	25.00		Bowl, 7", round nappy	22.00	
Bon bon, 6½", handled	25.00	37.50	Bowl, 8", cupped, nappy	30.00	
Bottle, toilet, 5 oz.	25.00	50.00	Bowl, 8", ftd.	45.00	
Bowl, 3", cranberry	17.00		Bowl, 8", hexagonal ftd., 2-handled	75.00	110.00
Bowl, 4", rose	50.00		Bowl, 8", pickle	30.00	
Bowl, 4½", finger	15.00		Bowl, 8", round nappy	35.00	
Bowl, 4½", round nappy	13.00	27.50	Bowl, 9", celery	32.00	
Bowl, 4½", sq. ftd., finger	15.00	35.00	Bowl, 10", flared	40.00	
Bowl, 5", round nappy	15.00	37.50	Bowl, 11", rolled edge	45.00	80.00
Bowl, 6", crimped dish	18.00		Bowl, 12", celery	35.00	
Bowl, 6", round nappy	1600		Bowl, 12", flange or console	50.00	
Bowl, 6", square nappy	16.00		Candlestick, 3½", rd. base	20.00	30.00

*Cobalt blue – 25 to 30 percent higher

Please refer to Foreword for pricing information

ENGLISH HOBNAIL (Cont.)

	Pink/Green	Turquoise/ *Ice Blue		Pink/Green	Turquoise/ *Ice Blue
Candlestick, 9", rd. base	40.00		Plate, 8½", rd.	12.50	25.00
Candy dish, 3 ftd.	55.00		Plate, 10", rd.	40.00	65.00
Candy, ½ lb. and cover, cone shaped	46.00	90.00	Plate, 14", rd., torte	55.00	
Cigarette box and cover, 4½" x 2½"	27.50	50.00	Puff box, w/ cover, 6", rd.	45.00	77.50
Cigarette jar w/cover, rd.	22.50	60.00	Saucer, demitasse, rd.	15.00	
Compote, 5", round, ftd.	25.00		Saucer, rd.	4.00	5.00
Compote, 6", honey, rd. ftd.	30.00		Shaker, pr., flat	125.00	200.00
Compote, 8", ball stem, sweetmeat	60.00		Shaker, pr., rd. ftd.	77.50	
Creamer, hexagonal, ftd.	22.50	45.00	Stem, 2 oz., sq. ftd., wine	30.00	60.00
Creamer, sq. ftd.	42.50		Stem, 3 oz., rd. ftd., cocktail	20.00	35.00
Cup	18.00	25.00	Stem, 5 oz., sq. ftd., oyster cocktail	16.00	
Cup, demitasse	55.00		Stem, 8 oz., sq. ftd., water goblet	30.00	50.00
Ice tub, 4"	47.50	80.00	Stem, sherbet, rd. low foot		12.00
Ice tub, 5½"	65.00	100.00	Stem, sherbet, sq. ftd., low	12.00	
Lamp, 6¼", electric	65.00		Stem, sherbet, rd. high foot	1500	
Lamp, 9¼", electric	135.00		Stem, sherbet, sq. ftd., high	15.00	35.00
Marmalade w/cover	40.00	65.00	Sugar, hexagonal, ftd.	22.50	45.00
Mayonnaise, 6"	20.00		Sugar, sq. ftd.	45.00	
Nut, individual, ftd.	13.00		Tid-bit, 2 tier	42.50	75.00
Pitcher, 23 oz., rounded	150.00		Tumbler, 5 oz., ginger ale	18.00	
Pitcher, 32 oz., straight side	185.00		Tumbler, 8 oz., water	22.00	
Pitcher, 38 oz., rounded	225.00		Tumbler, 10 oz., ice tea	25.00	
Pitcher, 60 oz., rounded	295.00		Tumbler, 12 oz., ice tea	27.50	
Pitcher, 64 oz., straight side	300.00		Urn, 11", w/cover (15")	350.00	
Plate, 5½", rd.	9.50		Vase, 7½", flip	75.00	
Plate, 6", sq. finger bowl liner	9.00		Vase, 7½", flip jar w/cover	100.00	
Plate, 6½", rd.	10.00		Vase, 8½", flared top	115.00	225.00
Plate, 6½, rd. finger bowl liner	9.50		Vase, 10" (straw jar)	95.00	
Plate, 8", rd.	12.50				

*Cobalt blue – 25 to 30 percent higher

FIRE-KING DINNERWARE "PHILBE" HOCKING GLASS COMPANY, 1937–1938

Colors: Blue, green, pink, and crystal.

We continue to revise Fire-King Dinnerware's repertoire of pieces. Recently, three green, high sherbet/champagnes were found in Ohio. Normally, Fire-King Dinnerware is found on Cameo shaped blanks, but these sherbets are on a Mayfair shaped blank! I guess that makes sense, because the 7¼", 9 ounce water goblet pictured in the *Very Rare Glassware of the Depression Years, Second Series* and the footed tumblers also share the Mayfair mould shape. Additional stems may be found. Keep an eye out for this rarely seen pattern. In 1972, I saw a locked display case full of blue Fire-King Dinnerware in the lobby at Anchor Hocking. At the time I was amazed to see a pattern the color of blue Mayfair with which I was not familiar! As an about-to-be-new author, I might have been more impressed with remembering the pieces displayed had I recognized the pattern!

Several **crystal** cup and saucer sets have been discovered in Fire-King Dinnerware. Note the one pictured has the platinum band that was on the blue set shown previously. That particular blue cup and saucer set were found in Washington Court House, Ohio, along with several other blue pieces in the middle 1970s. I was unable to acquire it for this photograph. You will have to find an earlier edition to view it. It's impossible to repeat everything in those earlier editions! I guess that's why they are now being marketed for premium prices when you can locate them!

Collectors, who try to own at least one piece of every pattern in my books, find that Fire-King Dinnerware is frequently one of the very last examples they find. It rates with "Cupid" as one of the two toughest patterns to capture! You can see additional pieces pictured in my *Very Rare Glassware of the Depression Years, Second Series*, including the blue candy dish and green cookie jar that are missing in the pictures here!

Speaking of green, has anyone found a candy lid? I have had two green candy bottoms and one complete blue, but I have never found the green top! I once had a lid brought to me that was supposed to fit the candy, but it turned out to be the lid for the cookie instead.

As mentioned previously, this Fire-King Dinnerware's blue is very similar to Mayfair's blue. Many pieces have that platinum trim that can be seen in the photograph. All the platinum banded blue pieces, except the pitcher, turned up in 1975 at the flea market mentioned above. I have never seen blue Mayfair trimmed in platinum. This seems strange since these patterns were contemporaries. Was this a special order production — which might account for its scarcity?

Many pieces shown here are the only ones ever found! Of the four pitchers shown on the right, only three other pitchers (two pink juice and a blue water without platinum band) have been found. The easiest to find blue items (but rare in other colors) include footed tumblers of which the tea seems twice as available as the water.

Oval vegetable bowls and the 10½" salver are the only commonly found pieces of pink. That oval bowl is also available in green and crystal. I have only found and sold 11 pieces in the past four years and five of them were bought at one time! So "commonly found" may be an inappropriate designation.

Green grill plates or luncheon plates might end up in your collection with more ease than anything else in "Philbe" if you are searching for only a sample. For once, any color 6" saucer/sherbet plate is rarer than these larger plates.

	Crystal	Pink, Green	Blue		Crystal	Pink, Green	Blue
Bowl, 5½" cereal	18.00	45.00	65.00	Plate, 10½" salver	22.50	55.00	80.00
Bowl, 7¼" salad	26.00	60.00	95.00	Plate, 10½" grill	22.50	45.00	75.00
Bowl, 10" oval				Plate, 11⅝" salver	22.50	62.50	95.00
vegetable	50.00	90.00	165.00	Platter, 12" closed			
Candy jar, 4" low,				handles	30.00	125.00	175.00
with cover	215.00	725.00	795.00	Saucer, 6" (same as			
Cookie jar with cover	600.00	950.00	1,500.00	sherbet plate)	30.00	55.00	75.00
Creamer, 3¼" ftd.	37.50	110.00	130.00	Sherbet, 4¾"		450.00	
Cup	55.00	110.00	140.00	Sugar, 3¼" ftd.	40.00	110.00	130.00
Goblet, 7¼", 9 oz.				Tumbler, 4", 9 oz.			
thin	75.00	185.00	235.00	flat water	40.00	105.00	130.00
Pitcher, 6", 36 oz.				Tumbler, 3½" ftd.			
juice	295.00	625.00	895.00	juice	40.00	150.00	175.00
Pitcher, 8½", 56 oz.	395.00	925.00	1,175.00	Tumbler, 5¼", 10 oz.			
Plate, 6" sherbet	30.00	55.00	75.00	ftd.	30.00	70.00	95.00
Plate, 8" luncheon	20.00	37.50	47.50	Tumbler, 6½", 15 oz.			
Plate, 10" heavy				ftd. iced tea	40.00	75.00	80.00
sandwich	22.50	65.00	100.00				

FLORAL, "POINSETTIA" JEANNETTE GLASS COMPANY, 1931–1935

Colors: Pink, green, Delphite, Jade-ite, crystal, amber, red, black, custard, and yellow.

I mentioned in the last book that we had received a call expounding that Floral was obviously a Hemp plant whose design was important for the war effort. I wondered for which war since the production years were 1931 to 1935, but Cathy took the call; so I didn't get to ask that. Well, I have received several letters since then, including one from a botanist, who explained that the Floral design is a passion flower of some genus. She even sent detailed drawings of passion flower leaves to prove her point! So now you know. Jeannette called this Floral. Perhaps "Passion Flower" was too risqué a name in those straighter-laced times! As a matter of fact, I doubt many collectors ever gave this much thought until I mentioned the "weed" angle in the twelfth edition.

The newest discovery in Floral is a 6" flat shaker with a rounded base instead of the normally found squared base style. After all these years of finding all those different pieces in green, a newly discovered piece pops up in pink! It is about time!

Green Floral pieces rarely found in the United States continue to be uncovered in England and Canada. As with Doric and Pansy, it is the **more unusual and previously thought to be rare pieces** that are being found. All the pieces shown in the photograph at the bottom of page 83 have been discovered in England. Many of these pieces have **only been found** in England! Some discoveries were brought back to the United States by furniture dealers. Now, many dealers have agents in England exploring for American-made glassware as well as fine European antiques. More and more of my books are being shipped to England as well as Australia and New Zealand. Yes, American glassware is being discovered "down under" — quite a bit of it, in fact! The green Floral, flat bottomed pitcher and tumblers are some of the pieces whose prices are presently stagnating because of these findings. Notice the color varieties of green Floral in the pictures. Floral found in Canada and England is usually a lighter green color, slightly paneled, and ground on the bottoms of flatware which normally means that this was an early production run of the pattern. Observe the oval vegetable bowl in the background that was placed on its side so you could see this paneled effect. The green cup has a ground bottom and is slightly footed. The base of the cup is larger than the normally found saucer indentation! If you have relatives in England who missed the Mayflower, better send them one of my books! Better yet, try a vacation to England to find Depression glass!

Lemonade pitchers are appearing mostly in the Northwest, but not as often as in previous years. There were only three at the recent Seattle show I attended. Pink lemonade pitchers significantly outnumber the green; that is one reason for price differences in these colors.

Floral is another of Jeannette's patterns in which the sugar and candy lids **are** interchangeable.

There are two varieties of pink Floral platters. One has a normal flat edge as shown in the back right of the top photo; the other has a sharp inner rim like the platter in Cherry Blossom. Few collectors deem both necessary for their collections. The style similar to Cherry Blossom is rarer than the normally found platter, and therefore priced higher.

For new collectors, in the pink Floral pictured on page 81, the 9" comport is the piece on the right in the bottom row. For a description of the lamp shown in the top row, be sure to read about a similarly made lamp under Adam on page 6.

Smaller Floral shakers have **now been reproduced** in pink, cobalt blue, and a very dark green color. Cobalt blue and the dark green Floral shakers are of little concern since they were originally never made in these colors. The green is darker than the original green shown here but not as deep a color as forest green. The new pink shakers, however, are not only a very good pink, but they are also a fairly good copy! There are many minor variations in design and leaf detail to someone who knows glassware well, but there is one easy way to tell the Floral reproductions. Take off the top and look at the threads where the lid screws onto the shaker. On the old there are a **pair of parallel threads** on each side or at least a pair on one side that end right before the mould seams down each side. The new Floral has **one continuous line** thread that starts on one side and continues around the shaker until it ends above the beginning line on the other side. There is approximately one inch of overlapped thread making two lines for that inch; but the whole thread is **one continuous line** and not two separate ones as on the old. No other Floral reproductions have been made as of May 1997.

Unusual items in Floral (so far) include the following:
a) an entire set of **Delphite**
b) a **yellow** two-part relish dish
c) **amber** and **red** plate, cup, and saucer
d) green and crystal juice pitchers w/ground flat bottoms (shown)
e) ftd. vases in green and crystal, flared at the rim (shown); some
   hold **flower frogs with the Floral pattern on the frogs** (shown)
f) a crystal lemonade pitcher
g) lamps (shown in green and pink)
h) a green **grill** plate
i) an octagonal vase with patterned, octagonal foot (shown)
j) a **ruffled edge** berry and master berry bowl (shown in pink)
k) pink and green Floral **ice tubs** (shown in green)
l) oval vegetable with cover
m) **rose bowl** and **three ftd. vase** (shown)
n) two styles of **9" comports** in pink and green (shown in pink)
o) 9 ounce flat tumblers in green (shown)
p) 3 ounce ftd. tumblers in green (shown)
q) 8" round bowl in **beige** and **opaque red**
r) **caramel** colored dinner plate
s) **cream soups** (shown in pink)
t) **custard** creamer and sugar
u) green **dresser set** (shown)
v) **custard**, 8½" bowl (like Cherry Blossom)
w) black footed water tumbler

FLORAL, "POINSETTIA" (Cont.)

	Pink	Green	Delphite	Jadite
Bowl, 4" berry (ruffled $65.00)	20.00	22.00	50.00	
Bowl, 5½" cream soup	750.00	750.00		
* Bowl, 7½" salad (ruffled $150.00)	22.00	24.00	60.00	
Bowl, 8" covered vegetable	40.00	50.00	75.00 (no cover)	
Bowl, 9" oval vegetable	20.00	22.50		
Butter dish and cover	85.00	90.00		
Butter dish bottom	25.00	25.00		
Butter dish top	60.00	65.00		
Canister set: coffee, tea, cereal				
sugar, 5¼" tall, each				55.00
Candlesticks, 4" pr.	75.00	85.00		
Candy jar and cover	37.50	42.50		
Creamer, flat (Cremax $160.00)	14.00	15.00	77.50	
Coaster, 3¼"	15.00	11.00		
Comport, 9"	800.00	950.00		
*** Cup	13.00	14.00		
Dresser set		1,250.00		
Frog for vase (also crystal $500.00)		725.00		
Ice tub, 3½" high oval	850.00	895.00		
Lamp	250.00	275.00		
Pitcher, 5½", 23 or 24 oz.		495.00		
Pitcher, 8", 32 oz. ftd. cone	35.00	37.50		
Pitcher, 10¼", 48 oz. lemonade	245.00	265.00		
Plate, 6" sherbet	6.00	7.50		
Plate, 8" salad	10.00	12.00		
** Plate, 9" dinner	17.50	18.00	150.00	
Plate, 9" grill		250.00		
Platter, 10¾" oval	17.50	20.00	150.00	
Platter, 11" (like Cherry Blossom)	85.00			
Refrigerator dish and cover,				
5" square		65.00	65.00	22.00
*** Relish dish, 2-part oval	18.00	20.00	160.00	
**** Salt and pepper, 4" ftd. pair	45.00	50.00		
Salt and pepper, 6" flat	50.00			
*** Saucer	11.00	12.00		
Sherbet	17.50	20.00	85.00	
Sugar (Cremax $160.00)	10.00	12.00	72.50 (open)	
Sugar/candy cover	15.00	17.50		
Tray, 6" square, closed handles	17.50	20.00		
Tray, 9¼", oval for dresser set		195.00		
Tumbler, 3½", 3 oz. ftd.		175.00		
Tumbler, 4", 5 oz. ftd. juice	18.00	22.00		
Tumbler, 4½", 9 oz. flat		185.00		
Tumbler, 4¾", 7 oz. ftd. water	18.00	22.00	195.00	
Tumbler, 5¼", 9 oz. ftd. lemonade	50.00	55.00		
Vase, 3 legged rose bowl		525.00		
Vase, 3 legged flared (also in crystal)		495.00		
Vase, 6⅞" tall (8 sided)		435.00		

   * Cremax $125.00
  ** These have now been found in amber and red.
  *** This has been found in yellow.
 **** Beware reproductions!

Please refer to Foreword for pricing information

FLORAL AND DIAMOND BAND U.S. GLASS COMPANY, Late 1920s

Colors: Pink, green; some iridescent, black, and crystal.

Floral and Diamond was advertised by Sears in the late 1920s, but there is presently not enough available to accommodate a great number of collectors. Notice that half the ad for the berry set pictured below says Diamond and Floral and not vice versa. It was listed both ways in advertisements at the time. Please! You can not order these items shown in the old advertisement below! They were the prices for this pattern in the year 1928! I was astounded to get orders from people who assumed they could still buy at those prices!

Luncheon plates, sugar lids, pitchers, and iced tea tumblers (in both pink and green) are difficult to unearth in Floral and Diamond. Many Floral and Diamond butter bottoms have been "recycled" to be used on other U.S. Glass patterns such as Strawberry and Cherryberry. This has transpired because all U.S. Glass butter bottoms are plain and, thus, interchangeable since the patterns are found on the top only. Floral and Diamond butter dishes used to be inexpensive in contrast to Strawberry and Cherryberry; so, collectors bought the inexpensive Floral and Diamond butter dishes to use the bottoms for those more expensive patterns. These past collecting practices have now created a shortage of butter bottoms for Floral and Diamond!

You may find rough mould lines on many Floral and Diamond pieces. This heavy seamed pattern was not finished as well as many of the later patterns of this era. This is **normal** for Floral and Diamond and not considered an impairment by long-time collectors who have come to ignore **some** roughness. An additional difficulty in gathering U.S. Glass patterns is the varying shades of green. Some of the green is blue tinted. It is up to you to decide how serious you are about color matching.

Only the small creamer and sugar have been found in black. These sugars and creamers are often found with a cut flower over the top of the customarily found moulded flower design. You can find this cut flower on other colors also.

Crystal pitchers and butter dishes are rare in Floral and Diamond! Notice the crystal pitcher on the right in the bottom photograph. It is yellow in appearance and that is one problem in collecting crystal. The other is locating it!

Floral and Diamond pitchers with exceptional iridescent color bring premium prices from carnival glass collectors as a pattern called "Mayflower"! Dealers who sell both Depression and carnival glass have been buying these pitchers at Depression glass shows and reselling them at carnival glass conventions and auctions. Sometimes glassware that fits into two categories, as does Floral and Diamond, receives more respect from one group of collectors than it does the other.

	Pink	Green		Pink	Green
Bowl, 4½" berry	8.00	9.00	Sherbet	7.00	8.00
Bowl, 5¾" handled nappy	12.00	12.00	Sugar, small	9.50	11.00
Bowl, 8" large berry	15.00	15.00	Sugar, 5¼"	15.00	15.00
* Butter dish and cover	140.00	130.00	Sugar lid	55.00	65.00
Butter dish bottom	100.00	100.00	Tumbler, 4" water	20.00	25.00
Butter dish top	40.00	30.00	Tumbler, 5" iced tea	40.00	45.00
Compote, 5½" tall	17.00	18.00			
Creamer, small	10.00	11.00			
Creamer, 4¾"	17.50	19.00			
* Pitcher, 8", 42 oz.	95.00	100.00			
Plate, 8" luncheon	42.50	42.50			

* Iridescent – $275.00; Crystal – $125.00

Seven-Piece Berry Set

You'll really be most satisfied with the purchase of this set. It's very attractive, and affords a fitting and stylish addition to your present pieces. In green pressed glass, with diamond and floral design. Large bowl, 8 inches in diameter, and six sauce dishes to match, 4½ inches in diameter.
35N6838—Weight, packed, 7 pounds. Per set......**68c**

Seven-Piece   Water Set

Made from green pressed glass, with a floral and diamond design. You'll find that the sparkling scintillating pitcher and glasses as a set you'll be mighty proud to own when serving cold drinks. 3-pint pitcher. Six 8-ounce tumblers.
35N6837—Weight, packed, 12 pounds. Per set.. **$1.18**

Please refer to Foreword for pricing information

FLORENTINE NO. 1, "OLD FLORENTINE," "POPPY NO. 1"
HAZEL ATLAS GLASS COMPANY, 1932–1935

Colors: Pink, green, crystal, yellow, and cobalt blue. *See Reproduction Section.*

Florentine No.1 is often confused with Florentine No. 2 by new collectors. Notice the outlines of the pieces. The serrated edged pieces are hexagonal (six sided); this edging occurs on all flat pieces of Florentine No. 1. All footed pieces (such as tumblers, shakers, or pitchers) have the serrated edge on that foot. In Florentine No. 2, all pieces have a plain edge as can be seen in the photographs on page 89. Florentine No. 1 was once advertised as hexagonal and Florentine No. 2 was once advertised as round. Both Florentine patterns were advertised and sold together. Today, many collectors are following that lead and mixing the two patterns! Original sets have been found with the two patterns intertwined.

The 48 ounce, flat-bottomed pitcher was sold with both Florentine No. 1 and No. 2 sets. It was listed as 54 ounces in catalogs, but measures 6 ounces less. My inclination is to list this pitcher only with Florentine No. 1 using the handle shape as my criterion. In defiance of that logic, this pitcher is frequently found with flat-bottomed Florentine No. 2 tumblers, which forces me to list it with both Florentine patterns.

Speaking of flat tumblers, many with **paneled** interiors are being found in sets with Florentine No. 1 pitchers. These paneled tumblers could be considered Florentine No. 1 rather than Florentine No. 2. That information is for die-hard collectors. Paneled flat tumblers are harder to find, but few collectors seem to make this a "must have" style. The paneled tumblers do not mix well with the plainer style; so be forewarned of that!

Pink is the most difficult color in which to complete a set. Pink footed tumblers, covered oval vegetable bowl, and ruffled creamer and sugar are almost unavailable at any price. Sets can be collected in green, crystal, or yellow with effort. Serrated edges are readily damaged; that is the first place you should look when you pick up a piece to examine. Be sure to check **underneath those edges** and not just on the top.

An abundance of fired-on colors are materializing in luncheon sets, but there is little collector request for these at the moment. You can find all sorts of colors and colored bands on crystal if that strikes your fancy. There are even some banded designs found on colors other than crystal. A major detriment to these banded colors is finding enough to put a set together.

Many 5½" yellow ash trays have a VFW (Veterans of Foreign Wars) embossed in the bottom. I have seen more with this embossing than without it. I have not seen an embossed design on any color other than yellow!

Florentine No. 1 shakers have been reproduced in pink and cobalt blue. There may be other colors to follow. No original cobalt blue Florentine No. 1 shakers have ever been found; so those are no problem.

The reproduction pink shaker is somewhat more difficult to distinguish. When comparing a reproduction shaker to several old pairs from my inventory, the old shakers have a major open flower on each side. There is a top circle on this blossom with three smaller circles down each side. The **seven circles form the outside** of the blossom. The new blossom looks more like a strawberry with **no circles** forming the outside of the blossom. Do not use the threading test mentioned under Floral for the Florentine No. 1 shakers, however. It will not work for Florentine although these are made by the same importing company out of Georgia. The threads are correct on this reproduction pattern. The reproductions I have seen have been badly moulded, but that is not to say that it will not be corrected. As of May 1997, it has not been!

	Crystal, Green	Yellow	Pink	Cobalt Blue		Crystal, Green	Yellow	Pink	Cobalt Blue
Ash tray, 5½"	22.00	30.00	30.00		Plate, 8½" salad	7.50	12.00	11.00	
Bowl, 5" berry	12.00	15.00	15.00	20.00	Plate, 10" dinner	16.00	25.00	25.00	
Bowl, 5", cream soup or ruffled nut	22.00		18.00	57.50	Plate, 10" grill	12.00	15.00	20.00	
Bowl, 6" cereal	22.00	25.00	25.00		Platter, 11½" oval	20.00	25.00	25.00	
Bowl, 8½" large berry	25.00	30.00	30.00		** Salt and pepper, ftd.	37.50	55.00	55.00	
Bowl, 9½" oval vegetable and cover	55.00	65.00	65.00		Saucer	3.00	4.00	4.00	17.00
Butter dish and cover	125.00	160.00	160.00		Sherbet, 3 oz. ftd.	10.00	12.00	12.00	
Butter dish bottom	50.00	85.00	85.00		Sugar	9.50	12.00	12.00	
Butter dish top	75.00	95.00	75.00		Sugar cover	18.00	30.00	30.00	
Coaster/ash tray, 3¾"	18.00	20.00	25.00		Sugar, ruffled	35.00		35.00	55.00
Comport, 3½", ruffled	*40.00		15.00	65.00	Tumbler, 3¼", 4 oz. ftd.		16.00		
Creamer	9.50	18.00	17.00		Tumbler, 3¾", 5 oz. ftd. juice	16.00	25.00	25.00	
Creamer, ruffled	45.00		37.50	65.00	Tumbler, 4", 9 oz., ribbed	16.00		22.00	
Cup	9.00	10.00	9.00	85.00	Tumbler, 4¾", 10 oz. ftd. water	22.00	24.00	24.00	
Pitcher, 6½", 36 oz. ftd.	40.00	45.00	45.00	850.00	Tumbler, 5¼", 12 oz. ftd. iced tea	28.00	30.00	30.00	
Pitcher, 7½", 48 oz. flat, ice lip or none	75.00	195.00	135.00		Tumbler, 5¼", 9 oz. lemonade (like Floral)			125.00	
Plate, 6" sherbet	6.00	7.00	6.00						

*Crystal $15.00
**Beware reproductions

Please refer to Foreword for pricing information

FLORENTINE NO. 2, "POPPY NO. 2" HAZEL ATLAS GLASS COMPANY 1932–1935

Colors: Pink, green, crystal, some cobalt, amber, and ice blue. *See Reproduction Section.*

Read about the differences between the two Florentines in the first paragraph on page 86 (under Florentine No.1). Many collectors are now mixing the Florentines together. Some pieces of each pattern have been found in boxed sets over the years; so the factory must have mixed them as well. I should point out that pictured here in the top photograph is the green ruffled nut or cream soup. This piece fits Florentine No. 1 because it matches the other ruffled pieces (comport, creamer, and sugar) in that pattern that are not found in Florentine No. 2.

The **rarely found** 6¼", 24 oz., footed, cone-shaped pitcher is shown on the right in the top photograph. The more frequently found footed pitcher stands 7½" tall and is shown on the left. Measure from the base to the top of the spout. There is over an inch difference in height. Forget ounce capacities because they often vary due to the hand produced spout. There is a giant price difference in these pitchers!

That 7½" pitcher and water tumbler have been reproduced in cobalt blue, pink, and a dark green. This pitcher was never originally made in those colors; therefore, no one should believe these reproductions to be old. See page 232.

Custard cups or Jell-O molds remain the most elusive piece in Florentine No. 2, although the bulbous 76 oz. pitcher still escapes many collectors. The custard is similar to a small, flared out bowl and fits a 6¼" indented plate. You can see a crystal one pictured on a yellow indented plate in the lower photograph on page 89. I recently bought a couple of these plates mistakenly identified as saucers. The saucer curves up on the edges while the custard plate is flat with a larger indentation.

The 10" relish dish comes divided or plain. There are two divided styles; do not be alarmed if yours is different from the "Y" style pictured here. The other style has two curved, separate divisions, one on each side. There are no price differences on these three relish dishes, but the undivided is the most difficult to acquire if you want all three types.

Grill plates with the indent for the cream soup have surfaced in green or crystal but have yet to be seen in yellow. Considering they are newly discovered, it is logical to assume they are not very plentiful.

Green Florentine is more requested than crystal, but crystal is seldom found; consequently, prices for both are similar. Amber, shown in earlier editions, is the rarest Florentine color; but enough has never surfaced to collect a set. It may have been a special order or even a trial production. Most sizes of flat tumblers have been found in amber, but no pitcher has come to light.

Between the two Florentine patterns, the lid to the butter dish and the lid for the oval vegetable are interchangeable. However, if you buy a candy lid thinking you are getting a butter lid, you have a problem since they are not interchangeable. The candy lid measures 4¾" in diameter, but the butter dish lid measures 5" exactly. Those measurements are from **outside edge to outside edge**!

Fired-on blue shakers in Florentine were shown in an earlier book. Now, **luncheon sets** of red, orange, green, and blue have been reported. The fired-on colors are sprayed over crystal. Once it has been fired-on (baked, so to speak), the colors will not strip off even with paint removers as some collectors have learned. Fired-on colors are not common.

	Crystal, Green	Pink	Yellow	Cobalt Blue		Crystal, Green	Pink	Yellow	Cobalt Blue
Bowl, 4½" berry	12.00	17.00	22.00		Plate, 6" sherbet	4.00		6.00	
Bowl, 4¾" cream soup	14.00	16.00	22.00		Plate, 6¼" with indent	17.50		30.00	
Bowl, 5½"	33.00		42.00		Plate, 8½" salad	8.50	8.50	9.00	
Bowl, 6" cereal	30.00		40.00		Plate, 10" dinner	15.00		15.00	
Bowl, 7½" shallow			95.00		Plate, 10¼" grill	12.00		14.00	
Bowl, 8" large berry	25.00	32.00	35.00		Plate, 10¼", grill w/cream soup ring	35.00			
Bowl, 9" oval vegetable and cover	57.50		75.00		Platter, 11" oval	16.00	16.00	20.00	
Bowl, 9" flat	27.50				Platter, 11½" for gravy boat			45.00	
Butter dish and cover	100.00		150.00		Relish dish, 10", 3 part or plain	20.00	25.00	30.00	
Butter dish bottom	25.00		70.00		*** Salt and pepper, pr.	42.50		50.00	
Butter dish top	75.00		80.00		Saucer (amber 15.00)	4.00		5.00	
Candlesticks, 2¾" pr.	45.00		67.50		Sherbet, ftd. (amber 40.00)	10.00		11.00	
Candy dish and cover	100.00	135.00	155.00		Sugar	10.00		11.00	
Coaster, 3¼"	14.00	16.00	22.00		Sugar cover	15.00		25.00	
Coaster/ash tray, 3¾"	17.50		30.00		Tray, rnd., condiment for shakers, creamer/sugar			70.00	
Coaster/ash tray, 5½"	17.50		37.50		Tumbler, 3⅜", 5 oz. juice	12.00	12.00	21.00	
* Comport, 3½", ruffled	40.00	15.00		65.00	Tumbler, 3⁹⁄₁₆", 6 oz. blown	18.00			
Creamer	8.00		10.00		**** Tumbler, 4", 9 oz. water	13.00	16.00	21.00	70.00
Cup (amber 50.00)	7.50		9.50		Tumbler, 5", 12 oz., blown	20.00			
Custard cup or jello	60.00		85.00		**** Tumbler, 5", 12 oz., tea	35.00		50.00	
Gravy boat			60.00		Tumbler, 3¼", 5 oz. ftd.	15.00	17.50		
Pitcher, 6¼", 24 oz. cone-ftd.			175.00		Tumbler, 4", 5 oz. ftd.	15.00		17.00	
** Pitcher, 7½", 28 oz. cone-ftd.	32.00		30.00		Tumbler, 4½", 9 oz. ftd.	27.50		37.50	
Pitcher, 7½", 48 oz.	75.00	135.00	195.00		Vase or parfait, 6"	30.00		62.50	
Pitcher, 8¼", 76 oz.	100.00	225.00	425.00						

*Crystal – $15.00   **Ice Blue – $500.00   *** Fired-On Red, Orange or Blue, Pr. – $42.50   **** Amber – $75.00

FLOWER GARDEN WITH BUTTERFLIES, "BUTTERFLIES AND ROSES"
U.S. GLASS COMPANY, Late 1920s

Colors: Pink, green, blue-green, canary yellow, crystal, amber, and black.

Flower Garden with Butterflies was a pattern we collected for years. After selling our collection, I have had a difficult time re-capturing enough to photograph for the book! Notice the green heart-shaped candy pictured in front of the box. This box held a heart-shaped candy Valentine's Day gift. Incidentally, we sold this particular candy the day after Valentine's Day with the collector now searching for other colors. It is doubtful he will get lucky enough to find another one boxed; but stranger things have happened!

There are three Flower Garden with Butterflies powder jars, which may account for the oval and rectangular dresser trays being so plentiful! Those trays and 8" plates are the only regularly found pieces. Apparently, more powder jars than trays were damaged over the years. There are two different footed powders. The smaller, shown in the photograph in amber and green, stands 6¼" tall; the taller, not shown, stands 7½" high. Lids to these footed powders are interchangeable. The flat powder jar has a 3½" diameter. I should tell you that we never found a blue, flat powder in the 18 years we collected this pattern.

Note the crystal cologne with black stopper. I pictured a black cologne earlier, but it was missing the stopper. It's a shame I didn't find this cologne while I had access to the topless black one. To illustrate how desirable that two toned crystal cologne was, a collector called us before a show and asked us if we were bringing this cologne that he had heard we had bought! Cathy told him we were since we'd already photographed it for the book. We put it out at the show and one of the first customers through the door proceeded to our booth, grabbed the cologne and bought it. Cathy assumed it to be the spouse of the collector who had called; but guess who came in the next day looking for the cologne bottle? Some miscommunication, obviously — but definitely a desirable piece of glass!

I have previously written about the so-called "Shari" perfume or cologne set, but I continually get letters about it. It's a semi-circular, footed glass dresser box that holds five wedge (pie shaped) bottles. This box is often confused with Flower Garden because it has flower designs on it. I spotted one at a show recently that still had the original labels intact on the bottles. They touted the New York/Paris affiliation of "Charme Volupte" but nowhere was the word "Shari" mentioned on the labels. One bottle had contained cold cream, another vanishing cream, and three others once held parfumes. There are **dancing girls at either end of the box,** and flowers abound on the semi-circle. There are no dancing girls on Flower Garden. Other not-to-be-mistaken-for Flower Garden pieces include the 7" and 10" trivets with flowers all over them made by U.S. Glass. They were mixing bowl covers and they do not have butterflies.

I have only seen one piece of Flower Garden that did not contain the entire butterfly; one piece, a long while ago, was shown me which had only half a butterfly in its design!

	Amber Crystal	Pink Green Blue-Green	Blue Canary Yellow
Ash tray, match-pack holders	165.00	185.00	195.00
Candlesticks, 4" pr.	42.50	55.00	95.00
Candlesticks, 8" pr.	77.50	135.00	130.00
Candy w/cover, 6", flat	130.00	155.00	
Candy w/cover, 7½" cone-shaped	80.00	130.00	165.00
Candy w/cover, heart-shaped		1,250.00	1,300.00
* Cologne bottle w/stopper, 7½"		200.00	325.00
Comport, 2⅞" h.		23.00	28.00
Comport, 3" h. fits 10" plate	20.00	23.00	28.00
Comport, 4¼" h. x 4¾" w.			50.00
Comport, 4¾" h. x 10¼" w.	48.00	65.00	85.00
Comport, 5⅞" h. x 11" w.	55.00		95.00
Comport, 7¼" h. x 8¼" w.	60.00	80.00	
Creamer		70.00	
Cup		65.00	

	Amber Crystal	Pink Green Blue-Green	Blue Canary Yellow
Mayonnaise, ftd. 4¾" h. x 6¼" w., w/7" plate & spoon	67.50	80.00	125.00
Plate, 7"	16.00	21.00	30.00
Plate, 8", two styles	15.00	17.50	25.00
Plate, 10"		42.50	48.00
Plate, 10", indent for 3" comport	32.00	40.00	45.00
Powder jar, 3½", flat		80.00	
Powder jar, ftd., 6¼"h.	75.00	135.00	175.00
Powder jar, ftd., 7½"h.	80.00	145.00	195.00
Sandwich server, center handle	50.00	65.00	95.00
Saucer		27.50	
Sugar		65.00	
Tray, 5½" x 10", oval	50.00	55.00	
Tray, 11¾" x 7¾", rectangular	50.00	65.00	85.00
Tumbler, 7½" oz.	175.00		
Vase, 6¼"	70.00	95.00	160.00
Vase, 10½"		125.00	225.00

* Stopper, if not broken off, ½ price of bottle

Please refer to Foreword for pricing information

PRICE LIST FOR BLACK ITEMS ONLY

Bon bon w/cover, 6⅝" diameter	250.00
Bowl, 7¼", w/cover, "flying saucer"	375.00
Bowl, 8½", console, w/base	150.00
Bowl, 9" rolled edge, w/base	200.00
Bowl, 11" ftd. orange	225.00
Bowl, 12" rolled edge console w/base	200.00
Candlestick 6" w/6½" candle, pr.	395.00
Candlestick, 8", pr.	300.00
Cheese and cracker, ftd., 5⅜" h. x 10" w.	325.00
Comport and cover, 2¾" h. (fits 10" indented plate)	200.00
Cigarette box & cover, 4⅜" long	150.00
Comport, tureen, 4¼" h. x 10" w.	250.00
Comport, ftd., 5⅝" h. x 10" w.	225.00
Comport, ftd., 7" h.	175.00
Plate, 10", indented	100.00
Sandwich server, center-handled	125.00
Vase, 6¼", Dahlia, cupped	135.00
Vase, 8", Dahlia, cupped	200.00
Vase, 9", wall hanging	325.00
Vase, 10", 2-handled	225.00
Vase, 10½", Dahlia, cupped	250.00

FORTUNE HOCKING GLASS COMPANY, 1937–1938

Colors: Pink and crystal.

I am still receiving pictures of a crystal Fortune candy dish with a Royal Ruby lid after mentioning in the eleventh edition that I did not have one. Thanks to over a 100 collectors who have written or sent confirming photos. The lid is plain and rounded and not paneled as the normally found candy lid.

Luncheon plates are getting expensive and you ordinarily find them one at a time. Prices have increased on almost all pieces in this small set which indicates that there are collectors who are discovering and treasuring Fortune. With an undertaking of time and a little fortune (when contrasted with the expense of other patterns) a small pink set can be compiled. Remember that both tumblers and the luncheon plates are not plentiful.

A few pitchers are surfacing that are similar to Fortune, and many collectors are buying them for use with their sets. These "go-with" pitchers are selling in the $25.00 to $30.00 range. So far, no actual Fortune pitcher has turned up; but never, say never!

	Pink, Crystal		Pink, Crystal
Bowl, 4" berry	7.00	Cup	6.00
Bowl, 4½" dessert	9.00	Plate, 6" sherbet	3.00
Bowl, 4½" handled	9.00	Plate, 8" luncheon	22.00
Bowl, 5¼" rolled edge	12.00	Saucer	3.00
Bowl, 7¾" salad or large berry	18.00	Tumbler, 3½", 5 oz. juice	9.00
Candy dish and cover, flat	25.00	Tumbler, 4", 9 oz. water	11.00

FRUITS HAZEL ATLAS AND OTHER GLASS COMPANIES, 1931–1935

Colors: Pink, green, some crystal, and iridized.

Every Fruits collector I know has been pursuing the 3½" (5 ounce) juice and 5" (12 ounce) ice tea tumblers! Because of this solicitation, the prices for both of these tumblers have risen sharply! I have never personally seen either one in pink, yet a few have been reported to me over the years. However, if I do not receive some confirming photos by the next book, I will remove the pink juice and iced tea from the listing. Most collectors pursue green tumblers, since there has never been a pitcher forthcoming in pink.

Fruits patterned water tumblers (4") in all colors are the pieces usually seen. Iridized "Pears" tumblers are plentiful. These iridescent tumblers may have been made by Federal Glass Company while they were making iridescent Normandie and a few pieces in Madrid. These are **not carnival glass** as they are often designated. These tumblers were made over 20 years after the ending period designated for carnival glass. Tumblers with cherries or other fruits are regularly found in pink, but finding **any** green tumbler is more of a predicament.

Fruits berry bowls in both sizes are among the hardest to acquire in all Depression glass patterns. Since this is not one of the major cherished patterns and does not have thousands of collectors that some other patterns do, the paucity of both sizes of bowls is only just dawning on collectors.

Fruits pitchers only have cherries in the pattern. Sometimes they are mistaken for Cherry Blossom flat bottomed pitchers. Notice that the handle is shaped like that of the flat Florentine pitchers (Hazel Atlas Company) and not like Cherry Blossom (Jeannette Glass Company) flat pitchers. Crystal Fruits pitchers sell for less than half the price of green if they sell at all. Crystal pieces are seldom collected, but tumblers are available if you would like an economically priced beverage set!

	Green	Pink		Green	Pink
Bowl, 5" berry	30.00	22.00	Sherbet	9.00	7.00
Bowl, 8" berry	75.00	40.00	Tumbler, 3½" juice	50.00	40.00
Cup	8.00	7.00	* Tumbler, 4" (1 fruit)	17.50	15.00
Pitcher, 7" flat bottom	85.00		Tumbler, 4" (combination of fruits)	25.00	20.00
Plate, 8" luncheon	6.50	6.50	Tumbler, 5", 12 oz.	135.00	95.00
Saucer	5.50	4.00			

* Iridized $7.50

Please refer to Foreword for pricing information

GEORGIAN, "LOVEBIRDS" FEDERAL GLASS COMPANY, 1931–1936

Colors: Green, crystal, and amber.

Georgian was dubbed "lovebirds" because of those little birds perched side by side on most pieces. Birds are not found on either size tumbler or the hot plate; and, a few dinner plates are found without them. Most collectors seek dinner plates with birds, however. Baskets normally alternate with birds in the design on all other pieces. Sometimes you can find a deal on tumblers if the seller does not know about the absent birds. A reader enlightened me that those birds are parakeets. I never gave it much thought since it was being called "lovebirds" before I ever knew what Depression glass was! I wondered why Federal Glass Company produced two bird patterns at the same time. Parrot was the other pattern (early 1930s) made predominately in the same green color. Parrot was also made in amber; and coming full circle, an **amber** Georgian 6" sherbet plate recently turned up! It's my understanding that birds were popular designs in the late 1920s due to a sweeping Oriental influence in that period. In that culture they're tied to health, happiness, and well being.

Both sizes of Georgian tumblers are difficult to find. Another boxed set of water tumblers has been found in the Chicago area. In the 1930s, a newspaper gave the tumblers away to subscribers. Prices for iced teas have doubled the price of water tumblers. I have owned at least a dozen Georgian waters for every iced tea to give you an idea of how difficult teas are to find. No pitcher has ever been found to go with the tumblers.

Some Georgian pieces are commonly found. Berry bowls, cups, saucers, sherbets, sherbet plates, and luncheon plates can be easily accumulated. You will have to search for other pieces. There are not as many collectors buying this pattern, today, as there were in the mid-1970s when a set was donated to the Smithsonian by the Peach State Depression Glass Club in the name of then President Jimmy Carter. Those particular pieces were engraved and numbered. The extras were sold or given as prizes. If you run into such a prize, cherish it!

Georgian Lazy Susans or cold cuts servers are not found as easily as the Madrid ones that turn up infrequently at best! You can see one pictured on page 95. One walnut tray turned up in Ohio with an original decal label that read "Kalter Aufschain Cold Cuts Server Schirmer Cincy." That may be why so many have been found in Kentucky and southern Ohio. These Lazy Susans are made of walnut and are 18½" across with seven 5" openings for holding the so called hot plates. Somehow, I believe these 5" hot plates are misnamed since they are found on a cold cuts server! These cold cuts plates also have only the center motif design.

There is no real mug in Georgian as has been previously reported. Someone found a creamer without a spout and labeled it a mug. There are many patterns that have creamers or pitchers without a spout; and one other Federal pattern, Sharon, has at least one two-spouted creamer known! Spouts were applied by hand at most glass factories using a wooden tool. Quality control of this glass was not as precise as today.

Many of the Georgian serving pieces were heavily utilized; so be wary of pieces that are scratched and worn from usage. You **pay a premium for condition**! Remember that all prices listed in this book are for **mint condition** pieces. Damaged or scratched and worn pieces should fetch less depending upon the extent of damage and wear. If you are collecting the glass to use, some imperfection may not make as much difference as collecting for eventual resale. Mint condition glass will sell more readily and for a much better price if you ever decide to part with your collection. Many of you do not intend to, but circumstances sometimes dictate otherwise.

	Green		Green
Bowl, 4½" berry	8.50	** Plate, 6" sherbet	6.00
Bowl, 5¾" cereal	23.00	Plate, 8" luncheon	9.00
Bowl, 6½" deep	65.00	Plate, 9¼" dinner	25.00
Bowl, 7½" large berry	60.00	Plate, 9¼" center design only	22.00
Bowl, 9" oval vegetable	60.00	Platter, 11½" closed-handled	65.00
Butter dish and cover	72.50	Saucer	3.00
Butter dish bottom	40.00	Sherbet	12.00
Butter dish top	30.00	Sugar, 3", ftd.	10.00
Cold cuts server, 18½" wood with		Sugar, 4", ftd.	12.00
seven 5" openings for 5" coasters	850.00	Sugar cover for 3"	40.00
Creamer, 3", ftd.	12.00	Sugar cover for 4"	165.00
Creamer, 4", ftd.	15.00	Tumbler, 4", 9 oz. flat	57.50
Cup	10.00	Tumbler, 5¼", 12 oz. flat	115.00
* Hot Plate, 5" center design	47.50		

* Crystal – $20.00

** Amber – $40.00

HEX OPTIC, "HONEYCOMB" JEANNETTE GLASS COMPANY, 1928–1932

Colors: Pink, green, Ultra Marine, and iridescent in 1950s.

The flat bottomed Hex Optic pitcher has also been found in green. For years no one noticed these pitchers, but once it was pictured, they seemed to fall out of the sky! The footed pitcher is scarcely seen, but the flat bottomed one is a new discovery. This flat pitcher is 8" tall and holds 70 ounces. Last time I had the capacity as 96 ounces, but that was an error. Notice that the Hex Optic pitchers are thick! There are other "honeycomb" pretenders out there that are thin. **These thin pitchers are not Jeannette and are not rare!** Most companies made patterns in a "honeycomb" design, but this book only covers Jeannette's Hex Optic!

Kitchenware shoppers are more vigilant of Hex Optic than nearly all other patterns of Depression glass. Hex Optic sugar shakers, bucket reamers, mixing bowls, stacking sets, and butter dishes are coveted in green and pink. In fact, were it not for Kitchenware collectors becoming hooked on this pattern, Hex Optic might still be unnoticed and unappreciated.

Iridized tumblers, oil lamps, and pitchers were all made during Jeannette's iridized craze of the 1950s. I have never been able to verify when the company made the Ultra Marine tumblers. My guess would be in the late 1930s when the company was making Doric and Pansy, but that is only conjecture. You can also find that flat bottomed pitcher iridized according to a recent letter I received. I have not spotted one yet!

	Pink, Green		Pink, Green
Bowl, 4¼" ruffled berry	5.50	Plate, 8" luncheon	5.50
Bowl, 7½" large berry	7.50	Platter, 11" round	14.00
Bowl, 7¼" mixing	12.00	Refrigerator dish, 4" x 4"	10.00
Bowl, 8¼" mixing	17.50	Refrigerator stack set, 4 pc.	60.00
Bowl, 9" mixing	22.00	Salt and pepper, pr.	27.50
Bowl, 10" mixing	25.00	Saucer	2.50
Bucket reamer	55.00	Sugar, 2 styles of handles	5.50
Butter dish and cover, rectangular 1 lb. size	85.00	Sugar shaker	195.00
Creamer, 2 style handles	5.50	Sherbet, 5 oz. ftd.	4.50
Cup, 2 style handles	4.50	Tumbler, 3¾", 9 oz.	4.50
Ice bucket, metal handle	18.00	Tumbler, 5", 12 oz.	7.00
Pitcher, 5", 32 oz. sunflower motif in bottom	22.00	Tumbler, 4¾", 7 oz. ftd.	7.50
Pitcher, 9", 48 oz. ftd.	45.00	Tumbler, 5¾" ftd.	10.00
Pitcher, 8", 70 oz. flat	225.00	Tumbler, 7" ftd.	12.00
Plate, 6" sherbet	2.50	Whiskey, 2", 1 oz.	8.00

HOBNAIL HOCKING GLASS COMPANY, 1934–1936

Colors: Crystal, crystal w/red trim, and pink.

Hobnail patterns of some description were made by most Depression era glass companies, but Hocking's Hobnail is easier to recognize because its pieces are shaped like those found in Moonstone or Miss America. In fact, the 1940s Moonstone pattern is really Hocking's Hobnail design with an added white accent to the hobs and edges. Hobnail serving pieces are difficult to find, but beverage sets are abundant. Turn to page 98 to view Hobnail.

Notice how red-trimmed crystal Hobnail (see photo) stands out! Collectors have been bewitched by this red trim which is found mainly on the West Coast. The decanter and footed juices are the only red-trimmed pieces I see with any regularity. I acquired some duplicate pieces to those shown. They rapidly sold when we set them out at a glass show!

Footed juice tumblers were sold along with the decanter as a wine set; thus, it is also a wine glass. Wine glasses during this era usually held three ounces. Today, people think water goblets from the Depression era are wine goblets. Dealers need to check with customers when they ask for wines since they may really want water goblets! Three ounces of wine does not seem like much to today's connoisseurs! I try to include explanations of older glass terminology throughout the book, but that means you have to read the entire book to find them!

Only four pieces were made by Hocking in pink. Another pink Hobnail pattern, such as one made by MacBeth-Evans, can accompany Hocking's; that way, you add a pitcher and tumbler set, something unavailable in Hocking ware. Most other company's Hobnail patterns blend with Hocking's. Crystal Hobnail is not a problem to match, but pink tints can be.

	Pink	*Crystal		Pink	*Crystal
Bowl, 5½" cereal		4.00	Plate, 8½" luncheon	3.50	3.50
Bowl, 7" salad		4.50	Saucer/sherbet plate	2.00	1.50
Cup	4.50	4.50	Sherbet	3.50	3.00
Creamer, ftd.		3.50	Sugar, ftd.		4.00
Decanter and stopper, 32 oz.		27.50	Tumbler, 5 oz. juice		4.00
Goblet, 10 oz. water		7.00	Tumbler, 9 oz., 10 oz. water		5.50
Goblet, 13 oz. iced tea		8.00	Tumbler, 15 oz. iced tea		7.00
Pitcher, 18 oz. milk		20.00	Tumbler, 3 oz. ftd. wine/juice		6.50
Pitcher, 67 oz.		25.00	Tumbler, 5 oz. ftd. cordial		6.00
Plate, 6" sherbet	2.00	1.50	Whiskey, 1½ oz.		6.00

*Add 20 – 25% for red trimmed pieces

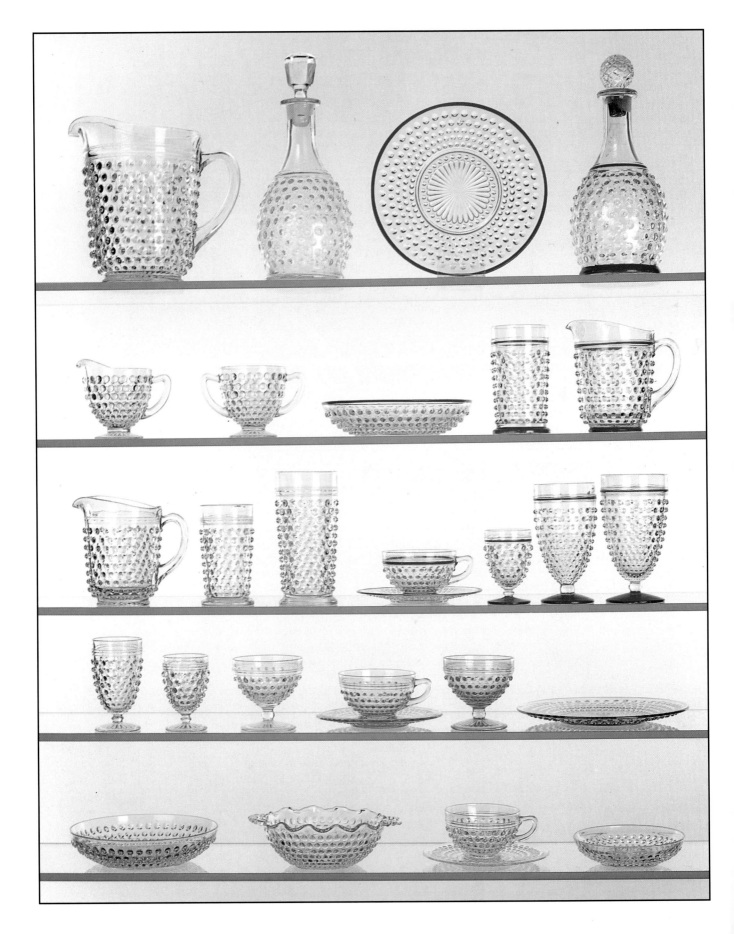

HOMESPUN, "FINE RIB" JEANNETTE GLASS COMPANY, 1939–1949

Colors: Pink and crystal.

I hope the Homespun tumblers pictured side by side on page 100 will help solve some of the difficulties in identification that have plagued collectors. There are six different flat tumblers and three footed ones. The footed juice is easily recognized, but there are two different 15 ounce footed teas. The taller, 6⅜", is on the right in the top row. Notice that it has a slight stem above the foot. The other iced tea on the left has no stem and stands only 6¼" tall. This tumbler appears to be fatter, but it still only holds 15 ounces! Over the years, the ⅛" difference has only been noticed by exacting collectors. You will need to specify which style you want if you order!

In the **middle** of the second row are two different styled flat teas. The one pictured on the right has ribs that run to the top edge. This tumbler stands 5⅜" tall and holds 12½ ounces. The other tea has a clear band of glass above the ribs, holds 13½ ounces, and stands 5⅞". Both of these tumblers have a waffle designed bottom.

There are four entirely different smaller, flat tumblers in that second row. In order (reading right to left) they include: a 4⅛", 8 ounce, ribs to top, flared, plain bottomed; a 3⅞", 7 ounce, ribs to top, straight, concentric ringed bottomed; a 4 5/16", 9 ounce, ribs to top, straight, waffle bottomed; and, after the teas, a 4¼", 9 ounce, band above ribs, waffle bottomed tumbler shown before the omnipresent footed juice! Banded tops are harder to find and most collectors seek the ribbed variety.

The cereal bowl has tab handles but are difficult to find without inner rim chips! Sherbets are disappearing.

Children's sets of Homespun are still in demand. There is no children's teapot in crystal and there are no sugar and creamers in this tea set. The teapot looks like a creamer with a sugar lid. You can see said teapot in the center below.

There is no sugar lid! The lid sometimes found on the Homespun sugar is a Fine Rib pattern powder jar top.

	Pink, Crystal		Pink, Crystal
Bowl, 4½", closed handles	11.00	Sherbet, low flat	17.50
Bowl, 5" cereal, closed handles	27.50	Sugar, ftd.	9.50
Bowl, 8¼" large berry	22.00	Tumbler, 3⅞", 7 oz. straight	20.00
Butter dish and cover	60.00	Tumbler, 4⅛", 8 oz. water, flared top	20.00
Coaster/ash tray	6.50	Tumbler, 4¼", 9 oz. band at top	20.00
Creamer, ftd.	10.00	Tumbler, 4 5/16", 9 oz., no band	20.00
Cup	10.00	Tumbler, 5⅜", 12½ oz. iced tea	30.00
Plate, 6" sherbet	6.00	Tumbler, 5⅞", 13½ oz. iced tea, banded at top	30.00
Plate, 9¼" dinner	16.00	Tumbler, 4", 5 oz. ftd.	7.00
Platter, 13", closed handles	15.00	Tumbler, 6¼", 15 oz. ftd.	27.50
Saucer	4.00	Tumbler, 6⅜", 15 oz. ftd.	27.50

HOMESPUN CHILD'S TEA SET

	Pink	Crystal		Pink	Crystal
Cup	30.00	20.00	Tea pot cover	75.00	
Saucer	10.00	8.00	Set: 14-pieces	325.00	
Plate	12.50	9.00	Set: 12-pieces		148.00
Tea pot	45.00				

99

INDIANA CUSTARD, "FLOWER AND LEAF BAND" INDIANA GLASS COMPANY 1930s; 1950s

Colors: Ivory or custard, early 1930s; white, 1950s.

Indiana Custard **is beginning** to attract new collectors who do not seem to be discouraged because it was so regionally distributed. Quantities of this pattern have been seen in the Ohio and Indiana area in the past, but even those areas are beginning to "dry up." However, this is the region to visit if you are earnestly searching for **any** Indiana glassware pattern! Collecting Indiana Custard will take work and luck, but it can be done! Many collectors never get a chance to see it in quantity. However, that is an advantage for those who do seek it. There is not a sufficient supply of this Indiana Custard to maintain immense collecting pressure!

Indiana Custard is the only Depression era pattern where cups and sherbets are the most troublesome items to find! Some collectors consider the sherbet overpriced; but others who have searched for years without acquiring one, would disagree! For me, cups have been more difficult to find than the sherbets, but I seem to find the sherbets in groups of six or eight and the cups one or two at a time. Both sell quickly; so there is a demand even at the expensive prices! A minor problem is consistent color. Some pieces have a whiter cast than the normally found beige color.

More Indiana Custard collectors are in the central Indiana area than any other place. Of course, it is more plentiful there, making it easier to get hooked!

I have been unable to establish if there is a full set available of yellow floral decorated pieces like the plate pictured on the left below. I have seen a set of Indiana Custard decorated like the saucer with the colored flowers standing behind the oval vegetable. After 60 years, a primary problem to collecting this set would be that the decorations flake rather freely. After all these years, gathering a set a piece or two at a time is a severe challenge! But, then, some people like the chase! One collector told me that he intentionally chose a rarely seen pattern so he could have greater enjoyment finding even one piece!

	French Ivory		**French Ivory**
Bowl, 5½" berry	10.00	Plate, 7½" salad	18.00
Bowl, 6½" cereal	24.00	Plate, 8⅞" luncheon	18.00
Bowl, 7½" flat soup	32.50	Plate, 9¾" dinner	27.50
Bowl, 9", 1¾" deep, large berry	32.50	Platter, 11½" oval	35.00
Bowl, 9½" oval vegetable	30.00	Saucer	8.00
Butter dish and cover	60.00	Sherbet	95.00
Cup	37.50	Sugar	12.00
Creamer	16.00	Sugar cover	23.00
Plate, 5¾" bread and butter	6.50		

Please refer to Foreword for pricing information

IRIS, "IRIS AND HERRINGBONE" JEANNETTE GLASS COMPANY, 1928–1932; 1950s; 1970s

Colors: Crystal, iridescent; some pink and green; recently bi-colored red/yellow and blue/green combinations, and white.

Iris is the most difficult pattern to situate in separating this book from the *Collectible Glassware from the 40s, 50s, 60s...* since it qualifies for both eras. Crystal production began in 1928. However, some crystal was made in the late 1940s into the 1950s, with some candy bottoms and vases appearing as late as the early 1970s. Iridescent **belongs** entirely within the time structure of *Collectible Glassware from the 40s, 50s, 60s....*

Prices for crystal Iris have finally steadied, but for a while diehard collectors helped inflate prices by buying into rising costs of harder-to-find pieces. There was a short supply of several Iris pieces because of heavy demand. That short supply became even shorter for a while. However, as prices increased, more collectors began to sell their sets and rare items again began to appear for sale. Had you bought a 12 place setting five years ago, you could have more than doubled your investment even if you sold it wholesale to a dealer! Today, many dealers are carrying hard-to-find cereals, soups, coasters, and demitasse sets that are not selling in the new rarefied strata created. Collectors can sometimes influence prices by refusing to buy when they deem items too costly. However, this can backfire on rare pieces! They can totally disappear into collections while collectors dither. I've heard collectors lamenting that they had an opportunity to buy such and so previously, but thought it too highly priced. Now, they can't find any for sale!

Iris **used to be** a plentiful pattern; now, there is so much in collections that only a few pieces are plentiful. There are enough pitchers, water tumblers, and wines to satisfy collectors! Demitasse **cups** are available; saucers are scarce. Many of these cups were originally sold on copper saucers instead of glass. The 11" flat fruit bowl is turning up in several variations including several degrees of pronouced or slight rolled edge.

Iridescent candy bottoms are a product of the 1970s when Jeannette made crystal bottoms and flashed them with two-tone colors such as red/yellow or blue/green. Many of these were sold as vases; and, over time, the colors have peeled off making them, again, crystal candy bottoms. **These later pieces can be distinguished by the lack of rays on the foot of the dish.** Similarly, white vases were made and sprayed outside in green, red, and blue. White vases sell in the area of $12.50–15.00. Yes, the colors can be removed. **These are not rare!** I saw a pink over white vase in an antique mall yesterday for $60.00 marked "rare Iris." I hope that no one believes that!

The decorated red and gold Iris that keeps turning up (see 4" sherbet, page 103) was called "Corsage" and "styled by Century" in 1946. This information was on a card attached to a 1946 wedding gift of this ware.

The 8 ounce water goblet, 5¾", 4 ounce goblet, 4" sherbet, and the demitasse cup and saucer are the most difficult pieces to find in iridescent. The 5¾", 4 ounce goblet is shown in the *Very Rare Glassware of the Depression Era, 4th Series*. Three iridescent 4" sherbets were found in Texas.

Good pink color in transparent Iris vases will bring the price below, but weakly colored pink will not! That red candlestick in the bottom photograph is flashed red and not truly red glass! A few other pieces have been found with this treatment.

	Crystal	Iridescent	Green/Pink
Bowl, 4½", berry, beaded edge	42.00	9.00	
Bowl, 5", ruffled, sauce	9.00	27.50	
Bowl, 5", cereal	120.00		
Bowl, 7½", soup	160.00	60.00	
Bowl, 8", berry, beaded edge	85.00	25.00	
Bowl, 9½", ruffled, salad	12.50	13.00	125.00
Bowl, 11½", ruffled, fruit	15.00	14.00	
Bowl, 11", fruit, straight edge	60.00		
Butter dish and cover	47.50	42.50	
Butter dish bottom	13.50	12.50	
Butter dish top	34.00	30.00	
Candlesticks, pr.	42.50	45.00	
Candy jar and cover	155.00		
Coaster	100.00		
Creamer, ftd.	12.00	12.00	110.00
Cup	15.00	14.00	
* Demitasse cup	35.00	150.00	
* Demitasse saucer	135.00	225.00	
Fruit or nut set	75.00		
Goblet, 4", wine		30.00	

	Crystal	Iridescent	Green/Pink
Goblet, 4½", 4 oz., cocktail	27.50		
Goblet, 4½", 3 oz., wine	17.00		
Goblet, 5½", 4 oz.	27.50	195.00	
Goblet, 5½", 8 oz.	26.00	195.00	
** Lamp shade, 11½"	85.00		
Pitcher, 9½", ftd.	37.50	40.00	
Plate, 5½", sherbet	15.00	14.00	
Plate, 8", luncheon	105.00		
Plate, 9", dinner	55.00	42.50	
Plate, 11¾", sandwich	32.00	32.00	
Saucer	12.00	11.00	
Sherbet, 2½", ftd.	27.50	15.00	
Sherbet, 4", ftd.	25.00	195.00	
Sugar	11.00	11.00	125.00
Sugar cover	12.00	12.00	
Tumbler, 4", flat	135.00		
Tumbler, 6", ftd.	18.00	16.00	
Tumbler, 6½", ftd.	35.00		
Vase, 9"	27.50	25.00	150.00

* Ruby, Blue, Amethyst priced as Iridescent   **Colors, $65.00

Please refer to Foreword for pricing information

JUBILEE LANCASTER GLASS COMPANY, Early 1930s

Colors: Yellow, crystal, and pink.

Jubilee luncheon sets consisting of cups, saucers, creamer, sugar, footed tumblers, and luncheon plates are easily acquired. The quantities of these items has caused a glut on the market and prices have declined a bit. However, you have a problem getting anything else. That, too, has caused the selling of common pieces to slow. New collectors look at the prices of the non common pieces and decide that collecting another pattern might not be such a bad idea! Gathering even four stems in each size, let alone eight or twelve, will put a dent in almost anyone's check book. You can see all known stems and tumblers except the oyster cocktail on page 105. The iced tea tumbler is included twice by mistake!

I have found more Jubilee in Florida than any place other than Ohio. Of course, Florida is where I have been searching for glass lately! Locating it has not been the problem, finding the right pieces to buy has! Crystal pieces are turning up in small batches. It's attractive, but hasn't the vibrancy of the yellow!

A dilemma in collecting Jubilee is all the look-alike items. Some Jubilee collectors exasperate dealers with their nit picking preciseness as to what constitutes Jubilee, while others are just happy to discover any similar flower cuttings on Lancaster blanks! There are other Lancaster look-alike patterns that have 16 petals or 12 petals with a smaller petal in between the larger ones. Most of my customers delight in buying look-alike pieces for less than prices paid for the real thing; then, purist collectors will accept nothing but the 12 petaled, open center pieces.

Accepted by more and more dealers and collectors now is that if the piece has a 12 or 16 petaled open centered flower, then it is Jubilee, regardless of the blank on which it is cut. The four pieces pictured below all fit this general criteria but are on different blanks than those normally used for Jubilee. A pink 12" vase previously listed only in yellow now has been discovered. It has a 4" top, 3½" base, and a bulbous 6" middle.

Several collectors report finding 11½", three-footed, scalloped, flattened bowls to go with the curved up 11½" bowl normally called a rose bowl in other elegant patterns. The 3", 8 ounce, non-stemmed sherbet has eleven petals as does the three-footed covered candy. You can see that sherbet and the oyster cocktail mentioned above in the *Very Rare Glassware of the Depression Years, Fourth Series*. Having only 11 petals on the candy and sherbet evidently came from cutting problems experienced when using the standard 6" cutting wheel. The foot of the sherbet and the knob on the candy were in the way when a petal of the design was cut directly up and down. The glass cutter had to move over to the side in order to cut a petal. Because of this placement, only an 11 petal flower resulted on these pieces. Yes! Those two 11 petal pieces **are** Jubilee. In those two cases, purists have to make allowances for the glass cutting problem being solved by eliminating one petal!

According to the catalog number, the liner plate to the mayonnaise is the same piece as the 8¾" plate. There is no indented plate for the mayonnaise shown in the catalogs. However, the plate under the mayonnaise in the photograph on page 105 has an indent. This mayonnaise has 16 petals! As I have mentioned before, true Jubilee should have 12 petals and an open-centered flower, but there are exceptions! The catalog sheets that show the mayonnaise picture one with 16 petals!

	Pink	Yellow
Bowl, 8", 3-ftd., 5⅛" high	250.00	200.00
Bowl, 9" handled fruit		125.00
Bowl, 11½", flat fruit	195.00	160.00
Bowl, 11½", 3-ftd.	250.00	250.00
Bowl, 11½", 3-ftd., curved in		225.00
Bowl, 13", 3-ftd.	250.00	225.00
Candlestick, pr.	185.00	185.00
Candy jar, w/lid, 3-ftd.	325.00	325.00
Cheese & cracker set	255.00	250.00
Creamer	35.00	17.50
Cup	40.00	12.00
Mayonnaise & plate	295.00	250.00
w/original ladle	310.00	265.00
Plate, 7" salad	22.50	13.00
Plate, 8¾" luncheon	27.50	12.00
Plate, 13½" sandwich, handled	85.00	50.00
Plate, 14", 3-ftd.		200.00
Saucer, two styles	12.00	4.00
Sherbet, 3", 8 oz.		70.00
Stem, 4", 1 oz., cordial		250.00
Stem, 4¾", 4 oz., oyster cocktail		75.00
Stem, 4⅞", 3 oz., cocktail		150.00
Stem, 5½", 7 oz., sherbet/champagne		95.00
Stem, 7½", 11 oz.		165.00
Sugar	35.00	17.50
Tray, 11", 2-handled cake	65.00	45.00
Tumbler, 5", 6 oz., ftd. juice		95.00

	Pink	Yellow
Tumbler, 6", 10 oz., water	75.00	33.00
Tumbler, 6⅛", 12½ oz., iced tea		150.00
Tray, 11", center-		
handled sandwich	195.00	200.00
Vase, 12"	350.00	350.00

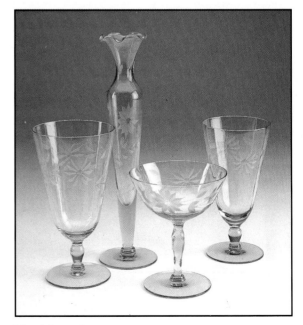

LACED EDGE, "KATY BLUE" IMPERIAL GLASS COMPANY, Early 1930s

Colors: Blue w/opalescent edge and green w/opalescent edge.

Laced Edge comes in a multitude of colors; only opalescent blue and green are being dealt with in this book. Most of the colors without the white edge were made into the 1950s; so, they creep out of the time frame (before 1940) handled in this book! The white edging technique was called "Sea Foam." Some "Sea Foam" treatment barely covers the edge of pieces while others have a ½" of bold, opalescent edging.

The opalescent blue is habitually called "Katy Blue" by its long time collectors, but I have never heard the green called "Katy Green." Blue and green pieces without the white sell for about half of the prices listed. Crystal pieces do not seem to be selling. I have never seen crystal pieces with white edging. Have you such a piece?

Some collectors do not accept the 12" cake plate (luncheon plate in Imperial catalog) or the 9" vegetable bowl (salad in ad) as Laced Edge because the edges are more open than those of the other items. Thanks to a Laced Edge collector from Illinois, for an original ad (page 107) showing a then-inflated retail price along with the cost in coupons for Laced Edge pieces. **Notice the bowl and cake plate are shown with this pattern!** The handwritten note below the ad states the coupons came from a margarine product (believed to be called "Oak Grove"). You could get six tumblers for fewer coupons than the platter or divided oval bowl!

The large accumulation I bought came from the family of a butter and eggs salesperson who stopped that occupation in 1941. The pieces purchased were left-over premiums he was to give out to his customers.

Notice the undivided oval vegetable bowl is missing from this ad and most collections today!

Creamers have several different styles of lips because they were individually made using wooden tools. Cereal bowls vary from 4⅞" to 5⅝"; soup bowls vary from 6⅞" to 7¼"; and berry bowls from 4⅜" to 4¾". Size differences are due to the turning out of the edge of the bowl. Some edges go straight up while others are flattened. Collectors will accept differences to have enough bowls!

If you are a recipe book collector, there's a 1937 Jell-O booklet with several pieces of Laced Edge pictured on the cover. A reader was kind enough to send me a photocopy!

	Opalescent		**Opalescent**
Basket bowl	225.00	Bowl, 9" vegetable	95.00
Bowl, 4⅜"–4¾" fruit	30.00	Bowl, 11" divided oval	115.00
Bowl, 5"	37.50	Bowl, 11" oval	150.00
Bowl, 5½"	37.50	Candlestick, double, pr.	165.00
Bowl, 5⅞""	37.50	Cup	35.00
Bowl, 7" soup	80.00	Creamer	40.00

	Opalescent		**Opalescent**
Mayonnaise, 3-piece	135.00	Platter, 13"	175.00
Plate, 6½" bread & butter	18.00	Saucer	15.00
Plate, 8" salad	32.00	Sugar	42.50
Plate, 10" dinner	85.00	Tidbit, 2-tiered, 8" & 10" plates	100.00
Plate, 12" luncheon (per catalog description)	80.00	Tumbler, 9 oz.	55.00

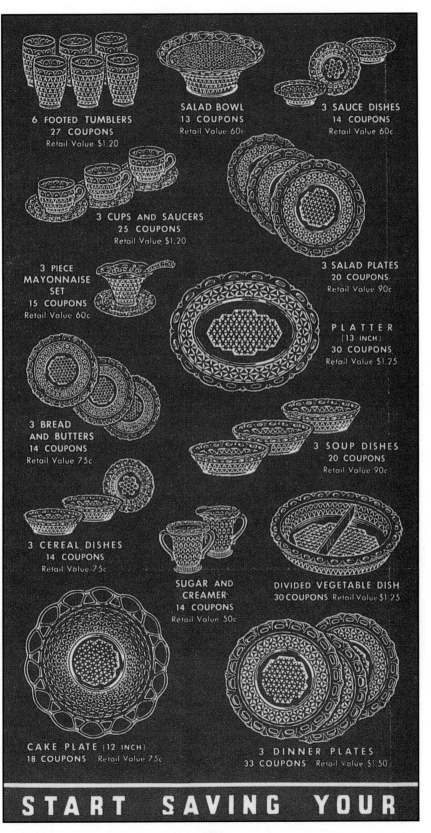

LACED EDGE

LAKE COMO HOCKING GLASS COMPANY, 1934–1937

Color: White with blue scene.

Lake Como has only 13 different pieces to garner and for the first time you can see every one of them pictured! The cereal bowl is standing up next to the sugar so you can see the pattern. Last fall, I bought a collection of glassware from the family of a former factory worker. There was a fairly large set of Lake Como included, but most of it was terribly worn. That is a dilemma for collectors. If it were ever used, the pattern is usually faded or even missing. The prices below are for **mint** condition Lake Como (full bright pattern). You should be able to buy worn Lake Como at 50% to 80% of the prices listed depending upon the amount of wear.

Lake Como is an elusive pattern that some collectors say they never see when out looking for glass. I find it occasionally and some pieces in all collections I have acquired have been worn. One collector told me that he had decided to buy less than mint glass in order to have some of the harder-to-find pieces. Items ordinarily found include shakers, sugars, and creamers. Rarely do other items present themselves. When exhibited, "like new" Lake Como sells very quickly!

Notice the flat soup standing up on the right of the middle row. The floral decoration on the edge is embossed (like the normally found Vitrock soup) instead of painted in blue. You will find platters and vegetable bowls are almost as difficult to find as soup bowls; but most collectors are looking for several soups, which creates a greater problem than finding only one platter or bowl. Finding either style cup will be a headache.

	White		White
Bowl, 6" cereal	25.00	Plate, 9¼" dinner	33.00
Bowl, 9¾" vegetable	65.00	Platter, 11"	70.00
Bowl, flat soup	100.00	Salt & pepper, pr.	42.50
Creamer, ftd.	32.50	Saucer	12.00
Cup, regular	30.00	Saucer, St. Denis	12.00
Cup, St. Denis	30.00	Sugar, ftd.	32.50
Plate, 7¼" salad	18.00		

LAUREL McKEE GLASS COMPANY, 1930s

Colors: French Ivory, Jade Green, White Opal, and Poudre Blue.

Laurel's Poudre Blue is the color most coveted by collectors, but it is the color least frequently found. Unfortunately, not all items were made in this powder blue color. That could be considered an advantage since you will not have to ferret out as many pieces to complete a set. A soup bowl in blue has recently been found. You can see it pictured in *Very Rare Glassware of the Depression Years, Fifth Series*. Some collectors are starting to search for Jade Green Laurel for variety. French Ivory (beige) excites few collectors; so prices there have remained stable for several years. Now might be the time to consider a set in that color before other collectors get that idea!

Serving pieces in all colors are inadequate for the demand. I will mention that some collectors of Depression glass are sending photos showing how they have **combined different colors of one pattern** to achieve ample serving capabilities. Paucity of pieces in a single color is giving birth to some artistic settings!

Children's Laurel tea sets are avidly sought. The Scotty Dog decorated sets are the most desired children's sets in Depression glass in both Jade Green and French Ivory! When have you seen a set or even one piece for sale? Collectors of Scotty Dog items have pushed the prices of these sets to double what they were selling for only a few years ago! Add to that all the collectors of children's dishes and there is not enough of this scarce set to accommodate all collecting fields!

Children's sets with edge trims of red, green, or orange are found in Laurel in limited quantity with orange being the most difficult color to discover. Watch for wear on these colored trims; it appears many children may have played with these dishes!

A few collectors are beginning to search for the trimmed dinner-sized ivory. Red trimmed Laurel is the most often found, but sets can also be built with green trim. As with the children's pieces, wear on the trim is a detriment. However, these dishes are past 60 years old now; so some usage wear is to be expected!

Laurel shakers are hard to find with **strong** patterns. Many Laurel shaker designs are vague and indistinct. Definitely, it's better to own a patterned Laurel shaker than one that has only the right shape! Doric and Pansy shakers are the only other Depression pattern that has this same problem! Jade shakers are quite rare, but there are not enough collectors buying them to expose this scarcity.

	White Opal, Jade Green	French Ivory	Poudre Blue		White Opal, Jade Green	French Ivory	Poudre Blue
Bowl, 4¾" berry	6.50	7.50	15.00	Plate, 6" sherbet	5.00	5.00	10.00
Bowl, 6" cereal	9.00	10.00	25.00	Plate, 7½" salad	10.00	9.00	14.00
Bowl, 6", three legs	12.50	15.00		Plate, 9⅛" dinner	15.00	13.00	25.00
Bowl, 7⅞" soup	35.00	35.00	75.00	Plate, 9⅛" grill, round or scalloped	12.00	12.00	
Bowl, 9" large berry	20.00	22.00	45.00	Platter, 10¾" oval	25.00	25.00	40.00
Bowl, 9¾" oval vegetable	25.00	25.00	50.00	Salt and pepper	60.00	45.00	
Bowl, 10½", three legs	30.00	35.00	65.00	Saucer	3.50	3.00	7.50
Bowl, 11"	33.00	38.00	70.00	Sherbet	10.00	11.00	
Candlestick, 4" pr.	40.00	35.00		Sherbet/champagne, 5"	45.00	40.00	
Cheese dish and cover	52.50	55.00		Sugar, short	8.50	9.00	
Creamer, short	10.00	10.00		Sugar, tall	11.00	11.00	35.00
Creamer, tall	12.00	12.00	35.00	Tumbler, 4½", 9 oz. flat	45.00	35.00	
Cup	7.50	7.00	20.00	Tumbler, 5", 12 oz. flat		50.00	

CHILDREN'S LAUREL TEA SET

	Plain	Green or Decorated Rims	Scotty Dog Green	Scotty Dog Ivory
Creamer	25.00	40.00	125.00	90.00
Cup	20.00	30.00	65.00	42.50
Plate	10.00	16.00	55.00	35.00
Saucer	8.00	10.00	55.00	25.00
Sugar	25.00	40.00	125.00	90.00
14-piece set	205.00	305.00	950.00	595.00

Please refer to Foreword for pricing information

LINCOLN INN FENTON GLASS COMPANY, Late 1920s

Colors: Red, cobalt, light blue, amethyst, black, green, green opalescent, pink, crystal, amber, and jade (opaque).

Lincoln Inn red and several shades of blue remain the most desirable colors. The good news is that those are the colors that are most often found! I've chosen this book to show the myriad of other colors you could collect. This fits very well with the rainbow collecting scheme that is beginning to mushroom in glass collecting circles. The rainbow of colors found in Lincoln Inn gives searchers a wide selection for collecting!

Champagne/sherbets are abundant in all colors. You can also find tumblers and stems easily; but obtaining a pitcher or serving pieces in **any** color is a task. Bear in mind that Fenton remade an iridized, dark carnival colored pitcher a few years ago! Any other **iridized** colored piece you might see in this pattern is of recent vintage! All light blue pitchers have been found in Florida; so watch for them there!

A 1930s catalog shows Lincoln Inn plates with a fruit design in the center. I have only found these in crystal; but I spoke with a collector at a recent show who had found several 8" pink plates with fruits design. It was the first report I have had of colored, fruit designed plates. I looked at a 9" crystal bowl with the fruit designs at an antique mall in Florida, but the bowl's owner valued it as Lalique — or better!

Lincoln Inn shakers continue to be difficult to find in all colors. There are collectors who only search for shakers. Although these are not the highest priced shakers in Depression glass, they are among the toughest to find. Red and black shakers are the most desired colors; but do not pass **any** color in your travels. I found a red pair sitting with Royal Ruby in a dark corner of a shop a few years ago! They were reasonably priced! You need to look in every nook and cranny in shops that do not specialize in Depression glass.

Many red pieces are more amberina in color. For novices, amberina is red glass that has a yellow tint to it. Older red glass was made by reheating glass that first came from the furnace as yellow glass. Then the glass was reheated to change it to red; irregular heating caused some parts of it to remain yellow. Some dealers have told collectors this is a rare color in order to sell it. In a certain sense, that may have an element of truth. Actually, it was a mistake; and the amounts of yellow on each piece make it hard to match colors. Many **expert** glass collectors reject amberina pieces. On the other hand, I have recently had calls for "any amberina glass." There are, then, collectors specifically looking for amberina glassware!

	Cobalt Blue, Red	**All Other Colors
Ash tray	17.50	12.00
Bon bon, handled square	15.00	12.00
Bon bon, handled oval	16.00	12.00
Bowl, 5" fruit	11.50	8.50
Bowl, 6" cereal	13.00	9.00
Bowl, 6" crimped	13.00	8.50
Bowl, handled olive	15.00	9.50
Bowl, finger	20.00	12.50
Bowl, 9", shallow		23.00
Bowl, 9¼" ftd.	65.00	30.00
Bowl, 10½" ftd.	55.00	35.00
Candy dish, ftd. oval	40.00	20.00
Comport	30.00	14.50
Creamer	22.50	14.50
Cup	20.00	10.00
Goblet, water	27.00	15.50
Goblet, wine	30.00	16.50
Nut dish, ftd.	20.00	12.00
Pitcher, 7¼", 46 oz.	800.00	700.00
Plate, 6"	7.50	4.50
Plate, 8"	12.50	7.50
Plate, 9¼"	35.00	11.50
Plate, 12"	40.00	15.50
* Salt/pepper, pr.	250.00	165.00
Sandwich server, center hdld.	150.00	90.00
Saucer	5.00	3.50
Sherbet, 4½", cone shape	17.00	11.50
Sherbet, 4¾"	19.00	12.50
Sugar	20.00	14.00
Tumbler, 4 oz. flat juice	30.00	9.50

	Cobalt Blue, Red	**All Other Colors
Tumbler, 9 oz. flat water		19.50
Tumbler, 5 oz. ftd.	30.00	11.00
Tumbler, 9 oz. ftd.	30.00	14.00
Tumbler, 12 oz. ftd.	45.00	19.00
Vase, 9¾"	135.00	75.00
Vase, 12" ftd.	150.00	95.00

* Black $300.00
** w/fruits, add 20 – 25%

Please refer to Foreword for pricing information

LORAIN, "BASKET," No. 615 INDIANA GLASS COMPANY, 1929–1932

Colors: Green, yellow, and some crystal.

Lorain has the ubiquitous problem of most of Indiana's Depression glassware, mould roughness on the seams. If you are inflexible about **mint** condition glassware, then you should concentrate on some other pattern. However, besides a formidable challenge, you **could** find collecting Lorain a stimulating experience that will reward you with beautiful arrangements of glass!

After buying and selling several collections of Lorain and talking with collectors who have hunted Lorain for years, I have arrived at several conclusions. Buy any cereal bowls you can find, but check the inner rims closely; they damage. The 8" deep berry is the next hardest piece to locate. Most collectors only want one of these, so that is not as big a obstacle as finding four or more cereals. Dinner plates are almost as scarce as cereals. Watch for scratches on the plates since they can be obscured by the pattern if you do not examine them closely! Oval vegetable bowls are infrequently found in both colors. Saucers are harder to come upon than cups because of mould roughness and wear and tear on them over the years. It is amazing how collecting has changed. Dealers used to refuse to buy saucers unless there were cups with them. Today, many of these once disdained saucers are eagerly bought whether there are cups or not! There are now a dozen or more patterns of Depression glass where saucers are more difficult to find than cups. Since Lorain is scarce, you might be tempted to buy pieces that are less than mint when you find them; just try to do so at less than the mint prices below!

Almost every Lorain price has risen since the last book. Many times only the rarer pieces of a pattern display that tendency. Recent collectors are starting green Lorain because of price and availability. Green is less expensive and more easily found. A few pieces are found in crystal, but I would not suggest you try to complete a set as I am not sure all pieces could be found in crystal. A few pieces could complement your colored sets, however.

Some crystal is found with colored borders of red, yellow, green, and blue. For those who have written to ask about the snack tray, one with yellow trim is pictured in the top photograph. It was made from the platter mould that had an indent added for a cup rest. Crystal cups are sometimes found trimmed in the four colors to match the snack tray, but frequently they are only crystal. To date, these snack trays have only been found in crystal or crystal with trims. A true green or yellow snack tray would be a find!

New collectors, please note that the white and green avocado colored sherbets (which have an open lace border) are a 1950s and later issue made by Anchor-Hocking. They were used regularly by florists for small floral arrangements and many are found with a tacky, clay-like substance in the bottom that was used to hold flowers. In the past they were accepted as an Indiana product; but several have been found with Anchor Hocking stickers. I have not been able to find these in catalogs, but Anchor-Hocking did affix labels in the late 1950s and early 1960s. If any one out there has more specific knowledge of these, please share!

	Crystal, Green	Yellow
Bowl, 6" cereal	45.00	65.00
Bowl, 7¼" salad	45.00	65.00
Bowl, 8" deep berry	100.00	155.00
Bowl, 9¾" oval vegetable	45.00	55.00
Creamer, ftd.	16.00	25.00
Cup	11.00	15.00
Plate, 5½" sherbet	7.50	11.00
Plate, 7¾" salad	10.00	15.00
Plate, 8⅜" luncheon	17.50	27.50
Plate, 10¼" dinner	45.00	60.00
Platter, 11½"	30.00	45.00
Relish, 8", 4-part	16.50	35.00
Saucer	4.50	6.00
Sherbet, ftd.	23.00	33.00
Snack tray, crystal/trim	21.00	
Sugar, ftd.	16.00	25.00
Tumbler, 4¾", 9 oz. ftd.	23.00	33.00

Please refer to Foreword for pricing information

MADRID FEDERAL GLASS COMPANY, 1932–1939; INDIANA GLASS COMPANY, 1980s

Colors: Green, pink, amber, crystal, and "Madonna" blue. (*See Reproduction Section.*)

Madrid has been controversial since 1976 when the Federal Glass Company reissued this pattern for the Bicentennial under the name "Recollection" glassware. Each piece was marked 1976 in the design; but it was manufactured in an amber color similar to the original. Collectors were informed and many assumed it would someday be collectible and even bought sets seeing future profits. Unfortunately, Indiana Glass bought the moulds for Madrid when Federal became insolvent and there have been headaches for collectors ever since. Indiana removed the 1976 date and made crystal. The old crystal butter was selling for several hundred dollars and the new one sold for $2.99. Prices plummeted!

Shortly afterwards, Indiana made pink; and even though it was a lighter pink than the original, prices nose-dived on the old pink Madrid. I keep seeing these pink Madrid sugar and creamers with high prices at flea markets and antique malls. Originally, there were no pink sugar and creamers made. Check my list for pieces made in pink. If no price is listed, then it was not made in the 1930s. Afterward, Indiana made blue; it is a brighter, harsher blue than the beautiful, soft blue of the original Madrid, but it had a devastating effect on the prices of the 1930s blue. (See the new pink in the Reproduction Section in the back.) All pieces made in pink have now been made in blue. Any blue pieces found not priced below is new! The latest color, teal, is the first color made that was not made in the 1930s.

Madrid gravy boats and platters have almost always been found in Iowa. I am betting it was a premium for some item used by rural folks — seed or chicken feed! I just spoke to a person from Iowa who attended a **recent** auction where a gravy boat and platter were sold! (See one in the foreground of the top photograph.) More platters for this boat are found than the gravy itself. These platters are selling in the $300.00 range by themselves.

Mint condition sugar lids in any color Madrid are a treasure. Footed tumblers are harder to find than flat ones. Amber footed shakers are harder to find than flat ones and have made a tremendous price increase! Footed shakers are the only style you can find in blue. Look at the shakers in the bottom photograph that shows both old styles available. Any heavy, flat ones you spot are new!

Collectors of green Madrid have turned out to be almost as sparse as the pattern! Green is almost as rare as blue!

Labels on the wooden Lazy Susans (found in eastern Kentucky and southern Ohio) say "Kalter Aufschain Cold Cuts Server Schirmer Cincy." One of these pictured in *Second Series, Very Rare Glassware of the Depression Years.*

	Amber	Pink	Green	Blue		Amber	Pink	Green	Blue
Ash tray, 6" square	225.00		195.00		Pitcher, 8½", 80 oz.	60.00		200.00	
Bowl, 4¾" cream soup	16.00				Pitcher, 8½", 80 oz. ice lip	60.00		225.00	
Bowl, 5" sauce	6.50	6.50	7.00	30.00	Plate, 6" sherbet	4.00	3.50	4.00	8.00
Bowl, 7" soup	15.00		16.00		Plate, 7½" salad	11.00	9.00	9.00	20.00
Bowl, 8" salad	14.00		17.50		Plate, 8⅞" luncheon	8.00	7.00	9.00	18.00
Bowl, 9⅜" lg. berry	20.00	20.00			Plate, 10½" dinner	45.00		40.00	70.00
Bowl, 9½" deep salad	30.00				Plate, 10½" grill	9.50		15.00	
Bowl, 10" oval veg.	15.00	15.00	20.00	40.00	Plate, 10¼" relish	15.00	12.50	16.00	
* Bowl, 11" low console	15.00	11.00			Plate, 11¼" rd. cake	14.00	10.00		
Butter dish w/lid	70.00		90.00		Platter, 11½" oval	15.00	14.00	16.00	24.00
Butter dish bottom	27.50		40.00		Salt/pepper, 3½" ftd., pr.	130.00		110.00	150.00
Butter dish top	37.50		50.00		Salt/pepper, 3½" flat, pr.	45.00		64.00	
* Candlesticks, pr., 2¼"	22.00	20.00			Saucer	4.00	5.00	5.00	10.00
Cookie jar w/lid	45.00	30.00			Sherbet, two styles	7.50		11.00	15.00
Creamer, ftd.	8.50		11.00	20.00	Sugar	7.50		8.50	15.00
Cup	6.50	7.50	8.50	16.00	Sugar cover	45.00		50.00	175.00
** Gravy boat and platter	1,200.00				Tumbler, 3⅞", 5 oz.	14.00		32.00	40.00
Hot dish coaster	40.00		40.00		Tumbler, 4¼", 9 oz.	15.00	15.00	20.00	30.00
Hot dish coaster w/Indent	40.00		40.00		Tumbler, 5½", 12 oz. 2 styles	22.00		30.00	40.00
Jam dish, 7"	25.00		20.00	40.00	Tumbler, 4", 5 oz. ftd.	28.00		40.00	
Jello mold, 2⅛" T	14.00				Tumbler, 5½", 10 oz. ftd.	30.00		40.00	
Pitcher, 5½" 36 oz. juice	40.00				Wooden lazy susan, cold cuts coasters	800.00			
***Pitcher, 8", sq. 60 oz.	45.00	35.00	135.00	160.00					

* Iridescent priced slightly higher
** Platter only – $450.00
*** Crystal – $150.00

Please refer to Foreword for pricing information

MANHATTAN, "HORIZONTAL RIBBED" ANCHOR HOCKING GLASS COMPANY, 1938–1943

Colors: Crystal, pink; some green, ruby, and iridized.

If you find a piece of Manhattan that does not fit the measurements in the list below, then you may have a piece of Anchor Hocking's newer line Park Avenue. Anchor Hocking was very careful to make pieces in different sizes or shapes than the old Manhattan! For new readers, I will repeat what I have said before for those who do not update books regularly.

Park Avenue was a new pattern line introduced by Anchor Hocking in 1987 to "re-create the Glamour Era of 1938 when Anchor Hocking first introduced a classic" according to the Inspiration '87 catalog issued by the company. Anchor Hocking went to the trouble to preserve the integrity of their older glassware, however! None of the pieces in this line are exactly like the old Manhattan! They are only similar and Manhattan was never made in blue as this line has been. Many collectors of Manhattan have bought this new pattern to use as everyday dishes. Thus, everyone remains happy, company and collector alike. Manhattan's collectibility has not been affected by the making of Park Avenue; however, it has caused some confusion with the older Manhattan cereal bowls. These older 5¼" cereals are rarely seen, particularly in **mint** condition; you need to be aware of the differences in these pieces. Park Avenue lists a small bowl at 6". All the original Manhattan bowls measure 1¹⁵⁄₁₆" **high.** If the bowl you have measures more than two inches, then you have a piece of Park Avenue! Be very suspicious if the bowl is mint! I hope this clears up the measuring problems that people ordering through the mail have had in buying the cereal bowls. You can see an original cereal in the right foreground (bottom photograph). You can also see the only known pink one in *Very Rare Glassware of the Depression Years, Fifth Series.*

The handled berry measures 5⅜". Cereals do not have handles! I mention the measurements because there is a vast price difference. In fact, the reason the 5⅜" handled berry has increased in price so much has come from dealers marketing these as cereals! Everyone wants costly cereals!

The price rise and scarcity of Manhattan comports can be attributed to margarita or martini drinkers! These were originally designed for candy or mints, but you cannot convince a drinker that these were not designed for him!

All metal accessories were made by sources outside the factory. Anchor Hocking sold their wares to other companies who made these accoutrements with tongs or spoons hanging or otherwise attached to them. There is a remote possibility that metal pieces were sold to Hocking; but years ago workers told me that they never assembled anything but glass at the factory. Of course, I have found that workers' memories are not always totally reliable!

Pink Manhattan cups, saucers, and dinner plates do exist, but are rarely seen. You can detect a cup in the top photograph, but I have never found a saucer to go with it. The saucer/sherbet plates of Manhattan are like many of Hocking's saucers; they have no cup ring. The pink dinner plate displayed at a Houston show years ago has been in someone's collection for some time now. Another Manhattan Royal Ruby juice pitcher was found last year in a northern Kentucky antique show. It is pictured with the pink!

The sherbet in Manhattan has a beaded bottom like the tumblers, but the center insert to the relish tray does not have these beads. Relish tray inserts can be found in crystal, pink, and Royal Ruby. The center insert is always crystal on these relish trays although I see a pink sherbet was placed in the center of the pink relish in the top picture by some helpful imp at the photo session!

Manhattan is one pattern that is aided by the many look-alike pieces that can be added to it! Some collectors buy Hazel Atlas shakers to use with Manhattan since they are round and look better to them than the original squared ones that Hocking made. However, I have intentionally left out all the look-alike Manhattan in these photographs! Too many new collectors were being confused by showing pieces that are not Manhattan. People tend to go by what they see pictured — rather than bothering to read!

	Crystal	Pink		Crystal	Pink
* Ashtray, 4" round	11.00		Relish tray, 14", 4-part	18.00	
Ashtray, 4½" square	18.00		Relish tray, 14" with inserts	50.00	50.00
Bowl, 4½" sauce, handles	9.00		*** Relish tray insert	5.50	6.00
Bowl, 5⅜" berry w/handles	18.00	20.00	**** Pitcher, 24 oz.	32.00	
Bowl, 5¼" cereal, no handles	50.00	95.00	Pitcher, 80 oz. tilted	45.00	65.00
Bowl, 7½" large berry	15.00		Plate, 6" sherbet or saucer	7.00	50.00
Bowl, 8", closed handles	22.00	25.00	Plate, 8½ salad	15.00	
Bowl, 9" salad	25.00		Plate, 10¼" dinner	20.00	175.00
Bowl, 9½" fruit open handle	35.00	35.00	Plate, 14" sandwich	22.00	
Candlesticks, 4½" (square) pr.	15.00		Salt & pepper, 2" pr. (square)	27.50	45.00
Candy dish, 3 legs		12.00	Saucer/sherbet plate	7.00	50.00
** Candy dish and cover	37.50		Sherbet	10.00	15.00
Coaster, 3½"	15.00		Sugar, oval	10.00	11.00
Comport, 5¾"	32.00	35.00	*****Tumbler, 10 oz. ftd.	17.00	17.00
Creamer, oval	10.00	11.00	Vase, 8"	20.00	
Cup	17.50	225.00	** Wine, 3½"	5.50	

*Ad for Hocking $15.00; ad for others $12.50   **Look-Alike   ***Ruby – $3.50   ****Ruby $400.00   ***** Green or iridized – $15.00

Please refer to Foreword for pricing information

MAYFAIR FEDERAL GLASS COMPANY, 1934

Colors: Crystal, amber, and green.

Federal had to redo their own "Mayfair" glass moulds into what ultimately became known as the "Rosemary" pattern because Hocking had copyrighted the name **Mayfair** first. I have divided the photographs into the "transitional period" and the old Federal "Mayfair" pattern before it was altered. The green and amber pieces pictured in the bottom photograph represent a "transitional period" of glassware made between the old Federal "Mayfair" pattern and what was to become known as the "Rosemary" pattern. Notice that these transitional pieces have arching in the bottom of each piece rather than the waffle design, and there is no waffling between the top arches. If you turn to the Rosemary (188–189) for reference, you will see that the design under the arches is entirely plain. Most collectors consider these transitional pieces a part of Federal Mayfair rather than Rosemary and that is why they are placed here. I suspect that after examining the conversion of the Mayfair moulds, someone decided that the revisions made were not changed enough, and they were redesigned a second time into the final pattern, Rosemary. That's only speculation, but it seems reasonable.

Federal's Mayfair was a very limited production, possibly because of pattern name obstacles. Amber and crystal are the colors that can be collected (in the true pattern form). Amber cream soups have been found in small numbers and platters in even fewer numbers. Crystal Mayfair can be collected as a set. Transitional crystal does not seem to exist. Green can only be bought in transitional form! Feel free to prove me wrong!

I, personally, prefer the scalloped lines of Mayfair to those of the plainer Rosemary. This is a challenging set to collect. Once you gather it, you will not be sorry. Mix the transitional with the regular pattern in amber. They go well together and only an experienced collector will detect the difference.

There are no sherbets in this pattern. The Mayfair sugar, like Rosemary, looks like a large sherbet since it does not have handles. I once bought six sugar bowls from a flea market dealer who sold them as sherbets. Both the Mayfair and the transitional pattern differences can easily be seen in the amber sugar.

Frequently you will find several pieces of Mayfair together, rather than a piece here and there. You can get a speedy beginning to a collection that way. Start a set! You'll like it!

	Amber	Crystal	Green		Amber	Crystal	Green
Bowl, 5" sauce	9.00	6.50	12.00	Plate, 9½" dinner	14.00	10.00	14.00
Bowl, 5" cream soup	18.00	15.00	18.00	Plate, 9½" grill	14.00	8.50	14.00
Bowl, 6" cereal	18.00	9.50	20.00	Platter, 12" oval	30.00	20.00	30.00
Bowl, 10" oval vegetable	30.00	18.00	30.00	Saucer	4.00	2.50	4.00
Creamer, ftd.	13.00	10.50	16.00	Sugar, ftd.	13.00	11.00	16.00
Cup	9.00	5.00	9.00	Tumbler, 4½", 9 oz.	30.00	15.00	33.00
Plate, 6¾" salad	7.00	4.50	9.00				

Please refer to Foreword for pricing information

MAYFAIR, "OPEN ROSE" HOCKING GLASS COMPANY, 1931–1937

Colors: Ice blue, pink; some green, yellow, and crystal. *(See Reproduction Section.)*

Hocking's Mayfair is possibly the most collected pattern in Depression glass. I spend hours answering questions and calls about reproductions and rare pieces in Mayfair. I noticed an inquiry on the Internet about reproduction shot glasses. Since 1977, I have explained how simple the originals are to distinguish from reproductions by the split stem on the flower design. That has never changed since they were first made at Mosser! I have updated the Reproduction Section in the back to take care of the odd colors of cookie jars and shakers now being found. Please read that section if you are having problems!

The four rarely found pieces pictured on page 123 were all discovered last year! The pink, three-footed bowl was found in West Virginia for a very reasonable price. The person that bought it took it to an antique mall where they laughed at her for trying to sell a $5,000.00 bowl! I bought it, photographed it, and sold it a few weeks later. I might mention that I visited that same mall and bought a Caprice blue ball jug for $22.00 less a discount. Bargains are available, if you search. The green, three-footed bowl is one of three known. It was bought from the family of an ex-worker at Hocking. I still own it, but it is for sale! The green cookie was found in the Cincinnati area last spring and the green pitcher was found in Illinois. There are rare pieces still being found!

I am frequently asked the value of frosted pieces in Mayfair and other Hocking patterns such as Princess. Originally, glass companies dipped glass items in camphoric acid to "satinize" them. Often, these frosted pieces were hand painted and sold by special order only. As you can see on page 125, there was an extensive line of satin-finished Mayfair. Today, these pieces are rarer than the unfrosted pieces, but there used to be only a few collectors searching for them; so the prices **were usually** lower than the normal Mayfair pieces. Having shown it in the last book, a demand has now started for **satinized pieces! They are presently selling about the same as regular pieces** or even more **with unworn (mint) original decorations!** I guess that picture of satinized glass awakened some interest!

Collectors of pink Mayfair have a predicament when selecting tumbler sizes and stems to collect. Most buy flat waters, footed teas, and water goblets to start. After they finish these, some pursue the harder to find stemware or tumblers. Mayfair has so many different pieces that you can approach collecting from many standpoints, be they getting everything or just buying enough for a small set!

Yellow and green Mayfair sets **can be collected,** but it takes considerable time and money to do so! Of course, that now holds true for pink or blue! A setting for four with all the pieces in easily found colors is expensive! However, if you try not to buy **everything** made, you can put a small set together for about the same money as most other patterns.

The 10" celery measures 11¼" handle to handle and the 9" one measures 10¼" handle to handle. The measurements in this book normally do not include handles unless so noted!

Those crystal items shown in the top photograph on page 125 are also rarely seen, but I have only met one collector of crystal Mayfair. Most commonly seen are the juice pitcher, shakers, and the divided platter. A reader writes that the divided platter was given as a premium with the purchase of coffee or spices in late 1930s. This platter is often found in a metal holder! The crystal footed vase is the only one known thus far, and I have confirmed a covered sugar. A rare piece in an uncollected color does not excite as many collectors as it does the owner. Collectors of pink Mayfair and collectors of sugar and creamers have not yet been too impressed over that report. Usually, the comment made had to do with asking if there were any way to dye crystal glass blue or green!

There are some significant details about this pattern that need to be pointed out. Some Mayfair stems have a plain foot while others are rayed. Footed iced teas vary in height. Some teas have a short stem above the foot and others have practically none. This stem causes the heights to vary to some extent. It is just a mould variation, but may account for capacity differences. Note under measurements on page 4 the listings of tumblers that I have taken from old Hocking catalogs. In two catalogs from 1935, these were listed as 13 ounce; but in 1936, both catalogs listed the tumbler as 15 ounces. I have never found a 13 ounce tumbler. (Catalog or measuring mistake?)

You may see a price advertised or displayed at shows for more (and sometimes less) than my listed price. You must ultimately decide the worth of an item to you! Mayfair is a great pattern with many collectors. Consider it!

	*Pink	Blue	Green	Yellow		*Pink	Blue	Green	Yellow
Bowl, 5" cream soup	52.50				Butter dish and cover or 7" covered vegetable	68.00	295.00	1,300.00	1,300.00
Bowl, 5½" cereal	26.00	50.00	85.00	85.00	Butter bottom with indent				300.00
Bowl, 7" vegetable	28.00	60.00	150.00	150.00	Butter dish top	40.00	235.00	1,150.00	1,150.00
Bowl, 9", 3⅛ high, 3 leg console	5,500.00		5,500.00		Cake plate, 10" ftd.	32.50	72.50	150.00	
Bowl, 9½" oval vegetable	30.00	70.00	125.00	135.00	Candy dish and cover	55.00	295.00	595.00	495.00
Bowl, 10" vegetable	28.00	70.00		135.00	Celery dish, 9" divided			195.00	195.00
Bowl, 10" same covered	125.00	135.00		995.00	Celery dish, 10"	45.00	65.00	125.00	125.00
Bowl, 11¾" low flat	57.50	72.50	45.00	195.00	Celery dish, 10" divided	245.00	65.00		
Bowl, 12" deep scalloped fruit	57.50	97.50	45.00	235.00					

*Frosted or satin finish items slightly lower if paint is worn or missing

Please refer to Foreword for pricing information

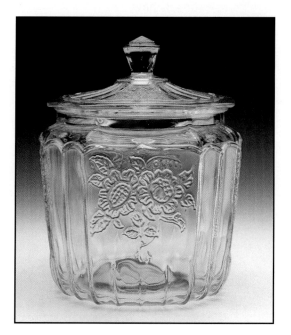

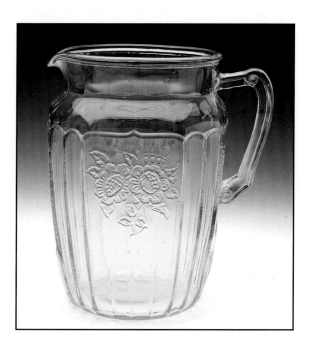

MAYFAIR (Cont.)

	*Pink	Blue	Green	Yellow
Cookie jar and lid	52.50	295.00	595.00	895.00
Creamer, ftd.	29.00	82.50	225.00	225.00
Cup	18.00	55.00	155.00	155.00
Cup, round	350.00			
Decanter and stopper, 32 oz.	195.00			
Goblet, 3¾", 1 oz. cordial	1,150.00		995.00	
Goblet, 4⅛", 2½ oz.	950.00		950.00	
Goblet, 4", 3 oz. cocktail	85.00		395.00	
Goblet, 4½", 3 oz. wine	95.00		450.00	
Goblet, 5¼", 4½ oz. claret	950.00		950.00	
Goblet, 5¾", 9 oz. water	67.50		495.00	
Goblet, 7¼", 9 oz. thin	225.00	195.00		
** Pitcher, 6", 37 oz.	55.00	150.00	550.00	550.00
Pitcher, 8", 60 oz.	55.00	175.00	525.00	525.00
Pitcher, 8½", 80 oz.	110.00	200.00	750.00	750.00
Plate, 5¾" (often substituted as saucer)	13.50	25.00	90.00	90.00
Plate, 6½" round sherbet	12.50			
Plate, 6½" round, off-center indent	25.00	27.50	135.00	135.00
Plate, 8½" luncheon	27.50	55.00	85.00	85.00
Plate, 9½" dinner	52.50	80.00	150.00	150.00
Plate, 9½" grill	40.00	52.50	85.00	85.00
Plate, 11½" handled grill				105.00
Plate, 12" cake w/handles	50.00	70.00	40.00	
*** Platter, 12" oval, open handles	30.00	70.00	165.00	165.00
Platter, 12½" oval, 8" wide, closed handles			235.00	235.00
Relish, 8⅜", 4-part	32.00	65.00	165.00	165.00
Relish, 8⅜" non-partitioned	225.00		295.00	295.00
**** Salt and pepper, flat pr.	65.00	295.00	1,100.00	875.00
Salt and pepper, ftd.	8,500.00			
Sandwich server, center handle	47.50	77.50	40.00	135.00
Saucer (cup ring)	32.50			150.00
Saucer (see 5¾"plate)				
Sherbet, 2¼" flat	175.00	125.00		
Sherbet, 3" ftd.	17.50			
Sherbet, 4¾" ftd.	77.50	77.50	165.00	165.00
Sugar, ftd.	30.00	82.50	210.00	210.00
Sugar lid	1,500.00		1,100.00	1,100.00
Tumbler, 3½", 5 oz. juice	45.00	120.00		
Tumbler, 4¼", 9 oz. water	30.00	110.00		
Tumbler, 4¾", 11 oz. water	195.00	135.00	200.00	200.00
Tumbler, 5¼", 13½ oz. iced tea	60.00	240.00		
Tumbler, 3¼", 3 oz. ftd. juice	85.00			
Tumbler, 5¼", 10 oz. ftd.	42.50	130.00		180.00
Tumbler, 6½", 15 oz. ftd. iced tea	42.50	250.00	220.00	
Vase (sweet pea)	145.00	115.00	295.00	
Whiskey, 2¼", 1½ oz.	67.50			

* Frosted or satin finish items slightly lower if paint is worn or missing
** Crystal – $15.00
*** Divided Crystal – $12.50
**** Crystal – $17.50 pr. – Beware reproductions.

MISS AMERICA (DIAMOND PATTERN) HOCKING GLASS COMPANY, 1935–1938

Colors: Crystal, pink; some green, ice blue, Jade-ite, and Royal Ruby. *(See Reproduction Section.)*

Pink Miss America became the center of attention at the recent Houston Depression glass show when the latest pink 5-part, 11¾" relish appeared after an absence of nearly five years! There have never been many of these around. I missed two at Washington Court House, Ohio, flea market in the early 1970s. They were $15.00 and sold for $25.00 for the pair! I've only seen two since then; they are rare! You will eventually be able to see it! This piece fits in a spinning metal holder creating a Lazy Susan. A crystal relish is pictured in the top row of page 128. Find another pink one and give me a call!

That pink relish will join the Royal Ruby Miss America set (pictured on page 129) in Arkansas. This red set was bought from the grandson of a former employee who retired in 1962. The 50 pieces contained some surprises! I discovered that there were two styles of water goblets, footed juices, and sherbets! Notice how one of the water goblets and one of the footed juices flare at the top. The sherbets do the same; but only one style was photographed. This set contained the first Miss America cups, sherbets, footed and flat juices I had seen in Royal Ruby. It was originally a basic set for eight with cups, saucers, and luncheon plates. A few other pieces turn up occasionally in the market. Butter dishes were reproduced in red in the late 1970s; but they were an amberina red. No original red butter has been seen! Enjoy this while you can, as it is doubtful this much will ever be pictured again!

There are pieces of Miss America found with metal lids. The relish dish is pictured on the bottom row of page 128 with a perfect fitting lid. These pieces were sold to some company who made lids to fit. They are not original factory lids.

Any time a glass pattern was made for several years, it will be possible to find pieces that deviate in design. Each item can vary as often as any mould was changed, reworked, or became worn.

Reproductions have been a small problem for the Miss America pattern since the early 1970s. Please refer to page 236 for a complete listing of Miss America reproductions and how to distinguish new from old!

Reproduction shakers have been perplexing! There are few green shakers available that are old. In fact, I haven't seen an older pair since the early 1970s before reproductions. There are at least four or five generations of reproduction Miss America shakers; it depends upon which one you find as to what to look for on them. There originally were two different moulds used for old shakers. The shakers that are fatter toward the foot are the best ones to buy, since that style has not been reproduced. The shakers that get thin (as shown in the photograph) are the style that has been reproduced. Buy shakers from a **reputable dealer**.

There are a few odd-colored or flashed pieces of Miss America that surface occasionally. Flashed-on red, green, or amethyst make interesting conversation pieces, but are not plentiful enough to collect a set. You can see an amethyst flashed goblet and a Jade-ite luncheon plate on the bottom of page 129. There may be more interest in odd colors in patterns now that rainbow collections are in vogue.

	Crystal	Pink	Green	Royal Ruby
Bowl, 4½" berry			12.00	
Bowl, 6¼" cereal	10.00	25.00	18.00	
Bowl, 8" curved in at top	40.00	75.00		450.00
Bowl, 8¾" straight deep fruit	35.00	65.00		
Bowl, 10" oval vegetable	15.00	30.00		
Bowl, 11", shallow				800.00
* Butter dish and cover	210.00	595.00		
Butter dish bottom	10.00	25.00		
Butter dish top	200.00	575.00		
Cake plate, 12" ftd.	26.00	45.00		
Candy jar and cover, 11½"	60.00	165.00		
*** Celery dish, 10½" oblong	15.00	32.50		
Coaster, 5¾"	15.00	30.00		
Comport, 5"	14.00	26.00		
Creamer, ftd.	10.00	19.00		175.00
Cup	10.00	24.00	12.00	225.00
Goblet, 3¾", 3 oz. wine	22.00	85.00		255.00
Goblet, 4¾", 5 oz. juice	27.00	90.00		255.00

	Crystal	Pink	Green	Royal Ruby
Goblet, 5½", 10 oz. water	21.00	45.00		255.00
Pitcher, 8", 65 oz.	46.00	125.00		
Pitcher, 8½", 65 oz. w/ice lip	65.00	185.00		
** Plate, 5¾" sherbet	6.00	10.50	7.00	47.50
Plate, 6¾"		7.50		
Plate, 8½" salad	7.50	23.00	9.50	150.00
*** Plate, 10¼" dinner	15.00	30.00		
Plate, 10¼" grill	11.00	25.00		
Platter, 12¼" oval	14.00	30.00		
Relish, 8¾", 4 part	11.00	25.00		
Relish, 11¾" round divided	25.00	3,250.00		
Salt and pepper, pr.	30.00	60.00		
Saucer	4.00	7.00		65.00
** Sherbet	800	15.00		125.00
Sugar	8.00	17.50		175.00
*** Tumbler, 4", 5 oz. juice	16.50	50.00		200.00
Tumbler, 4½", 10 oz. water	15.00	32.00	18.00	
Tumbler, 5¾", 14 oz. iced tea	25.00	85.00		

*Absolute mint price **Also in Ice Blue $50.00 ***Also in Ice Blue $150.00

Please refer to Foreword for pricing information

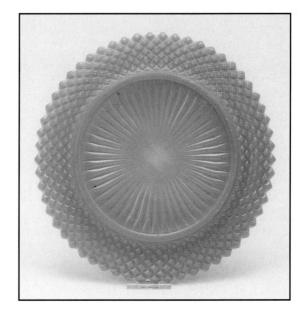

MODERNTONE HAZEL ATLAS GLASS COMPANY, 1934–1942; Late 1940s–Early 1950s

Colors: Amethyst, cobalt blue; some crystal, pink, and Platonite fired-on colors.

Cobalt blue Moderntone is highly collectible not only for its pattern but also for its color. Cobalt colored glassware is often exhibited in windows for the light to make a fantastic display of color.

Note the boxed set shown below. Many boxed sets of glass are found today, but few tell what pattern is found inside. These sets are more of a novelty than an outstanding discovery unless they give up some unknown facts.

There is no true Moderntone tumbler. Tumblers sold today as Moderntone were once advertised alongside this pattern, but they were never sold as a part of the set. There are even two different style tumblers that have been "adopted" for this set. The juice and water shown on page 133 are paneled and have a rayed bottom. Other cobalt tumblers are not paneled and have a plain bottom that is often marked **H** over top **A** which is the Hazel Atlas trademark. Either tumbler is acceptable, but the circular paneled one is chosen by most collectors. All sizes of these tumblers are hard to find except for the water. Green, pink, or crystal tumblers are also found, but there is little market for these except the shot or whiskey glass that is sought by those devotees.

I am repeatedly asked just which lid is the **real lid** for the Moderntone butter or sugar. There is no **true** sugar or butter lid. Evidently, the butter bottom and sugar were sold to some other company who made the tops. No one knows whether the lids are supposed to have black, red, or blue knobs, but I have seen all those colors on Moderntone! Red seems to be the dominate color. By adding a lid, mustards were made from the handle-less custard.

There is also a punch set being sold as Moderntone which uses a Hazel Atlas mixing bowl and the same roly poly cups found with the Royal Lace toddy set. This was not Hazel Atlas factory assembled; but some collectors accept it to go with Moderntone. I think It is merely a blue punch set; but if you want one for your Moderntone set, then by all means buy it! People should buy what they like! A similar punch set uses a Hazel Atlas cobalt blue mixing bowl in a metal holder with Moderntone custard cups sitting around the metal rim. That **is** being accepted as a Moderntone punch set by many collectors; it, at least, uses some Moderntone pieces to make up the set!

The boxed set with the crystal shot glasses in the metal holder came with a Colonial Block creamer. The box was marked "Little Deb" Lemonade Server Set. You can see the set in the bottom photograph on page 133. It's a shame the shot glasses and pitcher were not cobalt! That pitcher has turned up in cobalt and several have turned up with Shirley Temple's picture! These boxed crystal children's sets sell in the $70.00 range. These shots fetch $15.00 each! Other pieces of crystal Moderntone are found occasionally; and there are a few collectors for it. Price it about one-third the amethyst. It's a shame some of the crystal flat soups could not be changed into some other color. Now that collectors are combining colors, perhaps crystal soups will be more desirable!

Ruffled cream soups and sandwich plates are both approaching the $60.00 price; but both are successfully hiding from most collectors. Sandwich plates can be located, but nearly all are heavily scratched causing collectors to avoid them. When you pick up a blue plate that looks white in the center from use marks, that is not a good sign! The cheese dish lid has been moved to the side to show the wooden cheese plate that fits inside the metal lid. There have been some tremendous prices paid for these recently. This cheese dish is essentially a salad plate with a metal cover and wooden cutting board.

Both green and pink ash trays are found occasionally, but there is little demand for them now. Blue ash trays still command a hefty price for an ash tray. Finding any Moderntone bowls without inner rim damage is a problem. Prices below are for **mint** condition pieces. That is why bowls are so highly priced. Used, nicked, and bruised bowls are the norm; mint condition bowls are not!

Notice the premium certificate on the bottom of page 132 which offered a 36 piece setting with a money back guarantee for only $1.69 and flour coupons!

Platonite Moderntone has been moved into the *Collectible Glassware from the 40s, 50s, 60s...* since it better fits the glassware era covered by that book.

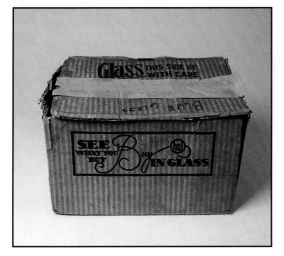

MODERNTONE (Cont.)

	Cobalt	Amethyst		Cobalt	Amethyst
* Ash tray, 7¾", match holder in center	165.00		Plate, 7¾" luncheon	12.50	9.00
Bowl, 4¾" cream soup	22.50	20.00	Plate, 8⅞" dinner	18.00	13.00
Bowl, 5" berry	26.00	24.00	Plate, 10½" sandwich	60.00	40.00
Bowl, 5" cream soup, ruffled	55.00	33.00	Platter, 11" oval	47.50	37.50
Bowl, 6½" cereal	75.00	75.00	Platter, 12" oval	77.50	50.00
Bowl, 7½" soup	140.00	100.00	Salt and pepper, pr.	40.00	35.00
Bowl, 8¾" large berry	50.00	40.00	Saucer	5.00	4.00
Butter dish with metal cover	100.00		Sherbet	13.00	12.00
Cheese dish, 7" with metal lid	450.00		Sugar	11.00	10.00
Creamer	11.00	10.00	Sugar lid in metal	37.50	
Cup	11.00	11.00	Tumbler, 5 oz.	55.00	32.00
Cup (handle-less) or custard	20.00	14.00	Tumbler, 9 oz.	37.50	27.50
Plate, 5⅞" sherbet	6.50	5.00	Tumbler, 12 oz.	110.00	90.00
Plate, 6¾" salad	12.50	10.00	** Whiskey, 1½ oz.	42.50	

* Pink $75.00; green $95.00
** Pink or green $17.50

Please refer to Foreword for pricing information

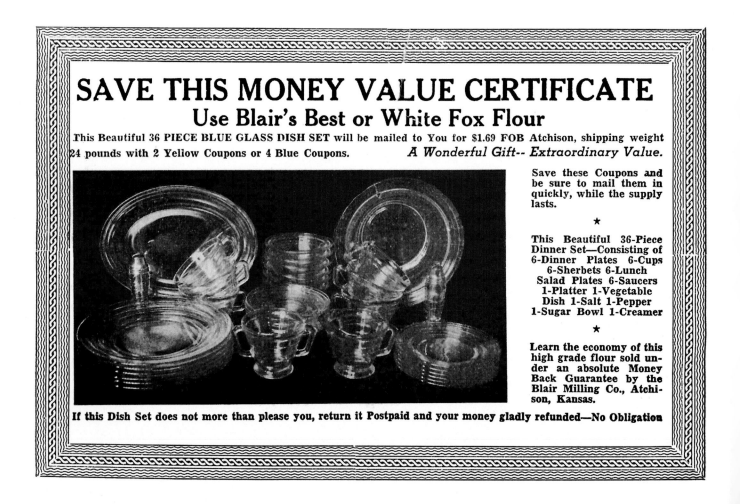
132

MOONDROPS NEW MARTINSVILLE GLASS COMPANY, 1932–1940

Colors: Amber, pink, green, cobalt, ice blue, red, amethyst, crystal, dark green, light green, Jade-ite, smoke, and black.

Collectors are relentless in their quest of red and cobalt blue Moondrops! Few collectors search for other colors. Every dealer knows that red and cobalt blue are expensive colors; therefore, prices are high even if they do not recognize Moondrops. On the other hand, other colors escape into the cracks and you may find a bargain or two. Amber seems to be the least preferred color. Perfume bottles, powder jars, mugs, gravy boats, and triple candlesticks are indications that this glassware is more elegantly oriented than most of its contemporaries. Bud vases, decanters, and "rocket style" stems (dark green bud vase, page 135) add a range of unusual pieces from which to choose.

New Martinsville evidently purposely mismatched some of their colors. I have seen two powder jars with crystal bottoms and cobalt blue tops in antique malls in Ohio and Florida. One was priced $45.00 and damaged badly; the other was $10.00; naturally, I bought that one!

The butter has to have a matching **glass** top to obtain the price listed below. The metal top with a bird finial found on butter bottoms sells for about $25.00. However, the metal top **with the fan finial** sells for approximately $55.00! Still, collectors prefer glass tops on their butter dishes!

	Blue, Red	Other Colors		Blue, Red	Other Colors
Ash tray	32.00	17.00	Goblet, 5¾" 8 oz.	33.00	19.00
Bowl, 4¼", cream soup	95.00	35.00	Goblet, 5⅛", 3 oz. metal stem wine	16.00	11.00
Bowl, 5¼" berry	18.00	10.00	Goblet, 5½", 4 oz. metal stem wine	20.00	11.00
Bowl, 5⅜" 3-ftd. tab hdld.	75.00	50.00	Goblet, 6¼", 9 oz. metal stem water	23.00	16.00
Bowl, 6¾" soup	90.00		Gravy boat	135.00	90.00
Bowl, 7½" pickle	22.00	14.00	Mayonnaise, 5¼"	55.00	32.00
Bowl, 8⅜" ftd., concave top	45.00	25.00	Mug, 5⅛", 12 oz.	40.00	23.00
Bowl, 8½" 3-ftd. divided relish	29.00	18.00	Perfume bottle, "rocket"	225.00	160.00
Bowl, 9½" 3-legged ruffled	65.00		Pitcher, 6⅞", 22 oz. small	165.00	90.00
Bowl, 9¾" oval vegetable	45.00	23.00	Pitcher, 8⅛", 32 oz. medium	185.00	115.00
Bowl, 9¾" covered casserole	195.00	100.00	Pitcher, 8", 50 oz. large, with lip	195.00	115.00
Bowl, 9¾" handled oval	52.50	36.00	Pitcher, 8⅛", 53 oz. large, no lip	185.00	125.00
Bowl, 11" boat-shaped celery	32.00	23.00	Plate, 5⅞"	11.00	8.00
Bowl, 12" round 3-ftd. console	85.00	32.00	Plate, 6⅛" sherbet	8.00	5.00
Bowl, 13" console with "wings"	120.00	42.00	Plate, 6" round, off-center sherbet indent	12.00	9.00
Butter dish and cover	440.00	275.00	Plate, 7⅛" salad	14.00	10.00
Butter dish bottom	65.00	50.00	Plate, 8½" luncheon	15.00	12.00
Butter dish top (glass)	375.00	225.00	Plate, 9½" dinner	25.00	16.00
Candles, 2" ruffled pr.	40.00	24.00	Plate, 14" round sandwich	40.00	18.00
Candles, 4½" sherbet style pr.	27.00	20.00	Plate, 14" 2-handled sandwich	45.00	23.00
Candlesticks, 5" ruffled, pr.	35.00	21.00	Platter, 12" oval	35.00	22.00
Candlesticks, 5" "wings" pr.	95.00	50.00	Powder jar, 3 ftd.	295.00	125.00
Candlesticks, 5¼" triple light pr.	125.00	65.00	Saucer	6.00	5.00
Candlesticks, 8½" metal stem pr.	40.00	30.00	Sherbet, 2⅝"	16.00	11.00
Candy dish, 8" ruffled	40.00	20.00	Sherbet, 4½"	30.00	16.00
Cocktail shaker with or without hdl.,			Sugar, 2¾"	15.00	10.00
metal top	60.00	35.00	Sugar, 3½"	16.00	11.00
Comport, 4"	27.50	18.00	Tumbler, 2¾", 2 oz. shot	16.00	10.00
Comport, 11½"	65.00	35.00	Tumbler, 2¾", 2 oz. handled shot	16.00	11.00
Creamer, 2¾" miniature	18.00	11.00	Tumbler, 3¼", 3 oz. ftd. juice	16.00	11.00
Creamer, 3¾" regular	16.00	10.00	Tumbler, 3⅜", 5 oz.	15.00	10.00
Cup	16.00	10.00	Tumbler, 4⅜", 7 oz.	16.00	10.00
Decanter, 7¾" small	67.50	38.00	Tumbler, 4⅜", 8 oz.	16.00	11.00
Decanter, 8½" medium	70.00	42.00	Tumbler, 4⅞", 9 oz. handled	30.00	16.00
Decanter, 11¼" large	100.00	50.00	Tumbler, 4⅞", 9 oz.	19.00	15.00
Decanter, 10¼" "rocket"	450.00	395.00	Tumbler, 5⅛", 12 oz.	30.00	14.00
Goblet, 2⅞, ¾ oz. cordial	40.00	27.50	Tray, 7½", for mini sugar/creamer	37.50	19.00
Goblet, 4", 4 oz. wine	22.00	13.00	Vase, 7¾" flat, ruffled top	60.00	57.00
Goblet, 4¾", "rocket" wine	60.00	30.00	Vase, 8½" "rocket" bud	265.00	185.00
Goblet, 4¾", 5 oz.	24.00	15.00	Vase, 9¼" "rocket" style	250.00	140.00

Please refer to Foreword for pricing information

MT. PLEASANT, "DOUBLE SHIELD" L. E. SMITH GLASS COMPANY, 1920s–1934

Colors: Black amethyst, amethyst, cobalt blue, crystal, pink, green, white.

People who buy cobalt blue and black glass often unknowingly buy Mt. Pleasant. At identification tables at shows I see many pieces of Mt. Pleasant brought in to be identified. Usually, the collector is excited to know that the pattern is even in a book! I often sell books to amateur glass buyers who wish to learn about what they already own!

The cobalt blue, leaf-shaped dishes attract non-collectors also. One person wrote, after seeing her cobalt leaf in a friend's book, that she had received a set of one large and six smaller plates as a wedding gift in 1931. The larger leaf measures 11¼", is being found sporadically, and is probably six times more rare than the small plate. The smaller, 8" leaf is available. It may even have been a premium item for buying a product!

A few undecorated white pieces of Mt. Pleasant have been reported, as were several pieces of color striped crystal. Decaled and enameled pieces are not often found. I have had only occasional reports of pink and green items. Usually these reports are sugars and creamers, but a few plates crop up once in a while.

A majority of cobalt blue Mt. Pleasant is found in the Midwest and in northern New York. Mt. Pleasant was promoted heavily at hardware stores in those areas; black predominates in other areas of the country. Many pieces are found with a platinum (silver) band around them. This decorated band faded with use. Price is generally less for decorated pieces.

Notice the black double candlestick in the center of the top photo on the next page. It is a souvenir piece of the Chicago World's Fair. World's Fair collectors also covet these labeled wares!

	Pink, Green	Amethyst, Black, Cobalt		Pink, Green	Amethyst, Black, Cobalt
Bonbon, 7", rolled-up, handled	16.00	23.00	Leaf, 11¼"		30.00
Bowl, 4" opening, rose	18.00	26.00	Mayonnaise, 5½", 3-ftd.	18.00	30.00
Bowl, 4⅞", square ftd. fruit	13.00	20.00	Mint, 6", center handle	16.00	25.00
Bowl, 6", 2-handled, square	13.00	18.00	Plate, 7", 2-handled, scalloped	9.00	15.00
Bowl, 7", 3 ftd., rolled out edge	16.00	25.00	Plate, 8", scalloped or square	10.00	15.00
Bowl, 8", scalloped, 2-handled	19.00	35.00	Plate, 8", 2-handled	11.00	18.00
Bowl, 8", square, 2-handled	19.00	35.00	Plate 8¼", square w/indent for cup		16.00
Bowl, 9", scalloped, 1¾" deep, ftd.		30.00	Plate, 9" grill		12.00
Bowl, 9¼", square ftd. fruit	19.00	32.00	Plate, 10½", cake, 2-handled	16.00	30.00
Bowl, 10", scalloped fruit		42.00	Plate, 10½", 1¼" high, cake		40.00
Bowl, 10", 2-handled, turned-up edge		32.00	Plate, 12", 2-handled	20.00	33.00
Cake plate, 10½", ftd., 1¼" high		37.50	Salt and pepper, 2 styles	24.00	42.00
Candlestick, single, pr.	20.00	30.00	Sandwich server, center-handled		40.00
Candlestick, double, pr.	26.00	45.00	Saucer	2.50	5.00
Creamer	18.00	19.00	Sherbet, 2 styles	10.00	17.50
Cup (waffle-like crystal)	4.50		Sugar	18.00	18.00
Cup	9.50	12.00	Tumbler, ftd.		23.00
Leaf, 8"		17.50	Vase, 7¼"		32.00

NEW CENTURY, and incorrectly, "LYDIA RAY" HAZEL ATLAS GLASS COMPANY, 1930–1935

Colors: Green; some crystal, pink, amethyst, and cobalt.

New Century is the **official** name for this pattern made by Hazel Atlas. "Lydia Ray" was the name used by collectors until an official name was found.

Green is the preferred color since sets can only be acquired in green. I have been told that it is impossible to collect a set in crystal by several who tried to do so. Crystal is so scarce that prices are on par with green even with little demand! Years ago, I ran into several crystal powder jars. They were made with a sugar lid on the top of a sherbet. The knob of the sherbet had glass marbles or beads attached by a wire. One of these is pictured on the next page. I have not seen these for a while. You can make a footed powder jar in many patterns (not all) by putting a sugar lid on a sherbet!

New Century is one of those patterns that a small number of collectors just cherish. Bowls are harder to find than for most patterns. I haven't had a berry bowl to sell for years. Cream soups, casseroles, wines, and cocktails are rarely seen. As with Adam, the casserole bottom is harder to find than the top. I saw one at an antique fair a couple of weeks ago that had turned white with use. It was priced $30.00, but I doubt a collector searching for it would have paid $2.00. I have never understood what some dealers are thinking when they price damaged or worn merchandise! That casserole bottom is a prime example. I bought some Mayfair tumblers for $25.00 each, but left the badly chipped and cracked ones priced for $22.00. Had they been "thrown in" on the deal I would still have left them since they were beyond repair! Nobody is going to pay $22.00 for damaged $25.00 pieces!

Pink, cobalt blue, and amethyst New Century have only been found in water sets and an occasional cup or saucer. Only flat tumblers have been encountered in these colors.

There are seven assorted tumblers if you count the whiskey; but only the nine and ten ounce **flat** tumblers are periodically found. Four of the five sizes of flat tumblers can be seen in amethyst. I seem to be missing a whiskey in all colors! Are they harder to find than I thought?

	Green, Crystal	Pink, Cobalt, Amethyst		Green, Crystal	Pink, Cobalt, Amethyst
Ash tray/coaster, 5⅜"	28.00		Plate, 8½" salad	10.00	
Bowl, 4½" berry	20.00		Plate, 10" dinner	18.00	
Bowl, 4¾" cream soup	20.00		Plate, 10" grill	12.00	
Bowl, 8" large berry	22.00		Platter, 11" oval	18.00	
Bowl, 9" covered casserole	65.00		Salt and pepper, pr.	35.00	
Butter dish and cover	55.00		Saucer	3.00	7.50
Cup	6.50	20.00	Sherbet, 3"	9.00	
Creamer	8.50		Sugar	8.00	
Decanter and stopper	60.00		Sugar cover	15.00	
Goblet, 2½ oz. wine	27.50		Tumbler, 3½", 5 oz.	12.00	15.00
Goblet, 3¼ oz. cocktail	25.00		Tumbler, 3½", 8 oz.	22.00	
Pitcher, 7¾", 60 oz. with or			Tumbler, 4¼", 9 oz.	15.00	18.00
without ice lip	35.00	35.00	Tumbler, 5", 10 oz.	18.00	20.00
Pitcher, 8", 80 oz. with or			Tumbler, 5¼", 12 oz.	28.00	30.00
without ice lip	40.00	42.00	Tumbler, 4", 5 oz. ftd.	20.00	
Plate, 6" sherbet	3.50		Tumbler, 4⅞", 9 oz. ftd.	22.00	
Plate, 7⅛" breakfast	9.00		Whiskey, 2½", 1½ oz.	20.00	

NEWPORT, "HAIRPIN" HAZEL ATLAS GLASS COMPANY, 1936–1940

Colors: Cobalt blue, amethyst; some pink, "Platonite" white, and fired-on colors.

Some Newport collectors are slightly irritated with me for exposing the 5⁄16" difference between a dinner and a luncheon plate! Most were upset because they now had another piece to find! Others had been trying to buy the dinners for luncheon plate prices. Actually, most found they had a mixture of the two sizes without realizing it. The dinner plate measures 8 13⁄16" while the luncheon plate measures 8½". I only brought the matter up because of problems that dealers who mail order were having! The only official listing I have states plates of 6", 8½", and 11½". However, after obtaining these plates, I found actual measurements quite different as you can see by the size listings in the price guide below. One of the problems with catalog measurements is that they are not always accurate and sometimes not even very close! One dealer informed me that he was now having trouble selling the dinners for $30.00 after I listed the differences in the book. He had been selling them through his ads before then! Strange things do happen in the glass business that defy logical thinking!

Amethyst Newport makes a great table setting! I personally like the shapes of this pattern more than Moderntone which is about the only other choice you have in accumulating a set of amethyst glassware from this era. Moroccan Amethyst came much later!

More collectors choose cobalt blue Newport than any other color! Of course, cobalt blue seems to be preferred in any pattern that comes in that color. Sets of pink Newport were given away as premiums for buying seeds from a catalog in the 1930s. Very few of these sets are entering the market but are not presently selling very well when they do. Why?

Cereal bowls, sandwich plates, large berry bowls, and tumblers have practically vanished from the market in any color. I finally found a large amethyst berry bowl; but I am having trouble replacing the large cobalt berry bowl that was "annihilated" **before** our photography session a few years ago. It is bad enough to lose pieces of glass, but losing them **before** they are pictured upsets me even more! Cathy did spot a damaged large cobalt blue bowl at an antique show for $25.00. I thought that would fill the hole in the picture, but it was missing an entire scallop! The dealer was willing to give a ten percent discount, but still owns it. After all, that **two inch missing piece** didn't hurt it, did it… because it **was** old?

1950s era Platonite Newport can be found in my book *Collectible Glassware from the 40s, 50s, 60s….*

	Cobalt	Amethyst		Cobalt	Amethyst
Bowl, 4¾" berry	20.00	15.00	Plate, 8 13⁄16", dinner	30.00	30.00
Bowl, 4¾" cream soup	20.00	18.00	Plate, 11¾" sandwich	40.00	35.00
Bowl, 5¼" cereal	37.50	32.50	Platter, 11¾" oval	45.00	40.00
Bowl, 8¼" large berry	42.50	40.00	Salt and pepper	47.50	40.00
Cup	12.00	10.00	Saucer	5.00	5.00
Creamer	16.00	13.00	Sherbet	15.00	13.00
Plate, 5⅞" sherbet	7.00	6.00	Sugar	16.00	14.00
Plate, 8½" luncheon	15.00	12.00	Tumbler, 4½", 9 oz.	40.00	35.00

No. 200. LADIES! Here's a gorgeous Dinner Set in that new shade Rose Crystal. It consists of 6 large plates, 6 small plates, 6 cups, 6 saucers, 6 cereal dishes, vegetable dish and large meat platter. This sparkling set, more beautiful than you can imagine, is given for one $4.00 order of Seeds. Weight 22 lbs. Sent Express collect.

32-Piece Rose Crystal Dinner Set

NORMANDIE, "BOUQUET AND LATTICE" FEDERAL GLASS COMPANY 1933–1940

Colors: Iridescent, amber, pink, crystal.

If you are one of those who like amber colored glassware, you might consider Normandie. Most basic items are available, and it is economical enough that you will not have to take out an equity mortgage to compile a setting for six, eight, or even twelve. Buy those hard-to-find items first or whenever you see them! That is good advice for collecting any pattern. Rarer, harder-to-find items increase in price much faster than commonly found items.

I have noticed there have been some fashion color shifts recently. Colors from the 1970s, including some Harvest Gold and Avocado Green, are once again appearing in ads. If some magazine were to feature amber glassware on the cover or a TV show use an amber set of glassware, we would probably encounter a push for amber like has never been seen! Witness the recent run on Jade-ite ware because of its exposure on a home and garden TV show!

Iridescent Normandie is presently displayed at Depression glass shows. That factor leads me to believe that people are asking for it, and dealers are heeding those solicitations. For years, iridescent Normandie sat on shelves unwanted at **any** price. Recently, however, hearsay circulated that it was getting hard to find and collectors started buying this iridescent color again. There were enough buyers to raise the prices a little. Iridescent is still fairly priced in contrast to the pink and amber.

Pink Normandie has been very evasive for years for those collectors hunting it. Amber has been available in most items; however, tumblers, sugar lids, and dinner-sized plates have become scarce even in this color. Those preceding items were never abundant in pink, even in the "good old days"! You will notice some soaring prices on pink Normandie. Tumblers are rare enough to approach prices of American Sweetheart; and Normandie collectors are vastly outnumbered by those of American Sweetheart. Pink Normandie pitchers can be bought reasonably when compared to those in American Sweetheart; collectors of Normandie come out ahead on that end!

The console bowl and candlesticks (occasionally found with sets of iridized Normandie) are Madrid! These were sold about the same time. That does not make it Normandie; it is still Madrid! The design on the glass determines pattern, not the color. See Madrid for pricing of these console sets.

	Amber	Pink	Iridescent
Bowl, 5" berry	6.50	8.00	5.00
* Bowl, 6½" cereal	28.00	33.00	8.50
Bowl, 8½" large berry	20.00	25.00	15.00
Bowl, 10" oval veg.	20.00	37.50	18.00
Creamer, ftd.	9.00	12.00	8.00
Cup	7.50	8.50	6.00
Pitcher, 8", 80 oz.	80.00	165.00	
Plate, 6" sherbet	4.50	4.00	3.00
Plate, 7¾" salad	8.50	11.00	52.50
Plate, 9¼" luncheon	8.50	14.00	15.00
Plate, 11" dinner	33.00	115.00	11.50
Plate, 11" grill	15.00	20.00	9.00
Platter, 11¾"	18.00	28.00	12.00
Salt and pepper, pr.	50.00	80.00	
Saucer	4.00	4.00	3.00
Sherbet	6.50	8.50	7.00
Sugar	8.00	9.00	6.00
Sugar lid	95.00	195.00	
Tumbler, 4", 5 oz. juice	32.00	90.00	
Tumbler, 4¼", 9 oz. water	20.00	55.00	
Tumbler, 5", 12 oz. iced tea	38.00	110.00	

* Mistaken by many as butter bottom.

No. 610, "PYRAMID" INDIANA GLASS COMPANY, 1926–1932

Colors: Green, pink, yellow, white, crystal, blue, or black in 1974–1975 by Tiara.

"Pyramid" is a collectors' name for Indiana's pattern No. 610. Indiana gave nearly all their patterns a number rather than a name. Collectors do not seem to tolerate calling patterns by numbers; so most of Indiana's patterns have been given an informal moniker. This art deco styled pattern has received plaudits in collecting realms outside Depression Glass and prices have risen with increased exposure for this glassware.

Even though there are fewer collectors searching for them, I should mention that crystal pitchers and tumblers in "Pyramid" are harder to find than any colored ones! Crystal pitchers are priced higher than all but yellow, even though yellow ones are found more often. There are so many collectors of yellow No. 610 that prices continue to increase! Ice buckets turn up often, even in yellow. However, the yellow **lid** to the ice bucket is nearly impossible to find! No other lids have yet been found for the other colors!

Optimistically, **I hope you are reading this paragraph about the crystal shaker shown on the next page** and not looking at the picture and saying, "I knew that shaker was 'Pyramid'!" This shaker was made by Indiana, and is often represented to be "Pyramid," but it is not. If you see one, look at it closely. The design is upside down from that of all No. 610 pieces and slightly different in make-up. It would serve as a great companion item since there are no shakers per se in this older Indiana pattern.

I might point out that the yellow stand in the top photo is not No. 610. The authentic stand has **squared** indentations on each side to fit the bottoms of the sugar and creamer. Thanks to a reader for pointing out that miscue!

Oval bowls and pickle dishes are sometimes confused since both measure 9½". The oval bowl has pointed edges as is shown by bowls in white, green, and yellow. The pickle dish is shown only in pink. The edges of that pickle dish are rounded instead of pointed.

Eight ounce tumblers come with two different bases. One has a 2¼" square foot while the other has a 2½" square foot. That discrepancy would not be noticed unless two tumblers with different bases were placed side by side.

No. 610 was and still is easily damaged. Be sure to examine all the ridged panels and all the corners on each piece. You will be amazed how often a chipped or cracked piece of "Pyramid" is sold as mint!

Blue and black pieces of "Pyramid" were made by Indiana for Tiara during the 1970s. You will see two sizes of black tumblers, blue berry bowls, and the 4-part center-handled relish in either color. If you like these colors, it is fine to buy them! Just realize that they are **not Depression era old**. Do not pay antique glass prices for them! That handled 4-part relish is sometimes mistaken for Tea Room, but it is not.

There are no new reports of any other green water sets with satinized panels this year! That satinization was rather carelessly done, but it was an eye catching set from a distance! It may have been an early designed piece because it had a different base than the one normally seen.

	Crystal	Pink	Green	Yellow
Bowl, 4¾" berry	11.00	20.00	22.00	35.00
Bowl, 8½" master berry	20.00	30.00	35.00	60.00
Bowl, 9½" oval, handled	27.00	35.00	35.00	55.00
Bowl, 9½" pickle, 5¾" wide	20.00	35.00	35.00	55.00
Creamer	17.50	30.00	30.00	40.00
Ice tub	75.00	95.00	100.00	200.00
Ice tub lid				650.00
Pitcher	350.00	215.00	200.00	450.00
Relish tray, 4-part handled	23.00	45.00	50.00	65.00
Sugar	17.50	30.00	30.00	40.00
Tray for creamer and sugar	25.00	30.00	30.00	55.00
Tumbler, 8 oz. ftd., 2 styles	55.00	40.00	45.00	70.00
Tumbler, 11 oz. ftd.	65.00	50.00	60.00	85.00

No. 612, "HORSESHOE" INDIANA GLASS COMPANY, 1930–1933

Colors: Green, yellow, pink, crystal.

The official name for this Indiana pattern is No. 612, but collectors christened it "Horseshoe."

A green "Horseshoe" butter dish is the piece most often missing from those collections, although the footed iced tea tumblers, both flat tumblers, grill plates, and pitchers are becoming scarce! I bought four grill plates at a yard sale in Florida. The unpatterned Depression glass there was priced "out of sight," but these inner rim rough grills were only $20.00 each. I had to buy them, because I had only owned two in the nearly 30 years I have been buying glass! The only "Horseshoe" butter I have seen at a show was priced about $500.00 above the price that they have been selling. That same butter has made the show tour for three years now without anyone buying it! The "Horseshoe" butter dish has always been highly priced. If you can find a first edition of my book, the butter dish was $90.00 back in 1972!

Yellow pitchers, grill plates, and the footed iced teas also create problems for collectors of that color! I have never pictured the yellow grill plate, but I have finally found one.

New collectors have avoided "Horseshoe" for years because it was so expensive. However, prices for other patterns have now caught up! Prices have risen on "Horseshoe" for the first time in several years because some newer collectors have stimulated prices exploring for hard-to-find pieces.

There are two types of plates and platters. Some are plain in the center, while others have a pattern. See the contrast on the standing plates on either side of the pitcher in the photo.

Candy dishes only have the pattern on the top. The bottom is plain. A few **pink** candy dishes have been found, but that candy is the only piece to ever surface in pink.

	Green	Yellow		Green	Yellow
Bowl, 4½" berry	28.00	23.00	Plate, 6" sherbet	8.00	9.00
Bowl, 6½" cereal	30.00	30.00	Plate, 8⅜" salad	12.00	12.00
Bowl, 7½" salad	25.00	25.00	Plate, 9⅜" luncheon	14.00	15.00
Bowl, 8½" vegetable	35.00	35.00	Plate, 10⅜" grill	100.00	125.00
Bowl, 9½" large berry	45.00	50.00	Plate, 11½" sandwich	22.50	22.50
Bowl, 10½" oval vegetable	25.00	30.00	Platter, 10¾" oval	27.50	27.50
Butter dish and cover	775.00		Relish, 3 part ftd.	25.00	40.00
Butter dish bottom	175.00		Saucer	5.00	5.00
Butter dish top	600.00		Sherbet	15.00	16.00
Candy in metal holder motif			Sugar, open	16.00	17.00
on lid	185.00		Tumbler, 4¼", 9 oz.	160.00	
also, pink	160.00		Tumbler, 4¾", 12 oz.	160.00	
Creamer, ftd.	17.00	18.00	Tumbler, 9 oz. ftd.	25.00	25.00
Cup	12.00	13.00	Tumbler, 12 oz. ftd.	150.00	160.00
Pitcher, 8½", 64 oz.	275.00	325.00			

No. 616, "VERNON" INDIANA GLASS COMPANY, 1930–1932

Colors: Green, crystal, yellow.

No. 616 attracts a few collectors. There is very little of this smaller pattern available. It was christened "Vernon" after another glass author's spouse. We once used crystal No. 616 as "every day" dishes. I warn you there are rough mould lines protruding from the tumblers. After a cut lip drinking from a tumbler, this set was sold.

Many crystal "Vernon" pieces are found trimmed in platinum (silver). Few of these decorated pieces have worn platinum. Evidently, Indiana's process for applying this trim was better than that of many other glass companies!

The 11½" sandwich plates make great dinner or barbecue plates when grilling out! They are certainly lighter than the Fiesta chop plates that are also great for grilled steaks and pizza. If you use this pattern, it is either sandwich plates or the little 8" luncheon. For healthy appetites, that is what is called a "no brainer"!

Our biggest problem is photographing the pattern! No. 616 is very delicate and light passes through without picking up the design well. I hope we have succeeded this time! My copy looks great!

Both yellow and green sets are difficult to complete, but there is even less green than yellow available. I have had difficulty locating a green tumbler and creamer.

Crystal **is** attractive in No. 616. You would be pleased displaying a set of it.

	Green	Crystal	Yellow		Green	Crystal	Yellow
Creamer, ftd.	25.00	12.00	25.00	Saucer	4.00	3.00	4.00
Cup	17.50	10.00	17.50	Sugar, ftd.	25.00	11.00	25.00
Plate, 8" luncheon	9.50	6.00	9.50	Tumbler, 5" ftd.	37.50	15.00	37.50
Plate, 11½" sandwich	25.00	12.00	25.00				

Please refer to Foreword for pricing information

No. 618, "PINEAPPLE & FLORAL" INDIANA GLASS COMPANY, 1932–1937

Colors: Crystal, amber; some fired-on red, green; late 1960s, avocado; 1980s pink, cobalt blue, etc.

Indiana has reissued No. 618 diamond-shaped comports and 7" salad bowls in a legion of colors. Many of these are sprayed-on colors, although the light pink is an excellent transparent color. Prices on these two older crystal pieces have diminished because of these remakes. Amber and fired-on red are safe colors to collect to avoid reproductions. In crystal, you just have to be careful of those two items for now.

The two-tier tidbit with a metal handle is not priced in my listings. These sell in the $25.00 range. Tidbits were occasionally made by the glass companies, but were more often made elsewhere. They can easily be made today if you can find the metal hardware. Many tidbits are a product of the early 1970s when a dealer in St. Louis would make up any pattern for $10.00 if you furnished the plates. He did a great job!

A crystal "Pineapple and Floral" set is not easily put together; but, it is not impossible either. You will find that tumblers, cream soups, and sherbets are the most troublesome pieces to find. As with most of Indiana's patterns, mould roughness on the seams is a "turn off" to some collectors. This is true on both sizes of tumblers! If this roughness does not bother you, then search for the harder-to-find pieces as soon as you can! The set is extraordinarily attractive as a whole!

There are two different plates that have an indented center ring. No one has discovered exactly what these pieces were intended to be, but a cheese dish is the idea most often proposed. The usual one seen is 11½" in diameter. You may see these advertised as a servitor — which I believe historically was a human servant!

Amber No. 618 is not collected as often as the crystal because there is so little of it available. It is one of the more attractive amber sets if you can find enough to display!

The fired-on red pitcher that has been found with fired red sets of "Pineapple and Floral" has also been found with a set of fired red Daisy. The color is dull and has no sheen, as is most of this fired-on red. There is a crosshatching design on the base of the pitcher similar to that of No. 618, but that is where the resemblance to "Pineapple and Floral" ends.

	Crystal	Amber, Red		Crystal	Amber, Red
Ash tray, 4½"	17.50	20.00	Plate, 11½" w/indentation	25.00	
Bowl, 4¾" berry	25.00	20.00	Plate, 11½" sandwich	17.50	16.00
Bowl, 6" cereal	28.00	22.00	Platter, 11" closed handles	17.50	18.00
* Bowl, 7" salad	2.00	10.00	Platter, relish, 11½" divided	20.00	
Bowl, 10" oval vegetable	25.00	20.00	Saucer	4.00	4.00
* Comport, diamond-shaped	1.00	8.00	Sherbet, ftd.	22.00	18.00
Creamer, diamond-shaped	7.50	10.00	Sugar, diamond-shaped	7.50	10.00
Cream soup	22.00	22.00	Tumbler, 4¼", 8 oz.	35.00	25.00
Cup	11.00	10.00	Tumbler, 5", 12 oz.	45.00	
Plate, 6" sherbet	5.00	6.00	Vase, cone-shaped	55.00	
Plate, 8⅜" salad	8.50	8.50	Vase holder (35.00)		
** Plate, 9⅜" dinner	17.50	15.00			

* Reproduced in several colors

**Green $35.00

OLD CAFE HOCKING GLASS COMPANY, 1936–1940

Colors: Pink, crystal, and Royal Ruby.

Old Cafe pitchers and dinner plates are the most difficult to find pieces. They are costly! Pitchers were pictured in the last edition. One collector called to thank me for finally showing him that the pitchers exist! He had the pitcher that many collectors are using with this set (evenly spaced panels, not alternating large panels with two small panels that constitute the accepted Old Cafe pitcher). Those pitchers (made by Hocking) can be spotted in green, a color never found in Old Cafe. Several collectors told me they are happy with these substitutes! The juice pitcher, shaped like the Mayfair juice pitcher, appears to be Old Cafe even though it is not shown in Hocking's catalogs; neither was the larger one!

A new listing turning up is a 6½" tab (closed) handled bowl. I had never seen one until about a year ago. All at once, I had letters and several brought into shows for verification. I bought one for future books. It is not listed in Hocking catalogs that I have. Bowls have been confusing. The 5" bowl has an open handle while the 4½" bowl has tab handles, as does the 3¾" berry. The **footed** sherbet (pictured in front) also measures 3¾".

The Royal Ruby Old Cafe cup is found on crystal saucers, as were Coronation's. No Old Cafe Royal Ruby saucers have been found. A 5½" crystal candy with a Royal Ruby lid is also pictured. No Royal Ruby bottom has been spotted. Few lamps have been seen. Lamps were made by drilling through the bottom of a vase, turning it upside down and wiring it. You can see a Royal Ruby one pictured on page 195.

The low candy is 8⅜" including handles and 6½" without. It was not considered to be a plate although readers seem to think that it is. You can see a pink one on the left and a crystal one standing behind the covered candy in the photograph.

Hocking made a cookie jar (a numbered line) which is an excellent companion piece. It is ribbed up the sides **similar** to Old Cafe but has a crosshatched lid that does not resemble Old Cafe.

	Crystal, Pink	Royal Ruby		Crystal, Pink	Royal Ruby
Bowl, 3¾" berry	5.00	7.00	Pitcher, 6", 36 oz.	80.00	
Bowl, 4½", tab handles	6.00		Pitcher, 80 oz.	100.00	
Bowl, 5½" cereal	20.00	13.00	Plate, 6" sherbet	2.50	
Bowl, 6½", tab handles	25.00		Plate, 10" dinner	55.00	
Bowl, 9", closed handles	12.00	16.00	Saucer	3.00	
Candy dish, 8" low, tab handles	12.00	16.00	Sherbet, ¾" low ftd.	12.00	12.00
Candy jar, 5½", crystal with ruby cover		18.00	Tumbler, 3" juice	12.00	14.00
Cup	7.00	9.00	Tumbler, 4" water	13.00	20.00
Lamp	25.00	35.00	Vase, 7¼"	20.00	25.00
Olive dish, 6" oblong	7.00				

OLD COLONY "LACE EDGE," "OPEN LACE" HOCKING GLASS COMPANY, 1935–1938

Colors: Pink and some crystal.

In December 1990, I spent a day at Anchor Hocking going through files and catalogs. I spotted these old store display photographs proclaiming the name of this glass as Old Colony. I was excited to find the **real** name of the pattern! Originally, this trip was for my book *Collectible Glassware from the 40s, 50s, 60s...*; but that trip aided this book also! Old Colony as the corrected pattern name for "Lace Edge" is being accepted by most collectors; but I still get an occasional letter asking why I removed the "Lace Edge" pattern from my book. I merely moved Old Colony to its appropriate alphabetical arrangement! I have received numerous compliments at shows and in letters on the store window photos pictured. Don't you wish that our ancestors had stocked up on those dime sherbets and underliners? Those underliners appear to be salad plates! No Old Colony sherbet plate has ever surfaced. However, one engineer wrote that he had tried to calculate the size of those plates and felt that they were the size of saucers. Will we ever know for sure? Keep looking!

The primary problem with collecting Old Colony (besides finding it) is the damaged "lace" on the outside of pieces. It chipped and cracked, and still does! Plates and bowls have to be stacked carefully because of that. Paper plates between each piece should be a consideration when packing or storing this pattern. Candlesticks, console bowls, and vases are hard to find in mint condition. You will discover some tremendous price increases on rarely found items of Old Colony.

I have separated items in the photographs in order to discuss them. The flower bowl with crystal frog in the top photograph on page 154 becomes the candy jar with a cover shown in the bottom photograph. The 7" comport pictured behind the sherbet in the top photo is the covered comport in the bottom photo. This piece was listed as a covered comport; but today, many dealers call it a footed candy jar. The top photograph shows both ribbed and plain 7¾" bowls. The plain is the same piece as the butter bottom although Hocking called this a covered bon bon and not a butter. The bottom photograph shows both styles of 9½" bowls. Prices for the ribbed bowls are beginning to rise above those of the plainer one, perhaps because it is associated with the smaller, rare one!

Ribs on the footed tumbler extend approximately half way up the side as they do on the cup. This tumbler is often confused with the Coronation tumbler that has a similar shape and design. See the Coronation photograph. Notice the fine ribbed effect from the middle up on the Coronation tumbler. This upper ribbing is missing on Old Colony tumblers.

Satinized or frosted pieces presently sell for a fraction of the cost of their unfrosted counterparts. Lack of demand is one reason; but in some pieces, they are more plentiful than non-frosted pieces. So far, only a few collectors think frosted Old Colony is beautiful; but I have noticed just lately that more are considering it because of price — or perhaps because "mixture" collecting has become more acceptable!

The true 9" comport in Old Colony has a **rayed base**. There is a similar comport that measures 9". This "pretender" has a plain foot and was probably made by Standard or Lancaster Glass. It has been shown in earlier editions. Hocking may have gotten the idea for Old Colony from one of these other companies' designs when they bought them. Both Lancaster and Standard had very similar designs, but their glass generally was better quality and rings when **gently** flipped on the edge with your finger. Hocking's Old Colony makes a clunk sound. If the piece is not shown in my listing, or is in any color other than pink or crystal, the likelihood of your having an Old Colony piece is slim at best.

		Pink
*	Bowl, 6⅜" cereal	24.00
	Bowl, 7¾" ribbed salad	50.00
	Bowl, 8¼" (crystal)	12.00
	Bowl, 9½", plain	26.00
	Bowl, 9½", ribbed	30.00
**	Bowl, 10½", 3 legs, (frosted, $65.00)	250.00
	Butter dish or bon bon with cover	67.50
	Butter dish bottom, 7¾"	27.50
	Butter dish top	40.00
**	Candlesticks, pr. (frosted $85.00)	255.00
	Candy jar and cover, ribbed	50.00
	Comport, 7"	25.00
	Comport, 7" and cover, ftd.	50.00
	Comport, 9"	795.00
	Cookie jar and cover (frosted $50.00)	70.00
	Creamer	22.50
	Cup	25.00
	Fish bowl, 1 gal. 8 oz. (crystal only)	30.00

		Pink
	Flower bowl, crystal frog	25.00
	Plate, 7¼" salad	25.00
	Plate, 8¼" luncheon	23.00
	Plate, 10½" dinner	33.00
	Plate, 10½" grill	22.00
	Plate, 10½", 3-part relish	25.00
	Plate, 13", solid lace	45.00
	Plate, 13", 4-part solid lace	45.00
	Platter, 12¾"	37.50
	Platter, 12¾", 5-part	35.00
	Relish dish, 7½", 3-part deep	65.00
	Saucer	11.00
**	Sherbet, ftd.	100.00
	Sugar	22.50
	Tumbler, 3½", 5 oz. flat	110.00
	Tumbler, 4½", 9 oz. flat	20.00
	Tumbler, 5", 10½ oz. ftd.	80.00
	Vase, 7" (frosted $90.00)	525.00

* Officially listed as cereal or cream soup; green – $75.00

** Price is for absolute mint condition

Please refer to Foreword for pricing information

OLD ENGLISH, "THREADING" INDIANA GLASS COMPANY, Late 1920s

Colors: Green, amber, pink, crystal, crystal with flashed colors, and forest green.

Old English can be collected in green or amber. All pieces seem to be found in green. An entire set in amber may not be attainable since some pieces have never been seen. That does not mean that they were never made! Amber Old English is a richer color more reminiscent of Cambridge or New Martinsville wares which collectors find more appealing.

Pink Old English is elusive with only the center handled server, cheese and cracker, and sherbets being found regularly. Additional pieces in pink exist, but do not often surface! See a pink pitcher and both sizes of tumblers on page 156. Did you see the pitcher and tumblers below with flashed-on black and red decorations? A vase and candy dish with similar decoration have also been spotted!

The Old English center-handled sandwich server is rarely seen! I have one pictured in pink, but it has been over 15 years since I have seen a green one! That one, shipped to a customer in Georgia, arrived flat with tire tracks on it! You do know to always double box any glass shipped, don't you?

Footed pieces of Old English are easier to find than flat items. Both large and small berry bowls and the flat candy dish are in short supply. Sugar and candy jar lids have the same cloverleaf-type knob as the pitcher. The flat candy lid is similar in size to the pitcher lid that is notched on the bottom rim to allow for pouring. You can not mix the two lids since the candy lid is not notched. That candy is also found in a metal holder.

Egg cups have only been found in crystal. The fan vase is the only piece I have ever seen in dark green! A flashed lavender footed candy bottom is reported.

	Pink, Green, Amber		Pink, Green, Amber
Bowl, 4" flat	17.50	Pitcher	65.00
Bowl, 9" ftd. fruit	30.00	Pitcher and cover	125.00
Bowl, 9½" flat	35.00	Plate, indent for compote	20.00
Candlesticks, 4" pr.	32.50	Sandwich server, center handle	55.00
Candy dish & cover, flat	50.00	Sherbet, 2 styles	20.00
Candy jar with lid	50.00	Sugar	17.50
Compote, 3½" tall, 6⅜" across, 2 handled	22.50	Sugar cover	35.00
Compote, 3½" tall, 7" across	22.00	Tumbler, 4½" ftd.	25.00
Compote, 3½" cheese for plate	16.00	Tumbler, 5½" ftd.	35.00
Creamer	17.50	Vase, 5⅜", fan type, 7" wide	47.50
Egg cup (crystal only)	8.00	Vase, 8" ftd., 4½" wide	45.00
Fruit stand, 11" ftd.	40.00	Vase, 8¼" ftd., 4¼" wide	45.00
Goblet, 5¾", 8 oz.	32.50	Vase, 12" ftd.	60.00

"ORCHID" PADEN CITY GLASS COMPANY, Early 1930s

Colors: Yellow, cobalt blue, crystal, green, amber, pink, red, and black.

"Orchid" items, as other Paden City patterns, have made enormous price hikes in the last two years! Orchid growers may have aided this push. It seems many of them have completed or nearly completed their sets of Heisey "Orchid" and now are tuning their attention to other Orchid patterns such as that of Paden City. This "Orchid" pattern was not produced in hundreds of thousands of pieces as was Heisey, but more like hundreds or perhaps a few thousand. It will not stand the collecting pressure without prices increasing at a rapid rate. So far, for over a year, every piece of "Orchid" we have displayed at shows has sold not long after the show opened — if not to a dealer before it opened!

It was believed that "Orchid" etched pieces turned up only on #412 Line, the square, Crow's Foot blank made by Paden City, and not the rounded style #890 Line. Well, the cobalt blue comport on the bottom of page 158 is #890 and the red 8" vase in the top photograph does not belong to either of these lines. That red vase reminds me that Cathy spotted a black one at a flea market in Florida. It was mislabeled Tiffin, but it is the only piece of black "Orchid" I have seen! A yellow mayonnaise is shown below as a pattern shot. The design photographs better on transparent pieces.

There are conceivably three different "Orchid" designs found on Paden City blanks. Collectors do not mind mixing these different "Orchid" varieties because so little of any is found.

"Orchid" prices have not yet reached the range of those in "Cupid," even though there are a few pieces of "Orchid" being found. However, at the rate it is going, it will not be long before it catches prices of "Cupid!"

	All Other Colors	Red Black Cobalt Blue		All Other Colors	Red Black Cobalt Blue
Bowl, 4⅞" square	22.00	50.00	Comport, 6⅝" tall, 7" wide	65.00	135.00
Bowl, 8½", 2-handled	75.00	135.00	Creamer	40.00	85.00
Bowl, 8¾" square	75.00	125.00	Ice bucket, 6"	95.00	195.00
Bowl, 10", ftd., square	95.00	195.00	Mayonnaise, 3 piece	75.00	165.00
Bowl, 11", square	85.00	185.00	Plate, 8½", square		75.00
Cake stand, square, 2" high	75.00	150.00	Sandwich server, center handled	65.00	125.00
Candlesticks, 5¾" pr.	95.00	195.00	Sugar	40.00	85.00
Candy with lid, 6½", square, three part	95.00	195.00	Vase, 8"	95.00	275.00
Candy with lid, cloverleaf, three part	95.00	195.00	Vase, 10"	125.00	295.00
Comport, 3¼" tall, 6¼" wide	25.00	50.00			

"ORCHID"

OVIDE, incorrectly dubbed "NEW CENTURY" HAZEL ATLAS GLASS COMPANY, 1930–1935

Colors: Green, black, white Platonite trimmed with fired-on colors in 1950s.

Decorated sets of Ovide come in various types. Separating those decorations into time periods for my books has been a colossal pain. I have chosen black and red decorations for this book. Just call one "Windmills" and the other "Black, Red, and Gold Trim" for lack of actual names. These are priced under the decorated white pattern below.

Hazel Atlas used a multitude of decorating schemes on this popular Platonite. One of the more popular is the black floral design with red and yellow edge trim. That set encompassed kitchenware items (stacking sets and mixing bowls) as well as a dinnerware line. Evidently, many people found these patterns acceptable judging from the profusion of pieces now being found. You can see later patterns in *Collectible Glassware from the 40s, 50s, 60s....* For most of those later patterns I have found documentation and they are properly named!

The "Flying Ducks" (geese) set is priced under "Decorated White" and not as "Art Deco." Only the "Art Deco" pieces are priced under that column. You will never be able to sell other decorated Ovide for those prices! The egg cup in the "Flying Ducks" pattern is selling in the $12.00 range. It is strange that no other patterns have had egg cups reported. I would not bet against their existence!

Very little black, transparent green, or yellow Ovide are being found. A luncheon set in black or yellow can be assembled; but it would be easier to put together the same set in black or yellow Cloverleaf. However, Cloverleaf would cost three or four times as much! Depression glass dealers are inclined to bring the Cloverleaf pattern to shows, but few handle undecorated Ovide. Thus, if you want this, you'll have to start requesting it at shows!

	Black	Green	Decorated White	Art Deco		Black	Green	Decorated White	Art Deco
Bowl, 4¾" berry			7.00		Plate, 8" luncheon		3.00	14.00	45.00
Bowl, 5½" cereal			13.00		Plate, 9" dinner			20.00	
Bowl, 8" large berry			22.50		Platter, 11"			22.50	
Candy dish and cover	45.00	22.00	35.00		Salt and pepper, pr.	27.50	27.50	24.00	
Cocktail, ftd. fruit	5.00	4.00			Saucer	3.50	2.50	6.00	18.00
Creamer	6.50	4.50	17.50	85.00	Sherbet	6.50	3.00	14.00	50.00
Cup	6.50	3.50	12.50	60.00	Sugar, open	6.50	4.00	17.50	85.00
Plate, 6" sherbet		2.50	6.00		Tumbler			16.50	85.00

Please refer to Foreword for pricing information

OYSTER AND PEARL ANCHOR HOCKING GLASS CORPORATION, 1938–1940

Colors: Pink, crystal, Royal Ruby, white, and white with fired-on pink, blue, and green.

Royal Ruby Oyster and Pearl can be seen under the Royal Ruby pattern shown on page 195, but prices are also included here. Many collectors use Oyster and Pearl as accessory pieces for other patterns. Both the pink relish dish and candlesticks sell well since they are reasonably priced in comparison to other patterns. These pieces make wonderful gifts because they have an attractive design. Be informed in advance that giving presents of glass can create new collectors! We always try to start newlyweds off with an attractive gift of Depression glass. It helps to enclose a note explaining the pedigree of the piece. We found this practice to be well received! Let all those other relatives duplicate toasters and can openers!

The Oyster and Pearl relish dish measures 11½" including the handles. I mention that because of letters I receive wondering what piece is 11½" when I list a 10¼" relish. All measurements in this book are calculated without handles unless otherwise mentioned. Glass companies rarely measured the handles. I have made a point to talk about measurements with handles in my commentary since I have been getting so many letters about measurements on pieces that I have already listed. There is no divided bowl in Oyster and Pearl; it was listed as a relish!

I have not received pictures of a lamp made from several candlesticks, but it was reported. Many patterns had lamps made out of candle holders or vases. Sometimes these were factory made; more often, these were assembled by some other company. Lamps do add interest to your collection; if you would like one, then buy it!

Red decorated crystal pieces are rarely found, but they sell faster than undecorated crystal. The 10½" fruit bowl is a great salad bowl and the 13½" plate makes a wonderful server; several collectors have told me they also make an ideal small punch bowl and liner! You decide what punch cups to use!

The pink color fired-on over white was called Dusty Rose; the fired-on green was designated Springtime Green by Hocking. Collectors either love them or hate them. The undecorated white is more scarce, but not as desirable. I have a letter from a collector who has found this pattern with opaque blue; I would love a picture!

The pink, 6½", deep, bowl with the metal attached to the handle was another of the marketing ploys of that time. With tongs it could serve as a small ice bowl or serving dish. It was another way to retail this bowl!

The spouted, 5¼" bowl is often referred to as heart shaped. It might serve as a gravy or sauce boat although most people use them for candy dishes. The same bowl is found without the spout. Although pictured in Dusty Rose and Springtime Green, this bowl has never been found without a spout in those particular colors.

	Crystal, Pink	Royal Ruby	White and Fired-On Green Or Pink
Bowl, 5¼" heart-shaped, 1-handled	12.00	17.00	10.00
Bowl, 5½", 1-handled	10.00	15.00	
Bowl, 6½" deep-handled	15.00	25.00	
Bowl, 10½" deep fruit	25.00	55.00	14.00
Candle holder, 3½" pr.	25.00	55.00	15.00
Plate, 13½" sandwich	20.00	50.00	
Relish dish, 10¼" oblong, divided	12.00		

"PARROT," SYLVAN FEDERAL GLASS COMPANY, 1931–1932

Colors: Green, amber; some crystal and blue.

Prices for green "Parrot" have at last reached a plateau! "Parrot" pitchers steadied after more than doubling in price over a two year period! Everyone willing to pay the price did and other collectors are balking at the current $2,700.00 price. After years of pitchers selling in the same price range, suddenly everyone wanted one and there were few to be found! Now, those that wanted them have them; so, the price has momentarily leveled! Originally, there were 37 pitchers found in the basement of an old hardware store in central Ohio. Today, there are over 30 still in existence. Doubling in price in so short a time is the extraordinary part since the price was already "out there" for a majority of collectors. However, I believe we could see more of that happening in future Depression glass markets because collectors searching for rare items greatly outnumber their supply!

Both types of hot plates are pictured in the bottom photograph! One is shaped like the Madrid hot plate with the pointed edges. The other is round, and more like the one in Georgian pattern. The round hot plate may be the harder to find; but presently, finding **any** hot plate is vexatious! Prices for hot plates have also leveled at present! A collector in Tennessee has found an **amber hot plate with pointed edges**. That is the only one known! I have seen it, but have been unable to obtain a printable photograph!

Continuing their concealment are high sherbets/champagnes. Less than a dozen green Parrot sherbets are known. The one pictured is the only one I have ever owned. At a show in Indianapolis in the early 1970s, I saw six at one time! They sold to a dealer from Pennsylvania and I never saw or heard of them again.

Yes, I know that shaker is cracked! It's my way of preserving otherwise useless old glass by giving it a function. Actually, many dealers have offered me damaged, but hard to find pieces at reasonable prices so I can photograph them for my books. It seems better than having them thrown away or my having a good pair stored that some collector could really be enjoying!

Increased even more than green "Parrot" prices are amber ones! The amber butter dish, creamer, and sugar lid are all harder to find than green. There has been only one **mint** condition butter dish top found in amber. The commonly found butter bottom has an indented ledge for the top. The jam dish is the same as the butter bottom, but without the ledge; it has never been found in green. Additionally, very few **mint** amber sugar lids have been discovered. Considering there are fewer collectors of amber "Parrot," prices are not as adversely swayed by demand as are the prices for green.

Most collectors recognize "Parrot" shapes as those found on Madrid. Notice that "Parrot" tumblers are found on Madrid-like moulds except for the heavy footed tumbler. Evidently, the thin, moulded, footed tumbler did not accept the "Parrot" design successfully and a heavier styled tumbler was made. This thin, 10 ounce footed tumbler has only been found in amber. When you see one of these, you will understand what I mean when I say it does not accept the design well! The supply of heavy, footed tumblers in both colors, green water tumblers, and thin, flat iced teas in amber have more than met the demand of collectors. Prices for those last two tumblers have remained steady during the other "Parrot" price increases. Heavy tumblers are often damaged on the points which is the first place to look for problems on any "Parrot."

There are quantities of sugar and butter lids found. The major concern is finding **mint** condition lids. The pointed edges and ridges on "Parrot" chipped! You should carefully check these points when buying "Parrot." Damaged or **repaired** glassware should not bring **mint** prices. I emphasize that here because many sugar and butter lids have been repaired. If it has been reworked, it should be sold as repaired and priced accordingly!

	Green	Amber		Green	Amber
Bowl, 5" berry	25.00	18.00	Plate, 9" dinner	52.50	40.00
Bowl, 7" soup	45.00	35.00	Plate, 10½" round grill	32.00	
Bowl, 8" large berry	85.00	75.00	Plate, 10½" square grill		30.00
Bowl, 10" oval vegetable	55.00	70.00	Plate, 10¼" square (crystal only)	26.00	
Butter dish and cover	365.00	1,250.00	Platter, 11¼" oblong	52.00	75.00
Butter dish bottom	65.00	200.00	Salt and pepper, pr.	250.00	
Butter dish top	300.00	1,050.00	Saucer	15.00	15.00
Creamer, ftd.	50.00	65.00	*Sherbet, ftd. cone	25.00	25.00
Cup	40.00	40.00	Sherbet, 4¼" high	1,100.00	
Hot Plate, 5", pointed	850.00	900.00	Sugar	35.00	40.00
Hot plate, 5", round	975.00		Sugar cover	140.00	450.00
Jam dish, 7"		35.00	Tumbler, 4¼", 10 oz.	135.00	110.00
Pitcher, 8½", 80 oz.	2,700.00		Tumbler, 5½", 12 oz.	160.00	125.00
Plate, 5¾" sherbet	35.00	23.00	Tumbler, 5¾" ftd. heavy	125.00	110.00
Plate, 7½" salad	35.00		Tumbler, 5½", 10 oz. ftd. (Madrid mould)		150.00

*Blue – $195.00

162

PATRICIAN, "SPOKE" FEDERAL GLASS COMPANY, 1933–1937

Colors: Pink, green, crystal, and amber ("Golden Glo").

Amber Patrician was a nationally distributed Depression pattern which makes it available to all! Amber is the most collected color. The plentiful 10½" dinner plates were given away in 20 pound sacks of flour as cake plates! These plates have always been designated as dinner plates since I started buying Depression glass. My mom had stacks of Patrician plates and sent food home on one most Friday nights with the individual who helped in her day care center. When I found out about Depression glass, that practice stopped!

The jam dish is a butter bottom *without* **the indented ledge** for the top and measures 6¾" wide and stands 1¼" high. Cereal bowls are confused with jam dishes; cereals are 6" in diameter and 1¾" deep. Prices differ!

Green Patrician is collected (and found) more than pink or crystal. However, green dinner plates are few and far between! To complete a set in pink is difficult, but not yet an unattainable goal. I think it might be in crystal. Not all pieces have shown up in crystal.

Pitchers were made in two styles. The one pictured has a moulded handle and is easier to find in amber than the one with an applied handle, which I have not seen in years! In crystal, the applied handled pitcher is easiest to find!

Only the applied handled pitcher can be considered rare in amber; but mint condition sugar lids, cookie or butter bottoms, and footed tumblers are harder to find than other pieces. Check sugar lids for signs of repair. Many a glass repairer has cut his teeth on those. That cookie **bottom** is rare in green. There are several lids found for each bottom. Saucers are also harder to find than cups.

There is a green vase that was made from stretching a cookie bottom, probably a worker's experiment. It was shown in *Very Rare Glassware of the Depression Years, Fourth Series.*

	Amber, Crystal	Pink	Green		Amber, Crystal	Pink	Green
Bowl, 4¾" cream soup	16.00	18.00	20.00	Plate, 6" sherbet	10.00	8.00	8.00
Bowl, 5" berry	12.50	12.00	12.00	Plate, 7½" salad	15.00	15.00	14.00
Bowl, 6" cereal	25.00	24.00	27.50	Plate, 9" luncheon	12.00	10.00	11.00
Bowl, 8½" large berry	45.00	25.00	40.00	Plate, 10½" dinner	6.50	40.00	45.00
Bowl, 10" oval vegetable	30.00	25.00	35.00	Plate, 10½" grill	13.50	15.00	15.00
Butter dish and cover	90.00	225.00	110.00	Platter, 11½" oval	30.00	25.00	25.00
Butter dish bottom	60.00	175.00	60.00	Salt and pepper, pr.	55.00	85.00	60.00
Butter dish top	30.00	50.00	50.00	Saucer	9.50	9.50	9.50
Cookie jar and cover	85.00		550.00	Sherbet	13.00	14.00	14.00
Creamer, footed	10.00	12.00	12.00	Sugar	9.00	9.00	9.00
Cup	8.00	11.00	11.00	Sugar cover	60.00	65.00	60.00
Jam dish	33.00	30.00	40.00	Tumbler, 4", 5 oz.	30.00	30.00	30.00
Pitcher, 8", 75 oz. moulded				Tumbler, 4¼", 9 oz.	28.00	26.00	25.00
handle	115.00	110.00	125.00	Tumbler, 5½", 14 oz.	45.00	35.00	45.00
Pitcher, 8¼", 75 oz., applied				Tumbler, 5¼", 8 oz. ftd.	50.00		60.00
handle	150.00	135.00	150.00				

"PATRICK" LANCASTER GLASS COMPANY, Early 1930s

Colors: Yellow and pink.

Yellow "Patrick" luncheon sets are being found, but other pieces are difficult. A few **pink** "Patrick" luncheon sets have turned up, but the price has scared away all but serious collectors. There has been some easing on prices for pink; but I have not seen much available recently which could account for that. This is a very limited pattern; production was small. The already infinitesimal supply of "Patrick" is rapidly dwindling! Jubilee was distributed heavily in the Northwest and Florida, but "Patrick" is scarcely found anywhere.

Yes! Pink "Patrick" sugar or creamers are really selling for $75.00 each! That is not a misprint! The "Patrick" three-footed candy is shaped just like the one shown in Jubilee.

Serving dishes are rare! There are additional floral patterns made by Lancaster with the mould shapes of "Patrick" and Jubilee that can be combined with these sets! Most of these similar patterns will be priced reasonably.

	Pink	Yellow		Pink	Yellow
Bowl, 9", handled fruit	175.00	125.00	Mayonnaise, 3-piece	195.00	135.00
Bowl, 11", console	140.00	125.00	Plate, 7" sherbet	20.00	12.00
Candlesticks, pr.	150.00	150.00	Plate, 7½" salad	25.00	20.00
Candy dish, 3-ftd	150.00	150.00	Plate, 8" luncheon	45.00	27.50
Cheese & cracker set	150.00	125.00	Saucer	20.00	12.00
Creamer	75.00	37.50	Sherbet, 4¾"	60.00	50.00
Cup	65.00	35.00	Sugar	75.00	37.50
Goblet, 4" cocktail	80.00	80.00	Tray, 11", 2-handled	75.00	60.00
Goblet, 4¾", 6 oz. juice	80.00	75.00	Tray, 11", center-handled	155.00	110.00
Goblet, 6", 10 oz. water	90.00	70.00			

"PEACOCK REVERSE" PADEN CITY GLASS COMPANY, LINE #412 & #991, 1930s

Colors: Cobalt blue, red, amber, yellow, green, pink, black, and crystal.

Paden City's Line #412 ("Crow's Foot") and Line #991 ("Penny Line") constitute the blanks on which "Peacock Reverse" has been found. Paden City lines were used for many different patterns; it is not unusual to recognize a blank only to find that it does not have the etched design you want! (Those designs that show white in the photograph have been highlighted so you can see them better!)

The pink, eight-sided plate previously reported is pictured. This is the only one I have seen and the only piece I have found in pink. Note that we have found two colored sugars, but have yet to spot a creamer in ten years of searching. A newly discovered, lipped, footed comport measures 4¼" tall and 7⅜" wide. There are two styles of candy dishes. Notice that both have patterns only on the lids. The plain bottoms can be discovered with lids sporting other etches or even without an etch. That should make bottoms easier to find; but does it?

All colors are attractive, but most collectors are drawn to cobalt blue and red. Obligingly, those are the colors that frequently turn up. Prices for "Peacock Reverse" are not determined by color as much as other patterns. Collectors embrace any piece in any color they can discover!

"Peacock Reverse" could be found etched on almost any piece listed under "Crow's Foot" (squared) or "Orchid." Let me know what, as yet, unlisted pieces or colors you encounter!

	All Colors		All Colors
Bowl, 4⅞" square	40.00	Plate, 5¾" sherbet	22.50
Bowl, 8¾" square	110.00	Plate, 8½" luncheon	60.00
Bowl, 8¾" square with handles	100.00	Plate 10⅜", 2-handled	95.00
Bowl, 11¾" console	125.00	Saucer	20.00
Candlesticks, 5¾" square base, pr.	125.00	Sherbet, 4⅝" tall, 3⅜" diameter	65.00
Candy dish, 6½" square	175.00	Sherbet, 4⅞" tall, 3⅝" diameter	65.00
Comport, 3¼" high, 6¼" wide	75.00	Server, center-handled	75.00
Comport, 4¼" high, 7⅜" wide	85.00	Sugar, 2¾" flat	85.00
Creamer, 2¾" flat	85.00	Tumbler, 4", 10 oz. flat	85.00
Cup	85.00	Vase, 10"	195.00

"PEACOCK & WILD ROSE" "NORA BIRD" PADEN CITY GLASS COMPANY, LINE #300, 1929–1930s

Colors: Pink, green, amber, cobalt blue, black, light blue, crystal, and red.

While studying Paden City's "Peacock and Wild Rose" last year, Cathy made an interesting observation. "Nora Bird" is actually a condensed (or sectioned off) version of the "Peacock and Wild Rose" design. If you look closely at the tall vases pictured at the bottom of page 168, you will see the small bird at the bottom of the design that appears on the pieces formerly known as "Nora Bird." The bird on each piece can be found in flight or getting ready to fly. Obviously, the whole pattern would not fit on the smaller pieces; and so, a condensed version was etched! That is why creamers, sugars, and luncheon pieces have never been discovered in "Peacock and Wild Rose." These pieces have been attributed to another pattern, "Nora Bird." Both are found on Line #300 which is the same line on which most "Cupid" etched pieces occur. Thus, I have now combined both patterns into "Peacock and Wild Rose." Although there are several other bird designs in Paden City patterns, there is more recognition for the peacock patterns than for any other.

Now all the abundant serving pieces of "Peacock and Wild Rose" can combine with the cups, saucers, creamers, sugars, and luncheon plates of "Nora Bird" to give a fairly complete pattern! I suggested a mixture of these two Paden City peacock patterns in the last book, but not for this excellent, same pattern reason! I just thought they went well together!

Some collectors have suggested this bird is actually a pheasant which is probably true since several pheasant patterns made by other glass companies were available during this era. There's an Eastern connection of health and happiness associated with a pheasant which would also fit this time when America was enchanted with influences from the Orient.

Note the pink **octagonal** lid on the flat candy dish in that photograph! This is not a part of the #300 line as are the other three candy dishes pictured on the page. The 5¼" footed, pink candy dish, and the flat, open handled, three part, green candy are both shaped like the candy dishes in "Cupid" pattern. The lids to these two candy dishes are interchangeable. Finding a candy in "Peacock and Wild Rose" should be easier now with three from which to choose! Sadly, finding even one is not an easy accomplishment. Make note of the 11" console bowl in light blue and the fan and elliptical vases in pink. These pieces are rare!

There are two styles of creamers and sugars in pink. These two types are also found with "Cupid" etch. So far, we have only found the round handled set in green "Peacock and Wild Rose." Additionally, a collector in Texas has found two green tumblers that are different from those listed. They are 2¼", 3 ounces; and 5¼", 10 ounces.

There may be more pieces in this pattern than I have listed; please let me know if you find something else. A pitcher to go with the five different tumblers discovered would be enchanting!

	All Colors		**All Colors**
Bowl, 8½", flat	125.00	Ice bucket, 6"	195.00
Bowl, 8½", fruit, oval, ftd.	195.00	Ice tub, 4¾"	185.00
Bowl, 8¾", ftd.	175.00	Ice tub, 6"	175.00
Bowl, 9½", center-handled	165.00	Mayonnaise and liner	97.50
Bowl, 9½", ftd.	185.00	Pitcher, 5" high	250.00
Bowl, 10½", center-handled	125.00	Plate, 8"	25.00
Bowl, 10½", ftd.	195.00	Plate, cake, low foot	145.00
Bowl, 10½", fruit	185.00	Relish, 3-part	110.00
Bowl, 11", console	175.00	Saucer	15.00
Bowl, 14", console	195.00	Sugar, 4½", round handle	55.00
Candlestick, 5" wide, pr.	165.00	Sugar, 5", pointed handle	55.00
Candlesticks, octagonal tops, pr.	175.00	Tray, rectangular, handled	195.00
Candy dish w/cover, 6½", 3 part	175.00	Tumbler, 2¼", 3 oz.	50.00
Candy dish w/cover, 7"	225.00	Tumbler, 3"	55.00
Candy with lid, ftd., 5¼" high	175.00	Tumbler, 4"	65.00
Cheese and cracker set	185.00	Tumbler, 4¾", ftd.	75.00
Comport, 3¼" tall, 6¼" wide	125.00	Tumbler, 5¼", 10 oz.	75.00
Creamer, 4½", round handle	55.00	Vase, 8¼" elliptical	395.00
Creamer, 5", pointed handle	55.00	Vase, 10", two styles	250.00
Cup	65.00	Vase, 12"	295.00

PETALWARE MacBETH-EVANS GLASS COMPANY, 1930–1940

Colors: Monax, Cremax, pink, crystal, cobalt and fired-on red, blue, green, and yellow.

Red trimmed Petalware is the most desired decoration of all the different Petalware designs. A couple of boxed sets of sherbets with this decoration have been found in the last year. Both of these boxed sets have named the design "Mountain Flowers"! From now on it will be so identified in my books. While scouting the trail of "Mountain Flowers," many collectors have become smitten with other decorated Petalware patterns. That's good since the supply of "Mountain Flowers" is rapidly diminishing. Many collectors seek Florette which is the pointed petal, red flower decoration (sans red trim) pictured on the bottom two shelves on page 171. Notice the flat soup on the bottom row. Soups are rarely seen in Petalware, let alone decorated as Florette!

Monax and Cremax are names given the colors by MacBeth-Evans. Cremax refers to the opaque beige colored Petalware shown at the bottom of 172 and Monax is the whiter color shown in all the other pictures. Cremax will glow green under a black light, but Monax does not. Quite a large number of Petalware devotees are beginning to collect pastel decorated Cremax shown at the bottom of page 172. I have been asked for it at several different shows recently. Since little of it is found, prices are climbing! Notice the crystal tumbler with matching pastel bands in that photo. These are found in three sizes, all selling in the $7.00 to $10.00 range to collectors wanting additional pieces to go-with their sets. No pitchers or tumblers were originally made.

Red trimmed Petalware has three sizes of decorated tumblers, a pitcher, and sherbets to match it. These are possibly Libbey decorated since many of these tumblers are found in northern Ohio. I have listed the two sizes of tumblers pictured. You can find these tumblers both frosted or unfrosted. I have seen a decorated pitcher which is a frosted Federal Star juice pitcher. Somebody send the measurements on the other water tumbler, please!

I have tried to show as wide a variety of decorated Petalware as possible. On page 171 and the bottom of page 173 are plates from different series of fruits, birds, and flowers. The fruit-decorated Petalware with the names of fruit printed on the plate is found in sets of eight. One such set consists of plates showing cherry, apple, orange, plum, strawberry, blueberry, pear, and grape. You may find other sets with different fruits. Some plates have stickers (bottom of page 173 in row with blue bird plates) which read "Rainbow Hand Painted." Others have colored bands or 22K gold trim. All **series** of fruit- and bird-decorated Petalware are now fair game at $18.00–$20.00 each!

Pink Petalware has attracted the eyes of collectors. I have previously suggested that pink Petalware was inexpensive and an excellent pattern for beginning collectors. This pink is still less costly than most other pink patterns in Depression glass.

The cobalt mustard (foreground at top of 173) has a metal lid and it is Petalware! A few additional pieces of cobalt blue Petalware turned up in the mid-1970s, but they all were absorbed into collections and have not since been seen! The 9" berry bowl varies from 8¾" at times. You will find other quarter inch variances on many larger pieces in this pattern. It was made for a long time and replacing worn moulds caused some size discrepancies. Very few 4" Monax sherbets have been seen in recent years. The last one I owned (in 1976) was a casualty of my concrete basement floor!

PETALWARE (Cont.)

	Crystal	Pink	Monax Plain	Cremax, Monax Florette, Fired-On Decorations	Red Trim Floral
Bowl, 4½" cream soup	4.50	12.50	12.00	14.00	
Bowl, 5¾" cereal	4.00	11.00	8.00	14.00	37.50
Bowl, 7" soup			60.00	75.00	
*Bowl, 9" large berry	8.50	20.00	18.00	35.00	135.00
Cup	3.00	7.00	5.00	10.00	27.50
**Creamer, ftd.	3.00	8.00	6.00	12.50	35.00
Lamp shade (many sizes) $8.00 to $15.00					
Mustard with metal cover in cobalt blue only, $10.00					
Pitcher, 80 oz. (crystal decorated bands)	25.00				
Plate, 6" sherbet	2.00	2.50	2.50	6.00	20.00
Plate, 8" salad	2.00	5.00	4.00	10.00	25.00
Plate, 9" dinner	4.00	14.00	9.00	16.00	37.50
Plate, 11" salver	4.50	15.00	10.00	18.00	
Plate, 12" salver		11.00	18.00		40.00
Platter, 13" oval	8.50	20.00	15.00	25.00	
Saucer	1.50	2.00	2.00	3.50	10.00
Saucer, cream soup liner			18.00		
Sherbet, 4" low ftd.			30.00		
**Sherbet, 4½" low ftd.	3.50	10.00	8.00	12.00	38.00
**Sugar, ftd.	3.00	7.50	6.00	10.00	35.00
Tidbit servers or lazy susans, several styles 12.00 to 17.50					
Tumbler, 3⅝", 6 oz.					35.00
Tumbler, 4⅝", 12 oz.					37.50
***Tumblers (crystal decorated pastel bands) 7.50 to 10.00					

*Also in cobalt at $45.00   **Also in cobalt at $30.00   ***Several sizes

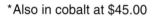

PRIMO, "PANELED ASTER" U.S. GLASS COMPANY, EARLY 1930s

Colors: Green and yellow.

Primo is another Depression glass pattern where little catalog information has surfaced. That is why I am excited to report two new finds. An 11", three-footed console bowl and a 6¼" sherbet plate are both pictured and listed for the first time. The bowl was beat up, but I paid $20.00 because "it had to be rare since it wasn't in Gene Florence's book," according to the proprietor of a small shop in Pennsylvania. I bought the sherbet plates, but had to take the sherbets to get them. A collector asked me to watch for this pattern and for over three years, I have looked for Primo. Some conclusions reached include that bowls, dinner, grill, and cake plates will take some searching. I have not found a green berry bowl to photograph either!

An annoyance to collecting Primo is mould roughness and inner rim damage on pieces that have rims. I have seen several sets in antique malls between Florida and Texas, but a majority of the pieces were very rough or chipped. Prices marked were for mint pieces! I wonder if anyone buys damaged Primo that way? Since the pieces were still on the shelves, I guess not. My theory is that if you see a piece priced for sale and it is still there, then no one has wanted to pay that price! When you see it a year or more later, then you know that for sure!

The tumbler exactly fits the coaster/ash tray! These coasters have been found in boxed Primo sets that were advertised as "Bridge Sets."

	Yellow, Green		Yellow, Green
Bowl, 4½"	18.00	Plate, 7½"	10.00
Bowl, 7¾"	30.00	Plate, 10" dinner	22.00
Bowl, 11", 3-footed	30.00	Plate, 10" grill	15.00
Cake plate, 10", 3-footed	30.00	Saucer	3.00
Coaster/ash tray	8.00	Sherbet	14.00
Creamer	12.00	Sugar	12.00
Cup	12.00	Tumbler, 5¾", 9 oz.	22.00
Plate, 6¼"	10.00		

PRINCESS HOCKING GLASS COMPANY, 1931–1935

Colors: Green, Topaz yellow, apricot yellow, pink, and blue.

Newly discovered pieces of Princess continue to surface! Just this week I received a picture confirming a blue 8¾" square, three-footed bowl which stands only 1½" high. It is like the pink one pictured in *Very Rare Glassware of the Depression Years, Fourth Series.* Unfortunately, it has been promised to someone else; so I will be unable to show it to you as I would have liked to do. Blue Princess pieces are discovered on rare occasions. The cookie jar and cup and saucer are coveted by collectors of those items. Blue Princess suffers the fate of many seldom-found patterns or colors of Depression glass. It is too rare to collect a set! Keep looking! You never know what will turn up!

Finding mint condition Princess bowls presents a problem due to inner rim roughness. If you see an ad that says "irr" next to the item, it means inner rim roughness. Some new collectors are always writing for explanations; I try to oblige, but you have to read each pattern for these trivialities. (They have to be worked into many different patterns because of space limitations.) Some of this "irr" damage was caused by stacking the bowls together over the years; but some destruction was created by the very sharply defined inner rim itself. The undivided relish is promoted as a soup bowl by some dealers. To me, it seems very shallow for a soup bowl.

Iced tea tumblers and bowls are hard to find in all colors of Princess. Besides the aforementioned items, green Princess collectors have to search long and hard for the undivided relish and the elusive, squared foot pitcher with tumblers to match. Collectors of pink Princess have problems finding coasters, ash trays, and the squared foot pitchers with matching tumblers. The hardest to find yellow pieces include the butter dish, juice pitcher, undivided relish, 10¼" handled sandwich plate, coasters, and ash trays.

Some dramatic price increases in the last few years have occurred in pink Princess. At this rate, a pink set will soon be as expensive as green.

There is some extensive color variation in yellow Princess. Topaz is the official color listed by Hocking, and it is a bright, attractive shade of yellow. However, some yellow turned out amber and has been termed "apricot" by collectors. Most favor the Topaz which makes the darker, amber shade difficult to sell. The colors are so different that it is almost as if Hocking meant to have two different colors. For some reason (probably distribution) yellow Princess bowls and sherbets abound in the Detroit area. Incidentally, almost all yellow Princess juice pitchers have been found in northern and central Kentucky.

The handled sandwich plate actually measures 10¼" (or 11¼" if measured including handles). These are rarely found in yellow Princess and have been fetching high prices when they do occasionally turn up. This plate is just like the handled grill plate without the dividers. You can see one in the background of the photograph at the bottom of page 176. These plates are common in pink and green; but since the yellow is so highly priced, prices have begun to creep up on the others. The grill plate without handles and dinner plate have been corrected to read 9½" in the listing instead of the 9" listed in Hocking catalogs. Measure perpendicularly and not diagonally!

PRINCESS (Cont.)

	Green	Pink	Topaz, Apricot
Ash tray, 4½"	70.00	85.00	100.00
Bowl, 4½" berry	25.00	25.00	50.00
Bowl, 5" cereal or oatmeal	35.00	35.00	32.00
Bowl, 9" octagonal salad	40.00	35.00	140.00
Bowl, 9½" hat-shaped	50.00	45.00	140.00
Bowl, 10" oval vegetable	30.00	28.00	65.00
Butter dish and cover	100.00	100.00	750.00
Butter dish bottom	35.00	35.00	250.00
Butter dish top	65.00	65.00	500.00
Cake stand, 10"	30.00	33.00	
Candy dish and cover	65.00	70.00	
Coaster	38.00	70.00	100.00
*Cookie jar and cover	58.00	70.00	
Creamer, oval	14.00	15.00	14.00
**Cup	12.00	12.00	8.00
Pitcher 6", 37 oz.	52.00	65.00	595.00
Pitcher, 7⅜", 24 oz. ftd.	525.00	475.00	
Pitcher, 8", 60 oz.	55.00	55.00	95.00
***Plate, 5½" sherbet	10.00	10.00	3.00
Plate, 8" salad	14.00	14.00	15.00
Plate, 9½" dinner	26.00	25.00	15.00

	Green	Pink	Topaz, Apricot
**Plate, 9½" grill	15.00	15.00	5.50
Plate, 10¼" handled sandwich	16.00	28.00	175.00
Plate, 10½" grill, closed handles	10.00	12.00	5.50
Platter, 12" closed handles	25.00	25.00	65.00
Relish, 7½" divided	26.00	28.00	100.00
Relish, 7½" plain	145.00	195.00	250.00
Salt and pepper, 4½" pr.	55.00	55.00	75.00
Spice shakers, 5½" pr.	40.00		
***Saucer (same as sherbet plate)	10.00	10.00	3.00
Sherbet, ftd.	24.00	24.00	35.00
Sugar	10.00	12.00	8.50
Sugar cover	22.00	22.00	17.50
Tumbler, 3", 5 oz. juice	30.00	30.00	30.00
Tumbler, 4", 9 oz. water	26.00	25.00	25.00
Tumbler, 5¼", 13 oz. iced tea	40.00	30.00	30.00
Tumbler, 4¾", 9 oz. sq. ftd	65.00	60.00	
Tumbler, 5¼", 10 oz. ftd.	30.00	28.00	21.00
Tumbler, 6½", 12½ oz. ftd.	95.00	95.00	165.00
Vase, 8"	35.00	40.00	

*Blue $895.00
**Blue $125.00
***Blue $60.00

QUEEN MARY (PRISMATIC LINE), "VERTICAL RIBBED"
ANCHOR HOCKING GLASS COMPANY, 1936–1949

Colors: Pink, crystal, and some Royal Ruby.

Crystal Queen Mary is attracting as many new collectors as pink. Price is one reason, but availability and its somewhat "Deco" look could be others. Currently, several crystal pieces have become more elusive; but, nothing can come close to being as vexing to get as pink dinner plates and footed tumblers. Prices for those items in crystal are increasing, but will have a way to go to catch the pink! A crystal set can be finished at reasonable prices!

I still have not confirmed the pink **footed** creamer and sugar that I showed in earlier editions as Anchor Hocking's. A set was found in crystal and is pictured in *Very Rare Glassware of the Depression Years, Fifth Series*. They have all the characteristics of Queen Mary!

The 6" cereal bowl has the same shape as the butter bottom. Butter dishes were called preserve dishes in Hocking catalogs. There are two sizes of cups. The smaller sits on the saucer with cup ring. The larger cup rests on the combination saucer/sherbet plate. Lately, the pink, smaller cup and saucer have outdistanced the larger in price.

The frosted butter dish pictured with a metal band looks somewhat like a crown. I was told that these were made about the time of the English Coronation hoopla in the mid 1930s. I have seen these priced as high as $150.00 in an Art Deco shop, but had to think before paying $25.00 for the one pictured! A pair of lamp shades were found made from frosted candy lids (with metal decorations similar to the butter).

In the 1950s, the 3½" ash tray in the Queen Mary pattern was made in forest green and Royal Ruby. The 2" x 3¾" ash tray and oval cigarette jar have been found together labeled "Ace Hi Bridge Smoking Set" and may be Hazel Atlas manufactured!

	Pink	Crystal		Pink	Crystal
Ash tray, 2" x 3¾" oval	5.00	3.00	Creamer, ftd.	40.00	20.00
*Ash tray, 3½" round		3.00	Creamer, oval	7.50	5.50
Bowl, 4" one handle or none	5.00	3.50	Cup, large	7.00	5.50
Bowl, 4½", berry	6.00	4.00	Cup, small	10.00	8.00
Bowl, 5" berry	12.00	6.00	Plate, 6" and 6⅝"	5.00	4.00
Bowl, 5¾", two handles	6.00	5.50	Plate, 8¾" salad		5.50
Bowl, 6" cereal	25.00	6.50	Plate, 9¾" dinner	60.00	18.00
Bowl, 7" small	12.00	7.00	Plate, 12" sandwich	16.00	9.00
Bowl, 8¾" large berry	16.00	10.00	Plate, 14" serving tray	22.00	12.00
Butter dish or preserve and cover	135.00	25.00	Relish tray, 12", 3-part	18.00	9.00
Butter dish bottom	35.00	6.50	Relish tray, 14", 4-part	20.00	12.00
Butter dish top	100.00	18.50	Salt and pepper, pr.		19.00
Candy dish and cover	40.00	22.00	Saucer/cup ring	5.00	2.50
**Candlesticks, 4½" double branch, pr.		15.00	Sherbet, ftd.	9.00	5.00
Celery or pickle dish, 5" x 10"	25.00	11.00	Sugar, ftd.	40.00	20.00
Cigarette jar, 2" x 3" oval	7.50	5.50	Sugar, oval	7.50	4.50
Coaster, 3½"	4.00	2.50	Tumbler, 3½", 5 oz. juice	10.00	4.00
Coaster/ash tray, 4¼" square	6.00	5.00	Tumbler, 4", 9 oz. water	15.00	6.00
Comport, 5¾"	15.00	8.00	Tumbler, 5", 10 oz. ftd.	65.00	30.00

*Royal Ruby $5.00;   Forest Green $3.00;   ** Royal Ruby $75.00

RADIANCE NEW MARTINSVILLE GLASS COMPANY, 1936–1939

Colors: Red, cobalt and ice blue, amber, crystal, pink, and emerald green.

Radiance punch, cordial, and condiment sets remain elusive. You can see a red punch set below. The punch ladle is the Achilles' heel of this set. The ladle was made from a punch cup by adding a long handle. If not broken years ago, collectors and dealers have added to their demise over recent years. I have been told that the handle comes loose from the cup very easily. That dealer should know; he did it — twice! The (amber) cordial set pictured is difficult to find in any color!

The crystal punch bowl sets being found on emerald green plates were made by Viking after they bought out New Martinsville. One such set was pictured previously. These are found frequently — unlike their older counterparts! I saw a black punch bowl in Seattle. I suspect that too is Viking! If Viking, it probably has a crystal plate and cups; this is only speculation! A Texas reader reports a crystal **cake stand**, 11½" x 4" tall.

A few collectors have firmly suggested that Radiance is too elegant a glassware to be included in this book, that it was more superior glassware than those mass-produced wares of the Depression era and belongs in my *Elegant Glassware of the Depression Era*!

Red and ice blue are the colors most sought. The most troublesome pieces to find in red and ice blue include the butter dish, pitcher, handled decanter, and the five-piece condiment set. Vases have been found made into lamps. I question this being a factory project, but it could have been.

There is no way a set could be collected in cobalt since only a few items were made in this beautiful color. All known pieces have an asterisk in the price listing below.

A few pieces are being found in pink including creamer, sugar, tray, cup, saucer, vase, and shakers. These are selling in the same range as the red since they are scarce at this time.

Price crystal about 50 percent of amber. Only crystal pieces that item collectors seek sell very well. These include pitchers, butter dishes, shakers, sugars, creamers, and cordials.

	Ice Blue, Red	Amber			Ice Blue, Red	Amber
Bowl, 5", nut 2-handled	20.00	10.00		Goblet, 1 oz., cordial	42.00	27.50
Bowl, 6", bonbon	30.00	15.00		Ladle for punch bowl	135.00	95.00
Bowl, 6", bonbon, footed	32.00	17.50		Lamp, 12"	110.00	56.00
Bowl, 6", bonbon w/cover	95.00	45.00		Mayonnaise, 3 piece, set	95.00	40.00
Bowl, 7", relish, 2-part	30.00	18.00	***	Pitcher, 64 oz.	235.00	150.00
Bowl, 7", pickle	25.00	15.00		Plate, 8", luncheon	16.00	10.00
Bowl, 8", relish, 3-part	35.00	25.00	****	Plate, 14", punch bowl liner	85.00	45.00
* Bowl, 9", punch	200.00	100.00		Salt & pepper, pr.	95.00	50.00
Bowl, 10", celery	30.00	18.00		Saucer	8.50	5.50
Bowl, 10", crimped	45.00	25.00		Sugar	25.00	15.00
Bowl, 10", flared	42.00	22.00		Tray, oval	30.00	24.00
Bowl, 12", crimped	50.00	30.00	*****	Tumbler, 9 oz.	30.00	20.00
Bowl, 12", flared	47.50	27.50	******	Vase, 10", flared or crimped	80.00	45.00
Butter dish	465.00	200.00		Vase, 12", flared or crimped	95.00	
Candlestick 6" ruffled pr.	175.00	80.00				
Candlestick 8" pr.	125.00	60.00				
Candlestick 2-lite, pr.	150.00	70.00				
Cheese/cracker, (11" plate) set	50.00	30.00				
Comport, 5"	30.00	18.00				
Comport, 6"	35.00	22.00				
Condiment set, 4-piece w/tray	295.00	160.00				
Creamer	25.00	15.00				
Cruet, indiv.	75.00	36.00				
Cup, ftd.	18.00	12.00				
Cup, punch	15.00	7.00				
** Decanter w/stopper, handled	175.00	90.00				

  * Emerald Green $125.00
  ** Cobalt blue $185.00
  *** Cobalt blue $350.00
  **** Emerald green $25.00
  ***** Cobalt blue $28.00
  ****** Cobalt blue $75.00

Please refer to Foreword for pricing information

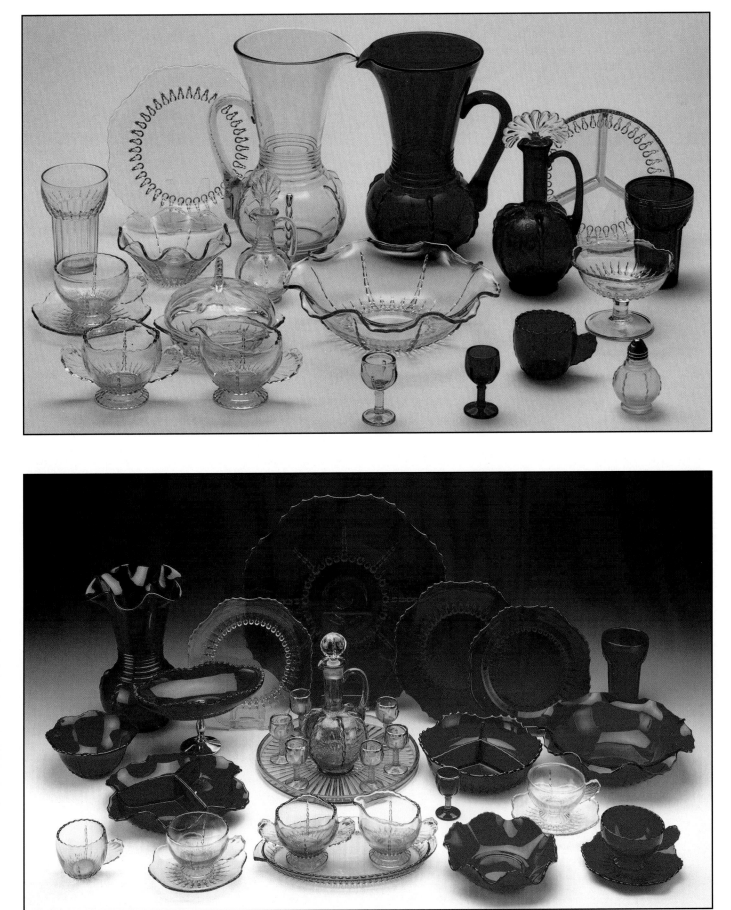

RAINDROPS, "OPTIC DESIGN" FEDERAL GLASS COMPANY, 1929–1933

Colors: Green and crystal.

Apropos of the subject matter, raindrops are falling outside my office window as I start writing about the Raindrops pattern. For beginning collectors please notice that Raindrops has rounded bumps and not elongated ones. Elongated bumps belong to another pattern usually referred to as "Thumbprint." Nearly all Raindrops pieces are embossed on the bottom with Federal's trademark of an **F** inside a shield.

The 7½" berry bowl price has overtaken that of the sugar bowl lid. However, both of these pieces have to take a back seat to the shakers. In reality, Raindrops sugar lids have turned out to be common in comparison to shakers! Subsequently, the price of shakers has soared over the last few years. A couple of shaker collectors have told me that these are harder to find than yellow and green Mayfair! That is quite a statement; but both collectors had at least one of those colors in Mayfair. I asked! I have never seen a Raindrops shaker for sale at any show I have attended if that makes any kind of impression on you as to how rare it is. I have owned the one footed Mayfair shaker and have held both genuine pairs of pink Cherry Blossom shakers known. One Raindrops shaker is all I have **seen**, though I have had reports of a few others!

Raindrops makes a great little luncheon or bridge set. It even has a few accessory pieces that other smaller sets do not. You can find three sizes of bowls in Raindrops. The 7½" bowl will be the one you will probably find last. Raindrops will blend well with many other green sets.

There are two styles of cups. One is flat bottomed and the other has a slight foot. The flat bottomed is 2⁵⁄₁₆" high and the footed is 2¹¹⁄₁₆" (reported by a Raindrops collector). Prices for crystal tumblers run from 50 to 60 percent less than for green.

	Green		Green
Bowl, 4½" fruit	6.00	Sugar	7.50
Bowl, 6" cereal	9.00	Sugar cover	40.00
Bowl, 7½" berry	45.00	Tumbler, 3", 4 oz.	5.00
Cup	5.50	Tumbler, 2⅛", 2 oz.	5.00
Creamer	7.50	Tumbler, 3⅞", 5 oz.	6.50
Plate, 6" sherbet	2.50	Tumbler, 4⅛", 9½ oz.	9.00
Plate, 8" luncheon	5.50	Tumbler, 5", 10 oz.	9.00
Salt and pepper, pr.	300.00	Tumbler, 5⅜", 14 oz.	12.00
Saucer	2.00	Whiskey, 1⅞", 1 oz.	7.00
Sherbet	6.50		

"RIBBON" HAZEL ATLAS GLASS COMPANY, Early 1930s

Colors: Green; some black, crystal, and pink.

Prices for "Ribbon" bowls are skyrocketing! Several collectors told me that they drooled over the sight of both the berry and the cereal in my last book. Some went so far as to tell me that they thought that these bowls really did not exist! My artistic photographer's helper placed the cereal and berry on their sides at an angle so that they could be better seen. I guess it worked for doubting collectors! I bought four of the berry bowls and kept one for photography. A dealer bought the other three for her sister's collection. Maybe I should have sold one each to three collectors!

The black bowl was turned over to show the pattern that is on the outside. Most black glass has to be turned over to see the pattern. I rarely see "Ribbon" for sale at shows. "Ribbon" is another of the patterns that is not seen in the West.

Tumblers, sugars, and creamers are not yet as difficult to find as bowls, but even they are starting to be in shorter supply. The candy dish remains the most frequently seen piece of "Ribbon." Easily found and economically priced, it makes a perfect gift for non-collectors. It is also serviceable!

Two bowl designs were made. The normally found smaller bowls have evenly spaced small panels on them while the panels on larger bowls expand in size as it approaches the top of the bowl. This makes the larger bowl flare at the top while the smaller bowls are more straight sided. This is evident on both the large green and black bowls pictured when compared to the cereal and berry. It is also obvious on the tumbler, creamer, and sugar which are all larger at the top than the bottom! I have reports of larger bowls with sides straight up like the cereal. This bowl is comparable to a Cloverleaf bowl. I have only seen pictures, but they measure 8" according to reports.

Shakers are the only pieces in pink that have been reported to me.

	Green	Black		Green	Black
Bowl, 4" berry	25.00		Plate, 8" luncheon	5.00	14.00
Bowl, 5" cereal	35.00		*Salt and pepper, pr.	30.00	45.00
Bowl, 8" large berry	33.00	35.00	Saucer	2.50	
Candy dish and cover	38.00		Sherbet, ftd.	5.50	
Creamer, ftd.	15.00		Sugar, ftd.	14.00	
Cup	5.00		Tumbler, 6", 10 oz.	30.00	
Plate, 6¼" sherbet	2.50				

* Pink — $35.00

Please refer to Foreword for pricing information

RING, "BANDED RINGS" HOCKING GLASS COMPANY, 1927–1933

Colors: Crystal, crystal w/pink, red, blue, orange, yellow, black, silver, etc. bands; green, pink, "Mayfair" blue, and Royal Ruby.

Ring with colored bands seems to capture more collectors than the more abundant plain crystal. Crystal with platinum (silver) bands is the second most collected Ring. Worn trims plague collectors of this decoration. Colored rings do not seem to suffer from that problem. It may be because the rings do not decorate the rims; but I suspect that painted trims proved more durable than metal ones.

Ring enthusiasts usually start by collecting one particular color sequence. There is a predominant scheme involving black, yellow, red, and orange colored rings in that order. Those other varieties drive the perfectionists crazy! Of course, some people consider perfectionists a bit crazy already!

A reader informed me that obtaining a subscription to *Country Gentleman* in the 1930s got you a green Ring berry bowl set consisting of an 8" berry and six 5" berry bowls. That must not have been too enticing since I have seen few green bowls over the years. You could put a set of green together over an interval of time, say 15 to 20 years. You will notice that my accumulation is not piling up very fast, though thanks to a reader I now have the two berry bowls!

Pitcher and tumbler sets seem to be the only pieces found in pink. I received a letter from a Wisconsin collector who reported that the pink pitchers were given away as a dairy premium. The tumblers were packed with cottage cheese and she could not remember how you ordered the pitcher! Pink sets are abundant only in that part of the country!

A few pieces of Ring are discovered in Royal Ruby and "Mayfair" blue. The luncheon plate and 10 ounce tumbler are rather common in Royal Ruby, but flat juice tumblers and cups have turned up in limited quantities. I have had no reports of saucers to go with the cups. Let me know if you spot any of those.

	Crystal	Decor., Green		Crystal	Decor., Green
Bowl, 5" berry	3.50	6.00	Plate, 11¼", sandwich	7.00	14.00
Bowl, 7" soup	10.00	14.00	****Salt and pepper, pr., 3"	20.00	40.00
Bowl, 5¼", divided	12.00	35.00	Sandwich server, center handle	16.00	27.50
Bowl, 8" large berry	7.00	12.00	Saucer	1.50	2.00
Butter tub or ice tub	22.00	35.00	Sherbet, low (for 6½" plate)	8.00	15.00
Cocktail shaker	20.00	27.50	Sherbet, 4¾" ftd.	5.00	9.00
** Cup	4.50	5.00	Sugar, ftd.	4.50	5.50
Creamer, ftd.	4.50	6.00	Tumbler, 3", 4 oz.	4.00	6.00
Decanter and stopper	25.00	40.00	Tumbler, 3½", 5 oz.	5.00	6.50
Goblet, 7¼", 9 oz.	10.00	15.00	Tumbler, 4", 8 oz., old fashion	15.00	17.50
Goblet, 3¾", 3½ oz. cocktail	11.00	18.00	Tumbler, 4¼", 9 oz.	4.50	10.00
Goblet, 4½", 3½ oz., wine	13.00	20.00	* Tumbler, 4¾", 10 oz	7.50	
Ice bucket	20.00	35.00	Tumbler, 5⅛", 12 oz.	7.00	10.00
Pitcher, 8", 60 oz.	17.50	25.00	Tumbler, 3½" ftd. juice	6.00	10.00
* Pitcher, 8½", 80 oz.	20.00	33.00	Tumbler, 5½" ftd. water	6.00	10.00
Plate, 6¼" sherbet	2.00	2.50	Tumbler, 6½", ftd. iced tea	8.00	15.00
Plate, 6½", off-center ring	5.00	6.00	Vase, 8"	17.50	35.00
***Plate, 8" luncheon	2.50	4.50	Whiskey, 2", 1½ oz.	6.00	10.00

* Also found in pink. Priced as green. Red $7.50   ** Red $65.00. Blue $45.00   ***$17.50   **** Green $55.00

182

ROCK CRYSTAL, "EARLY AMERICAN ROCK CRYSTAL" McKEE GLASS COMPANY,
1920s and 1930s in colors

Colors: Four shades of green, aquamarine, Canary yellow, amber, pink and frosted pink, red slag, dark red, red, amberina red, crystal, frosted crystal, crystal with goofus decoration, crystal with gold decoration, amethyst, milk glass, blue frosted or "Jap" blue, and cobalt blue.

Rock Crystal is a fascinating pattern to collect. Since crystal production started about 1915 and continued into the 1940s, catalogs showing **all** the pieces do not exist. Colored glassware production years are fairly well documented but a surprise or two awaits collectors. A red syrup pitcher has been discovered! The time period that red was supposedly made and the time period that syrup pitchers were made does not overlap. A red syrup pitcher should not exist; but it does; and that gives hope for red shakers and cruets. You can see this syrup in *Very Rare Glassware of the Depression Years, Fourth Series*. We bought flat candy bottoms as soups from a former McKee employee. I assume that may have been a way to get rid of excess stock to employees or maybe the public.

Red, crystal, and amber sets can be completed with perseverance. There are so many different pieces available that you need to determine how much you are willing to spend on a set by choosing what items to buy. Instead of buying every tumbler and stem made, you can pick a couple of each (choose which styles you prefer) and buy only them. Even collectors with limited budgets can start crystal or amber. Red will take a deeper pocket!

Rock Crystal can be amassed as a simple luncheon set, a dinner set, or a complete setting with many unusual serving and accessory pieces. In fact, Rock Crystal pieces are often bought by collectors of other patterns to use as accessory items with their own patterns. Vases, cruets, candlesticks, and an abundance of serving pieces are some of the items obtained. Serving pieces abound; so buy some to use!

In the photograph on page 185 are three styles of ice dishes. The one on the left is a combination of the others with a ring and three dividers outside the ring. The one in the center has only dividers and the one on the right has only a ring. The flat juice has been found in some of the ice dishes, but I suspect the liners could have been plain as were Fostoria's. Ice dishes were made to hold shrimp, crab, or juices with surrounding ice keeping the items cold (without diluting the contents or melting on the table). Icers were mostly found in the upper crust establishments of that day. They could afford to waste ice!

Remember, we believed there to be two different sizes of punch bowls? The recent purchase of a smaller-based bowl confirms this. The base for the larger bowl has an opening 5" across, and stands 6 1/16" tall. This base fits a punch bowl that is 4 3/16" across the bottom. The other style base has only a 4 1/8" opening but also stands 6 1/16" tall. The bowl to fit this base is only 3 1/4" across the bottom. This shoots down the theory that the base for the smaller-based bowl was actually an overturned vase!

ROCK CRYSTAL (Cont.)

	Crystal	All Other Colors	Red
* Bon bon, 7½" s.e.	22.00	35.00	60.00
Bowl, 4" s.e.	12.00	22.00	32.00
Bowl, 4½" s.e.	14.00	22.00	32.00
Bowl, 5" s.e.	16.00	24.00	42.00
** Bowl, 5" finger bowl with 7" plate, p.e.	30.00	45.00	85.00
Bowl, 7" pickle or spoon tray	25.00	40.00	65.00
Bowl, 7" salad s.e.	24.00	37.50	65.00
Bowl, 8" salad s.e.	27.50	37.50	75.00
Bowl, 8½" center handle			225.00
Bowl, 9" salad s.e.	25.00	50.00	110.00
Bowl, 10½" salad s.e.	25.00	50.00	90.00
Bowl, 11½" 2-part relish	30.00	50.00	75.00
Bowl, 12" oblong celery	27.50	45.00	85.00
*** Bowl, 12½" ftd. center bowl	75.00	125.00	295.00
Bowl, 12½", 5 part relish	45.00		
Bowl, 13" roll tray	35.00	60.00	125.00
Bowl, 14" 6-part relish	37.50	65.00	
Butter dish and cover	335.00		
Butter dish bottom	200.00		
Butter dish top	135.00		
**** Candelabra, 2-lite pr.	45.00	105.00	275.00
Candelabra, 3-lite pr.	52.50	125.00	350.00
Candlestick, flat, stemmed pr.	40.00	65.00	125.00
Candlestick, 5½" low pr.	40.00	65.00	175.00
Candlestick, 8" tall pr.	100.00	150.00	425.00
Candy and cover, ftd., 9¼"	60.00	90.00	250.00
Candy and cover, round	55.00	75.00	195.00
Cake stand, 11", 2¾" high, ftd.	35.00	52.50	125.00
Comport, 7"	35.00	52.50	95.00
Creamer, flat s.e.	37.50		
Creamer, 9 oz. ftd.	20.00	32.00	67.50
Cruet and stopper, 6 oz. oil	95.00		
Cup, 7 oz.	17.50	27.50	70.00
Goblet, 7½ oz., 8 oz. low ftd.	18.00	27.50	57.50
Goblet, 11 oz. low ftd. iced tea	20.00	30.00	67.50
Ice dish (3 styles)	35.00		
Jelly, 5" ftd. s.e.	18.00	27.50	52.50
Lamp, electric	195.00	325.00	650.00
Parfait, 3½ oz. low ftd.	25.00	37.50	75.00
Pitcher, qt. s.e.	165.00	225.00	
Pitcher, ½ gal., 7½" high	110.00	195.00	
Pitcher, 9" large covered	175.00	300.00	675.00
Pitcher, fancy tankard	195.00	595.00	950.00
Plate, 6" bread and butter s.e.	6.00	9.50	20.00
Plate, 7½" p.e. & s.e.	8.00	12.00	21.00
Plate, 8½" p.e. & s.e.	9.00	12.50	30.00
Plate, 9" s.e.	18.00	22.00	55.00
Plate, 10½" s.e.	25.00	30.00	65.00
Plate, 10½" dinner s.e. (large center design)	47.50	70.00	175.00
Plate, 11½" s.e.	18.00	25.00	57.50
Punch bowl and stand, 14" (2 styles)	595.00		
Punch bowl stand only (2 styles)	195.00		
Salt and pepper (2 styles) pr.	75.00	125.00	
Salt dip	40.00		
Sandwich server, center-handled	30.00	45.00	145.00

    * s.e. McKee designation for scalloped edge
   ** p.e. McKee designation for plain edge
  *** Red Slag – $350.00 Cobalt – $325.00
 **** Cobalt – $325.00

ROCK CRYSTAL (Cont.)

	Crystal	All Other Colors	Red
Saucer	7.50	8.50	22.00
Sherbet or egg, 3½ oz. ftd.	17.00	25.00	60.00
Spooner	45.00		
Stemware, 1 oz. ftd. cordial	22.00	45.00	65.00
Stemware, 2 oz. wine	20.00	30.00	52.50
Stemware, 3 oz. wine	20.00	30.00	52.50
Stemware, 3½ oz. ftd. cocktail	15.00	21.00	40.00
Stemware, 6 oz. ftd. champagne	16.00	23.00	35.00
Stemware, 7 oz.	16.00	25.00	52.50
Stemware, 8 oz. large ftd. goblet	18.00	26.00	57.50
Sundae, 6 oz. low ftd.	12.00	18.00	35.00
Sugar, 10 oz. open	15.00	22.00	40.00
Sugar, lid	35.00	50.00	135.00
Syrup with lid	150.00		750.00
Tray, 5⅜" x 7⅜", ⅞" high	65.00		
Tumbler, 2½ oz. whiskey	22.00	30.00	65.00
Tumbler, 5 oz. juice	16.00	25.00	57.50
Tumbler, 5 oz. old fashioned	18.00	27.50	60.00
Tumbler, 9 oz. concave or straight	18.00	26.00	52.50
Tumbler, 12 oz. concave or straight	25.00	35.00	67.50
Vase, cornucopia	75.00	95.00	
Vase, 11" ftd.	60.00	110.00	195.00

"ROMANESQUE" L. E. SMITH GLASS COMPANY, early 1930s

Colors: Black, amber, crystal, yellow, and green.

"Romanesque" is one of those smaller Depression glass patterns that reaches out and grabs my wife every time she walks by a piece. You can guess, then, how this tiny pattern came to be included. No matter how much I try to ignore "Romanesque," she either talks me into it or buys it herself! I even forced myself to buy a scalloped top sherbet she was missing when I saw it at a flea market in northern Ohio. We had the regular one and did not know it came in a different style. I am not sure what pieces may turn up in the future, but we have acquired several since we photographed last fall! Perhaps with all these geometric shapes, this pattern will grow on me. Cathy is charmed by the jeweled effect created by the crossed lines of the arches.

There is a console bowl that is not footed, but comes in two parts. The bowl rests on a separate base. I suspect this may have been unstable, and the attached foot style was designed. Mind you, that is just a guess; but it seems logical.

Green and amber seem to be the most prevalent colors, but we have, so far, only found plates in amber. The tri-cornered candles stand 2½" high.

Black pieces have the design on the bottoms, so the cake plate was turned upside down so you could see the pattern. I had previously only seen bowls in black before the cake plate appeared at a show. If you have any other information on pieces not listed in this pattern, please let me know!

	* All Colors		* All Colors
Bowl, 10", ftd., 4¼" high	55.00	Plate, 7", octagonal	7.00
Bowl, 10½"	40.00	Plate, 8", octagonal	10.00
Cake plate, 11½" x 2¾"	35.00	Plate, 8", round	9.00
Candlestick, 2½", pr.	25.00	Plate, 10", octagonal	22.00
Plate, 5½", octagonal	5.00	Sherbet, plain top	8.00
		Sherbet, scalloped top	10.00
		Vase, 7½", fan	40.00

*Black — add 50%

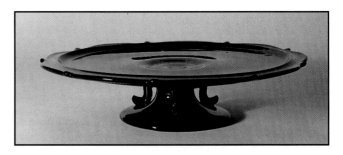

ROSE CAMEO BELMONT TUMBLER COMPANY, 1931

Color: Green.

Records indicate that Rose Cameo was patented in 1931 by Belmont Tumbler Company. I still believe that the rightful manufacturing was done by Hazel Atlas. Very seldom have glass shards of a pattern been found in excavations at a factory location where it was not made. Rose Cameo was dug up on the site of Hazel Atlas's plant in West Virginia. Maybe time will solve this mystery. Of course, a yellow Cloverleaf shaker was dug up at the site of Akro Agate's factory in Clarksburg, West Virginia; and we know that Akro had nothing to do with making Cloverleaf. (Did you know some glass collectors superficially engage in archaeology in pursuit of glass?)

All three bowls are difficult to find, with the smaller berry being the easiest. The straight sided 6" bowl is not being found by most collectors. This little set only has six pieces, but it will take at least six months of searching to assemble!

Rose Cameo is not confusing new collectors as it once did. Cameo, with its dancing girl, and this cameo encircled rose were often mixed up in bygone times. An informed collecting public rarely makes those mistakes today.

The difference in two styles of tumblers is recognized by noticing the flaring of the rims. One does not flare.

	Green		Green
Bowl, 4½" berry	10.00	Plate, 7" salad	12.00
Bowl, 5" cereal	17.00	Sherbet	12.00
Bowl, 6" straight sides	22.00	Tumbler, 5" ftd. (2 styles)	22.00

Please refer to Foreword for pricing information

ROSEMARY, "DUTCH ROSE" FEDERAL GLASS COMPANY, 1935–1937

Colors: Amber, green, pink; some iridized.

The story of Rosemary's becoming a separate pattern redesigned from Federal's Mayfair can be read on page 120. Rosemary pattern came about inadvertently because of Hocking's previous patent to the Mayfair name.

Collectors who saw gathering pink Rosemary as a challenge tell me they have been stymied. Pink is not being seen any more! It is impossible to collect a pattern that is not being seen at any price! I told you it was scarce!

On the other hand, an amber set can be assembled; it will take you some time to arrange for a green set. I cannot remember when I have seen an amber cereal or a green cream soup! They are missing in my photo, I noticed!

Cereal bowls, cream soups, grill plates, and tumblers are infrequently seen in any color. I viewed a want list for green Rosemary cream soups on the Internet last night! Wish I had a few! I might add for new collectors that grill plates are the divided plates usually associated with diners or grills (restaurants) in that time. Food was kept from running together by those raised divisions (normally three). These are especially tough to find in pink.

The sugar has no handles and is often mislabeled as a sherbet. There is no sherbet known in Rosemary! Those sugars could serve as large sherbets and dessert lovers could get an extra helping if you used it that way.

Rosemary is an intriguing pattern whether you are a beginning collector or a collector looking for a new set to collect!

	Amber	Green	Pink
Bowl, 5" berry	6.00	9.00	10.00
Bowl, 5" cream soup	17.00	20.00	30.00
Bowl, 6" cereal	27.50	30.00	37.50
Bowl, 10" oval vegetable	17.00	27.50	40.00
Creamer, ftd.	8.50	12.50	18.00
Cup	5.50	9.50	10.00
Plate, 6¾" salad	5.50	8.50	9.00
Plate, dinner	9.00	14.00	20.00
Plate, grill	7.50	15.00	22.00
Platter, 12" oval	17.00	22.00	32.00
Saucer	4.50	5.00	6.00
Sugar, ftd.	8.50	12.50	17.00
Tumbler, 4¼", 9 oz.	30.00	30.00	50.00

ROULETTE, "MANY WINDOWS" HOCKING GLASS COMPANY, 1935–1939

Colors: Green, pink, and crystal.

Roulette was discovered to be the authentic name of this pattern which collectors formerly had called "Many Windows." Several collectors have told me they favor that designation rather than the real name!

Only beverage sets can be found in pink. Pink pitchers and tumblers are easier to find than green ones. Pieces continue to be priced similarly because there are few collectors for the pink water set. All five sizes of pink **flat** tumblers are pictured, but I have never found a pink footed tumbler.

Cups, saucers, sherbets, and luncheon plates can be located in green. The 12" sandwich plate and fruit bowl are seldom encountered. After finding those items comes the fun of looking for the various six tumblers! Juice tumblers and the old fashioned are the most elusive. I still have not found a green juice tumbler or whiskey for my photograph.

Crystal tumbler and pitcher sets are rarely found; however, there is little demand for the few that have surfaced. Some crystal sets are decorated with colored stripes. In fact, this striped effect gives them an Art Deco look. I am more dazzled with these embellished crystal pitchers than with any other Roulette items I have seen!

	Crystal	Pink, Green		Crystal	Pink, Green
Bowl, 9" fruit	9.50	15.00	Sherbet	3.50	5.50
Cup	36.00	6.50	Tumbler, 3¼", 5 oz. juice	7.00	22.50
Pitcher, 8", 65 oz.	30.00	35.00	Tumbler, 3¼", 7½ oz. old fashioned	23.00	45.00
Plate, 6" sherbet	3.50	4.50	Tumbler, 4⅛", 9 oz. water	13.00	30.00
Plate, 8½" luncheon	5.00	6.00	Tumbler, 5⅛", 12 oz. iced tea	16.00	30.00
Plate, 12" sandwich	11.00	14.00	Tumbler, 5½", 10 oz. ftd.	14.00	30.00
Saucer	1.50	3.50	Whiskey, 2½", 1½ oz.	10.00	17.00

"ROUND ROBIN" MANUFACTURER UNKNOWN, Probably early 1930s

Colors: Green, iridescent, and crystal.

"Round Robin" is a small mystery pattern whose manufacturer has been obscured. In all the years that glassware has been collected, it never fails to astonish me how little we have found out about some of the patterns. Why hasn't someone found a boxed set, an ad, or a labeled piece?

The Domino tray is the unexpected piece in this small pattern. Hocking's Cameo is the only other pattern in Depression glass to offer a sugar cube tray. This tray has only been found in green. For new readers, the Domino tray held the creamer in the center ring with sugar cubes surrounding it. Sugar cubes were made by a famous sugar company, and the tray became synonymous with this name. I have only seen a couple of these in the last few years. Grab one if you can!

Sherbets and berry bowls are the hardest pieces to locate outside the Domino tray. I have not been able to round up a green berry bowl myself. Sherbets and berry bowls are particularly hard to find in green, but plentiful in iridescent. Saucers seem to be harder to find than the cups. Only a few patterns can claim that.

Some crystal "Round Robin" is found today. Crystal was sprayed and baked to achieve the iridized look. Obviously, not all the crystal was sprayed, since we sporadically find it.

The "Round Robin" cup is one of the few footed ones available in Depression glass. I have not found an iridescent cup and saucer. Do you have one?

	Green	Iridescent
Bowl, 4" berry	5.00	5.00
Cup, ftd.	5.00	5.50
Creamer, ftd.	7.50	6.50
Domino tray	37.50	
Plate, 6" sherbet	2.50	2.50
Plate, 8" luncheon	4.00	4.00
Plate, 12" sandwich	9.00	7.00
Saucer	2.00	2.00
Sherbet	5.00	6.00
Sugar	6.50	6.00

ROXANA HAZEL ATLAS GLASS COMPANY, 1932

Colors: "Golden Topaz," crystal, and some white.

For years, for some unknown reason Roxana always seemed to show up in Michigan. Thanks to a couple of Michigan collectors, we now know why! They supplied the information displayed on page 192. If you ate Star Brand Oats, you were able to receive one piece of "Golden Topaz" table glassware in every package. This "Golden Topaz" is what we now know as Roxana. This may clear up why the deep 4½" bowl and the 5½" plate are so hard to find. They were not packed as a premium in these oats! I am assuming that the plate shown on the ad is the 6" one for the sherbet.

The "saucer" listed in previous editions is actually a 5½" plate! All seven affirmed pieces are shown! For those who count eight, I also included a plate **with its design highlighted in gold** in hopes the pattern would show better in the photograph. This delicate pattern is difficult to capture on film since the light shade of yellow has a tendency to disappear under bright lights. Notice that the pattern nearly disappeared in the original advertisement! Well, now you know why shapes are important for identification.

Roxana was only cataloged by Hazel Atlas for one year. It is a limited pattern when compared to thousands of pieces in many other patterns made over years. Unfortunately, there are so few pieces available that most collectors avoid it. If your name is Roxana, how could you avoid collecting this pattern?

Only the 4½" deep bowl has been found in white.

	Yellow	White
Bowl, 4½" x 2⅜"	12.00	15.00
Bowl, 5" berry	11.00	
Bowl, 6" cereal	17.50	
Plate, 5½"	8.50	
Plate, 6" sherbet	7.50	
Sherbet, ftd.	12.00	
Tumbler, 4¼", 9 oz.	20.00	

Please refer to Foreword for pricing information

ROYAL LACE HAZEL ATLAS GLASS COMPANY, 1934–1941

Colors: Cobalt blue, crystal, green, pink; some amethyst.

Cobalt blue Royal Lace has **always** been one of the most desirable patterns in Depression glass. In the summer of 1970, when I found out dealers in the South and Midwest were paying big prices for this cobalt glass, I started buying as much as I could and shipping it. By 1971, you could sell a straight-sided blue Royal Lace pitcher for $30.00, and the most you could expect to pay in my area was $12.00 to $15.00. As I math teacher in Kentucky, I found doubling my meager moneys was an easy concept to embrace! Since teachers only received 10 paychecks, summers of buying and selling were important if we wanted to eat. I went to Springfield, Missouri, in May 1971 to attend my first Depression glass show. I delivered enough glass to dealers that I cleared several hundred dollars on that trip after all expenses; and that show was my crash course in glass buying and selling. There, first thing, I sold a Miss America butter dish for $35.00 and an extra top for $12.00! I did not know the top was the rare part! I had only paid a quarter for it; but, believe me, I was armed with knowledge the next time I found another top. Depression glass could be found in my area, there was a market for it — and Chad outgrew those costly toddler shoes every three months!

Since I have pictured cobalt blue in previous books, I am now showing green. There are almost as many collectors for green Royal Lace as for blue. England is becoming a new source for that color. An abundance of basic "tea" sets are there, i.e. cups, saucers, creamers, and sugars. I never received a sugar lid. Perhaps, the lid got in the way of spooning sugar in that strong tea! The straight-sided pitcher must be common in England as I bought six or seven in a couple of years. Shakers with original Hazel Atlas labels proclaiming "Made in America" were on several of the shakers I bought! You have to wonder if Hazel Atlas named this pattern specifically for this "royal" market!

There are five different pitchers made in Royal Lace: a) 48 ounce, straight side; b) 64 ounce, 8", no ice lip; c) 68 ounce, 8", w/ice lip; d) 86 ounce, 8", no ice lip; e) 96 ounce, 8½", w/ice lip. The 10 ounce difference in the last two listed is caused by the spout on the pitcher without lip dipping below the top edge of the pitcher. This causes the liquid to run out before you get to the top. All spouted pitchers will vary in ounce capacity (up to eight ounces) depending upon how the spout tilts or dips. Always measure ounce capacities until no more liquid can be added without running out.

Crystal, pink, and blue pitchers can be found in all five styles. Green can only be found in four styles. There is no 68 ounce with ice lip in green.

The 4⅞",10 ounce tumblers remain the most elusive; but the number of iced teas and juice tumblers is waning. This is true for all colors including crystal. Some collectors only purchase water tumblers and the straight-sided pitcher for their collections. This style of pitcher and water tumblers is more prolific and, therefore, more economically priced; but demand continues to drive up the price!

Both a rolled-edge console bowl and rolled-edge candlesticks have been found in amethyst! The only other amethyst pieces are the sherbets in metal holders and the cookie jar bottom used for toddy sets. There were **reports** of shakers.

Collectors prefer all glass sherbets to the ones found in metal holders!

	Crystal	Pink	Green	Blue
Bowl, 4¾" cream soup	12.00	25.00	32.00	45.00
Bowl, 5" berry	15.00	30.00	35.00	52.00
Bowl, 10" round berry	20.00	28.00	30.00	65.00
Bowl, 10", 3-legged straight edge	30.00	50.00	65.00	85.00
* Bowl, 10", 3-legged rolled edge	225.00	75.00	95.00	400.00
Bowl, 10", 3-legged ruffled edge	45.00	75.00	95.00	495.00
Bowl, 11" oval vegetable	25.00	35.00	40.00	65.00
Butter dish and cover	75.00	160.00	275.00	625.00
Butter dish bottom	45.00	105.00	180.00	425.00
Butter dish top	30.00	55.00	95.00	200.00
Candlestick, straight edge pr.	32.00	60.00	80.00	150.00
** Candlestick, rolled edge pr.	60.00	100.00	120.00	225.00
Candlestick ruffled edge pr.	40.00	110.00	115.00	250.00
Cookie jar and cover	35.00	60.00	90.00	375.00
Cream, ftd.	12.00	20.00	25.00	55.00
Cup	7.00	15.00	20.00	35.00
Nut bowl	225.00	400.00	400.00	1,500.00
Pitcher, 48 oz., straight sides	40.00	85.00	115.00	165.00

	Crystal	Pink	Green	Blue
Pitcher, 64 oz., 8", w/o/l	45.00	80.00	120.00	245.00
Pitcher, 8", 68 oz., w/lip	50.00	95.00		265.00
Pitcher, 8", 86 oz., w/o/l	50.00	125.00	175.00	325.00
Pitcher, 8½", 96 oz., w/lip	65.00	110.00	160.00	395.00
Plate, 6", sherbet	5.00	8.00	10.00	12.00
Plate, 8½" luncheon	8.00	15.00	16.00	35.00
Plate, 9⅞" dinner	16.00	30.00	35.00	42.50
Plate, 9⅞" grill	11.00	22.00	28.00	35.00
Platter, 13" oval	20.00	38.00	42.00	55.00
Salt and pepper, pr.	42.00	65.00	125.00	275.00
Saucer	5.00	7.00	9.00	12.50
Sherbet, ftd.	16.00	18.00	25.00	45.00
*** Sherbet in metal holder	3.50			35.00
Sugar	8.50	15.00	22.00	25.00
Sugar lid	20.00	50.00	55.00	150.00
Tumbler, 3½", 5 oz.	18.00	30.00	32.00	50.00
Tumbler, 4⅛", 9 oz.	14.00	20.00	30.00	45.00
Tumbler, 4⅞", 10 oz.	30.00	70.00	65.00	120.00
Tumbler, 5⅜", 12 oz.	30.00	60.00	55.00	100.00
****Toddy or cider set: includes cookie jar metal lid, metal tray, 8 roly-poly cups and ladle				250.00

* Amethyst $900.00   ** Amethyst $900.00   *** Amethyst $40.00   **** Amethyst $165.00

ROYAL RUBY ANCHOR HOCKING GLASS COMPANY, 1938–1940

Color: Ruby red.

Anchor Hocking introduced the Royal Ruby color in 1938 using their existing moulds. I am trying to include **only** pieces of Royal Ruby introduced **before 1940** in my list. Royal Ruby pieces made **after 1940** are in *Collectible Glassware from the 40s, 50s, 60s….*

Oyster and Pearl and Coronation were two of the patterns used to launch the Royal Ruby campaign in 1938. Inaugural pieces of Royal Ruby have been found in many of Anchor Hocking's lines including Colonial, Ring, Manhattan, Queen Mary, and Miss America. Most of these Royal Ruby pieces are rare in these patterns. Many of the pieces in the patterns not included in the listing below are of exceptional quality for Anchor Hocking having ground bottoms which are usually not found on mass-produced glassware. There were other designs made.

Again, you have to wonder if the name of the color didn't stem from the country's fascination with the English coronation of Edward VIII in 1936, and his subsequent abdication which riveted the eyes of the world! If Diana's face can insure magazine sales today, it's not hard to see that a hint of "royalty" might have sold glassware in 1938!

	Royal Ruby		Royal Ruby
Bonbon, 6½"	8.50	Creamer, ftd.	9.00
Bowl, 3¾" berry (Old Cafe)	7.00	Cup (Coronation)	6.50
Bowl, 4½", handled (Coronation)	7.00	Cup (Old Cafe)	9.00
Bowl, 4⅞", smooth (Sandwich)	12.50	Cup, round	5.50
Bowl, 5¼" heart-shaped, 1-handled (Oys & Prl)	17.00	Goblet, ball stem	10.00
Bowl, 5¼", scalloped (Sandwich)	20.00	Jewel box, 4¼", crys. w/Ruby cov.	12.50
Bowl, 5½" cereal (Old Cafe)	13.00	Lamp (Old Cafe)	35.00
Bowl, 5½", 1-handled (Oys & Prl)	15.00	Marmalade, 5⅛", crys. w/Ruby cov.	7.50
Bowl, 6½" deep-handled (Oys & Prl)	25.00	Plate, 8½", luncheon (Coronation)	10.00
Bowl, 6½", handled (Coronation)	12.00	Plate, 9⅛", dinner, round	11.00
Bowl, 6½", scalloped (Sandwich)	27.50	Plate, 13½" sandwich (Oys & Prl)	50.00
Bowl, 8", handled (Coronation)	15.00	Puff box, 4⅝", crys. w/Ruby cov.	9.00
Bowl, 8", scalloped (Sandwich)	37.50	Relish tray insert (Manhattan)	3.50
Bowl, 9", closed handles (Old Cafe)	16.00	Saucer, round	2.50
Bowl, 10½" deep fruit (Oys & Prl)	55.00	Sherbet, low ftd. (Old Cafe)	12.00
Candle holder, 3½" pr. (Oys & Prl)	55.00	Sugar, ftd.	7.50
Candle holder, 4½" pr. (Queen Mary)	75.00	Sugar, lid	11.00
Candy dish, 8" mint, low (Old Cafe)	16.00	Tray, 6" x 4½"	12.50
Candy jar, 5½", crys. w/Ruby cov. (Old Cafe)	18.00	Tumbler, 3" juice (Old Cafe)	14.00
Cigarette box/card holder, 6⅛" x 4" crys.		Tumbler, 4" water (Old Cafe)	20.00
w/Ruby top	65.00	Vase, 7¼" (Old Cafe)	25.00
		Vase, 9", two styles	16.00

"S" PATTERN, "STIPPLED ROSE BAND" MacBETH-EVANS GLASS COMPANY, 1930–1933

Colors: Crystal; crystal w/trims of silver, blue, green, amber; pink; some amber, green, fired-on red, Monax, and light yellow.

"S" Pattern with decorations, whether it be platinum or pastel banded receives more attention than does plain crystal. The dilemma in collecting pastel banded "S" Pattern is that there are limited amounts available! Amber, blue, or green banded crystal was made; you might follow an ever-growing trend and collect various colors! You can find crystal.

Variance in amber coloration causes some pieces to look more yellow than amber. The discrepancy is almost as distinct as in Hocking's Princess; however, amber "S" Pattern collectors **do** have a dinner plate to use! Neither crystal nor crystal-trimmed dinner plates have been found. Crystal luncheon plates would be striking against a colored dinner plate of some variety. I'm seeing photos where this type of thing is being done with eye-catching success!

A pink or green pitcher and tumbler set still turns up once in a while; but the demand for these has diminished. Years ago, there were a number of pitcher collectors; rare pitchers sold fast in the $200.00–500.00 range. Today, some are commanding prices of $1,500.00–2,500.00! One of the most stunning collections ever displayed was of pitchers on lighted glass shelves with mirrors behind the glass. It made the room a show place!

If you find a pink tumbler that has a moulded pattern, it will be a "Dogwood" moulded tumbler and not "S" Pattern. The only pink tumblers found in "S" Pattern have a silk screened design not moulded into the glass.

Fired-on red and true red "S" Pattern items both fit the rare category; however, there are fewer collectors who are excited by them. The first red "S" Pattern luncheon plates discovered sold for $65.00 each in the early 1970s. Today, those red "S" Pattern plates are a tough sell at $40.00.

	Crystal	Yellow, Amber, Crystal W/ Trims		Crystal	Yellow, Amber, Crystal W/ Trims
* Bowl, 5½" cereal	5.00	7.00	Plate, grill	6.50	8.00
Bowl, 8½" large berry	11.00	16.00	Plate, 11¾" heavy cake	40.00	50.00
* Creamer, thick or thin	6.00	7.00	*** Plate, 13" heavy cake	60.00	75.00
* Cup, thick or thin	3.50	4.50	Saucer	2.00	2.50
Pitcher, 80 oz. (like "Dogwood") (green or pink 550.00)	52.50	110.00	Sherbet, low ftd.	4.50	7.00
			* Sugar, thick and thin	5.50	6.50
Pitcher, 80 oz. (like "American Sweetheart")	65.00		Tumbler, 3½", 5 oz.	5.00	7.00
Plate, 6" sherbet (Monax 8.00)	2.50	3.00	Tumbler, 4", 9 oz. (green or pink 50.00)	6.00	8.00
** Plate, 8¼" luncheon	4.50	5.00	Tumbler, 4¾, 10 oz.	7.00	8.00
Plate, 9¼" dinner		9.00	Tumbler, 5", 12 oz.	9.00	15.00

* Fired-on red items will run approximately twice price of amber   **Red – $40.00; Monax – $10.00   ***Amber – $77.50

SANDWICH INDIANA GLASS COMPANY, 1920s–1980s

Colors: Crystal late 1920s–today; teal blue 1950s–1980s; milk white mid-1950s; amber late 1920s–1980s; red 1933,1969–early 1970s; Smokey Blue 1976–1977; pink, green 1920s–early 1930s.

Collecting Indiana's Sandwich pattern still excites some people who are very taken with this long-lived design. Most dealers and even more collectors avoid it like a disease because of the company's penchant for not protecting their older patterns by continually reissuing them in like colors! The pink and green shown here are from the Depression era, except for the light green decanter with the stopper which is the newer green that was named Chantilly and made for Tiara. Any green piece that has no price listed below is likely new! Indiana also made a lighter pink in recent years.

Only six items in red Sandwich date from 1933, i.e., cups, saucers, luncheon plates, water goblets, creamers, and sugars. In 1969, Tiara Home Products marketed red pitchers, 9 ounce goblets, cups, saucers, wines, wine decanters, 13" serving trays, creamers, sugars, salad, and dinner plates. Today, there is no difference in pricing red unless you have some marked 1933 Chicago World's Fair. I pictured a red wine in the older style made in the 1930s that was reissued in the late 1960s. Later (1980s), this mould was redesigned to make a fatter wine shaped more like Iris's cocktail. If you have any wine in this pattern shaped differently than the one pictured, it is less than 20 years old!

	Amber Crystal	Teal Blue	Red	Pink/ Green		Amber Crystal	Teal Blue	Red	Pink/ Green
Ash trays(club, spade, heart, diamond shapes, ea.)	3.25				Decanter and stopper	22.00		80.00	110.00
Basket, 10" high	35.00				Goblet, 9 oz.	13.00		45.00	
Bowl, 4¼" berry	3.50				Mayonnaise, ftd.	13.00			30.00
Bowl, 6"	4.00				Pitcher, 68 oz.	22.00		130.00	
Bowl, 6", hexagonal	5.00	14.00			Plate, 6" sherbet	3.00	7.00		
Bowl, 8½"	11.00				Plate, 7" bread and butter	4.00			
Bowl, 9" console	16.00			40.00	Plate, 8" oval, indent for cup	5.50	12.00		
Bowl, 11½" console	18.50			50.00	Plate, 8⅜" luncheon	4.75		20.00	
Butter dish and cover, domed	22.00	*155.00			Plate, 10½" dinner	8.00			20.00
Butter dish bottom	6.00	42.50			Plate, 13" sandwich	12.75	24.00	35.00	25.00
Butter dish top	16.00	112.50			Puff box	16.00			
Candlesticks, 3½" pr.	16.00			45.00	Salt and pepper pr.	17.50			
Candlesticks 7" pr.	26.00				Sandwich server, center	18.00		45.00	30.00
Creamer	9.00		45.00		Saucer	2.50	4.50	7.50	
Celery, 10½"	16.00				Sherbet, 3¼"	5.50	12.00		
Creamer and sugar on diamond shaped tray	16.00	32.00			Sugar, large	9.00		45.00	
Cruet, 6½ oz. and stopper	26.00	135.00		160.00	Sugar lid for large size	13.00			
Cup	3.50	8.50	27.50		Tumbler, 3 oz. ftd. cocktail	7.50			
*Beware recent vintage sell $22.00					Tumbler, 8 oz. ftd. water	9.00			
					Tumbler, 12 oz. ftd. iced tea	10.00			
					Wine, 3", 4 oz.	6.00		12.50	25.00

SHARON, "CABBAGE ROSE" FEDERAL GLASS COMPANY, 1935–1939

Colors: Pink, green, amber; some crystal. *(See Reproduction Section.)*

Prices for pink and green Sharon are rising again; and those for amber are up on harder-to-find pieces. Of course, that upward direction is true of **all major patterns** right now. That has not always been the case, but prices on rarely found items and collectible patterns have increased dramatically in the last two years. Amber footed teas are the most scarce of all Sharon tumblers; but fewer collectors of amber Sharon have been making this tumbler a priority at today's prices. Believe me, they are truly under priced for their paucity! Amber Sharon pitchers are more than twice as difficult to find as pink; but prices are not witness to that. Demand for pink Sharon by the multitude of collectors searching for it pushes up those prices.

Pink Sharon registered a loss of collectors for several years because of reproductions. Pink was the color attacked by the rip-off artists because it was the most collectible. Due to education of the differences between old and new (page 236–238), interest in Sharon has been revitalized! It was not that mankind stopped collecting as much as newer collectors did not risk starting it. Without new collecting blood, fundamental pieces stopped selling and dealers, in turn, stopped buying them. It becomes a vicious cycle with only the rarely found and bargain priced pieces selling. Today, every dealer who bought into this gloom and doom, is wailing that he cannot find enough pink or green Sharon to meet the demand! This rising market is a great sign, unless you are an author trying to keep your prices current!

I have pictured amber Sharon since I have a part of an ad showing a coupon exchange for amber Sharon. We only reproduced parts of this advertisement. The numbers in the right column under Golden Glow Tableware represent the number of coupons from large cans needed to order the item. Labels from small cans only were worth one half. The problem being that I have no idea as to cans of what. This ad was given to me, and I failed to mark some pertinent information on the back as I usually do. In any case, most of the items shown were for amber Sharon and Patrician or, as listed, Golden Glow Dinnerware. This ad also listed pieces from Hocking (Manhattan), Jeannette (Jennyware), and McKee (Glass Bake). The major portion of the ad was for Federal glassware. I would like to know for what canned product the manufacturer traded labels for glass!

The price for a pink Sharon cheese dish continues to climb toward the $1,000.00 range. The top for the cheese and butter dish are the same piece. The bottoms are different. The butter bottom is a 1½" deep bowl with an indented ledge while the cheese bottom is a salad plate with a raised band of glass on top of it. The lid fits inside this raised band! Amber cheese dishes can be found. There is no cheese dish in the original green.

Other Sharon pink pieces infrequently found include flat, thick iced teas and jam dishes. The jam dish is like the butter bottom except it has **no indentation** for the top. It differs from the 1⅞" deep soup bowl by standing only 1½" tall. Once in a while, you can still find a jam dish priced as a soup bowl if you keep your eyes peeled!

Green Sharon pitchers and tumblers in all sizes are difficult to find. Surprisingly enough, the green pitcher without ice lip is rarer than the one with an ice lip. There are no green soup bowls, only jam dishes.

You will find thick or thin flat iced teas and waters. The thick tumblers are easier to find in green; and the price reflects that. In amber and pink, the heavy iced teas are more rarely seen.

	Amber	Pink	Green		Amber	Pink	Green
Bowl, 5" berry	8.50	13.00	16.00	Pitcher, 80 oz. with ice lip	145.00	175.00	425.00
Bowl, 5" cream soup	28.00	47.50	55.00	Pitcher, 80 oz. without ice lip	140.00	165.00	450.00
Bowl, 6" cereal	22.00	27.50	27.50	Plate, 6" bread and butter	5.00	7.50	8.00
Bowl, 7¾" flat soup, 1⅞" deep	52.50	55.00		** Plate, 7½" salad	15.00	22.50	22.50
Bowl, 8½" large berry	6.00	32.00	35.00	Plate, 9½" dinner	11.00	20.00	22.50
Bowl, 9½" oval vegetable	20.00	32.00	35.00	Platter, 12½" oval	18.00	30.00	32.50
Bowl, 10½" fruit	21.00	40.00	42.50	Salt and pepper, pr.	40.00	50.00	70.00
Butter dish and cover	47.50	55.00	90.00	Saucer	6.50	12.00	12.00
Butter dish bottom	24.00	27.50	40.00	Sherbet, ftd.	13.00	16.00	37.50
Butter dish top	23.50	27.50	50.00	Sugar	9.00	14.00	15.00
* Cake plate, 11½" ftd.	27.50	42.50	65.00	Sugar lid	22.00	32.50	40.00
Candy jar and cover	45.00	50.00	160.00	Tumbler, 4⅛", 9 oz. thick	27.00	45.00	70.00
Cheese dish and cover	195.00	925.00		Tumbler, 4⅛", 9 oz. thin	27.00	45.00	75.00
Creamer, ftd.	14.00	18.00	22.50	Tumbler, 5¼", 12 oz. thin	52.00	50.00	100.00
Cup	9.00	14.00	20.00	Tumbler, 5¼", 12 oz. thick	65.00	85.00	95.00
Jam dish, 7½"	40.00	225.00	45.00	*** Tumbler, 6½", 15 oz. ftd.	125.00	55.00	

*Crystal $8.00   **Crystal $13.50   ***Crystal $15.00

Golden Glow Tableware

*101	Cup and Saucer	20
*102	Drinking Set, Ice Lip Jug and 6 Tumblers	110
*104	Salt and Pepper Shakers . . . . pair	22
*108	Bowl, 8½ inch	22
*113	Fruit Dish, 5 inch	8
*116	Plate, 6 inch	10
*117	Plate, 9½ inch	20
*118	Sherbet	10
*121	Sugar and Creamer	30
*122	Vegetable Dish, 9½ inch	22
*123	Meat Platter, 12½ inch	28
*124	Cream Soup, Handled	12
*127	Butter Dish	24

*Items not mailable. See page 31.
†Coupons from Small Cans count ½ Coupon.

"SHIPS" or "SAILBOAT" also known as "SPORTSMAN SERIES"
HAZEL ATLAS GLASS COMPANY, Late 1930s

Colors: Cobalt blue w/white, yellow, and red decoration, crystal w/blue.

"Ships" decorated Moderntone is not extensively found and sherbet plates are as hard to find as dinner plates! Prices below are for **mint** pieces (white, not discolored beige). Discolored items should sell for less.

The confusing "Ships" shot glass is shown in the top picture on page 201. It is the smallest (2¼", 2 ounce) tumbler in front on the right. It is **not** the heavy bottomed tumbler shown to its left that holds 4 ounce and is 3¼" tall. I have letters from people who purchased this 4 ounce tumbler believing (or having been told) it was a shot glass! You will notice there is a large price difference between the authentic 2 ounce shot and the 4 ounce tumbler! We had one of these $185.00 shot glasses stolen at a recent show. As a dealer, that makes my costs go up, and therefore, my prices.

The yellow "Ships" old-fashioned tumbler next to the ice bucket is not a discoloration. It really is "raincoat" yellow! Observe the pieces with red and white "Ships" or crystal tumblers with a blue boat.

Pictured below are other items in the "Sportsman Series." (My computer's grammar correction just told me to make that "sports lover" or "sport enthusiast" to be politically correct!) People who collect Dutch-related paraphernalia enjoy the "Windmills." There are nursery rhymes, dogs, fish, horses, skiing, golfing, or dancing!

The bottom photo on page 201 shows the cocktail shaker, ice tub, and several sizes of tumblers in a pattern designated as "fancy" ships. The cloud formation differs. Also shown here are some accessory pieces that can go with this "Ships" pattern which has its beginnings on the Moderntone blank. None of these are in the Hazel Atlas listing below; so I will put prices for these in parentheses as I mention them. The square or round ash trays ($60.00) and the three-sectioned box ($195.00) on the right may have been manufactured by the same company since the designs are very similar. The ash tray with the metal ship ($125.00) is more than likely Hazel Atlas. The smaller glass tray ($95.00) which has a tumbler with a sailor and matching anchor and rope design and the larger glass tray ($120.00) which has a matching tumbler are rarely seen. The crystal ash tray with light blue ship ($20.00 — set of 4) was a piece bought solely because it had a ship. The ceiling globe seems to match the ships found on McKee "Ships" pieces. I have seen many of these items priced higher; but these are selling prices... not "dust them once a year" ones! I might mention that **no red pitcher** has ever been found to go with the **red "Ships" tumblers** ($9.00)! I must get 40 letters a year regarding those!

	Blue/White		Blue/White		Blue/White
Cup (Plain) "Moderntone"	11.00	Plate, 8", salad	25.00	Tumbler, 5 oz., 3¾", juice	12.00
Cocktail mixer w/stirrer	27.50	Plate, 9", dinner	32.00	Tumbler, 6 oz., roly poly	10.00
Cocktail shaker	35.00	Saucer	17.00	Tumbler, 8 oz., 3⅜", old fashion	17.00
Ice bowl	35.00	Tumbler, 2 oz., 2¼" shot glass	185.00	Tumbler, 9 oz., 3¾", straight water	14.00
Pitcher w/o lip, 82 oz.	60.00	Tumbler, 3½" , whiskey	27.50	Tumbler, 9 oz., 4⅝", water	11.00
Pitcher w/lip, 86 oz.	70.00	Tumbler, 4 oz., heavy bottom	27.50	Tumbler, 10½ oz., 4⅞", iced tea	15.00
Plate, 5⅞", sherbet	28.00	Tumbler, 4 oz., 3¼" heavy bottom	27.50	Tumbler, 12 oz., iced tea	22.00

SIERRA, "PINWHEEL" JEANNETTE GLASS COMPANY, 1931–1933

Colors: Green, pink, and some Ultra Marine.

Prices for rare pieces of Sierra are following the elevating trend of all Depression glass. Both pink and green pitchers, tumblers, and oval vegetable bowls have disappeared into collections. You could chance upon one of these pieces in pink once in a while with persistent shopping, but finding them all, at any price, is a major task! Ardent Sierra collectors tell me that acquiring the green, oval vegetable is the most perplexing chore; but finding six or eight tumblers takes more time and a parcel of money! A greater problem is finding **mint condition** oval bowls. If they were used much, one of those pointed protrusions invariably became chipped, nicked, or chunked! The points have to be carefully inspected!

Sugar bowls have become harder to find than lids. It is the pointed tips on the sugar bowl (which chip so easily) that make this bowl so hard to obtain in mint condition. **Mint** is the flaw in collecting any Sierra. You need to carefully examine all pink Sierra butter dishes. You might run into the Adam/Sierra combination. That is the way I found my first one. Be sure to read about this under Adam. You can see one pictured in *Very Rare Glassware of the Depression Years, Fifth Series*.

Many times, the wrong cup is found on Sierra saucers. You always have to be on your toes when you are buying! Saucers are becoming harder to find than cups because of damaged points. The cups, pitchers, and tumblers all have smooth edges instead of the serrated edges of the other pieces. Without smooth edges, these cups and tumblers would be the forerunners of dribble glasses.

There have been three Sierra Ultra Marine cups found, but no one has seen a saucer! Why? These must have been an experimental run or more would be surfacing! Possibly a batch of Sierra was made at the time Jeannette was making Doric and Pansy or Swirl in Ultra Marine. You might even run into fired-on colors of Sierra!

	Pink	Green		Pink	Green
Bowl, 5½" cereal	15.00	18.00	Platter, 11" oval	45.00	52.50
Bowl, 8½" large berry	32.00	32.00	Salt and pepper, pr.	40.00	40.00
Bowl, 9¼" oval vegetable	50.00	125.00	Saucer	7.00	8.00
Butter dish and cover	62.50	67.50	Serving tray, 10¼", 2 handles	15.00	18.00
Creamer	20.00	22.50	Sugar	20.00	26.00
Cup	12.00	15.00	Sugar cover	16.00	16.00
Pitcher, 6½", 32 oz.	95.00	130.00	Tumbler, 4½", 9 oz. ftd.	60.00	80.00
Plate, 9" dinner	22.00	24.00			

SPIRAL HOCKING GLASS COMPANY, 1928–1930

Colors: Green, crystal, and pink.

Hocking's Spiral is one of many spiraling patterns from this Depression era. It is available in limited pieces, but can be collected. The difficulty lies in finding Hocking's Spiral among all the others. You might notice several pieces shaped like Cameo including the ice tub, platter, creamer, and sugar. The platter is not often found. It has closed or tab handles as do many patterns made by Hocking.

A luncheon set can be acquired rather inexpensively in Spiral! This is not a pattern that most dealers carry to glass shows; so you will have to ask for it.

Green Spiral is the color normally found, but there is a little pink available. You might even find a few pieces in crystal. However, I have never seen a collector searching for any color other than green.

The Spiral center-handled server has a solid handle and the Twisted Optic center-handled server has an open handle if you have trouble distinguishing those patterns from each other.

I have always included a Twisted Optic piece in my Spiral pictures for comparison to the Spiral. It is the covered candy on the left. Remember that Spiral swirls go to the left or clockwise while Twisted Optic spirals go to the right or counterclockwise. Green Twisted Optic pieces have a yellow tint missing from Spiral.

	Green		Green
Bowl, 4¾" berry	5.00	Preserve and cover	32.00
Bowl, 7" mixing	8.50	Salt and pepper, pr.	35.00
Bowl, 8" large berry	12.50	Sandwich server, center handle	25.00
Creamer, flat or ftd.	7.50	Saucer	2.00
Cup	5.00	Sherbet	4.00
Ice or butter tub	27.50	Sugar, flat or ftd.	7.50
Pitcher, 7⅝", 58 oz.	30.00	Tumbler, 3", 5 oz. juice	4.50
Plate, 6" sherbet	2.00	Tumbler, 5", 9 oz. water	7.50
Plate, 8" luncheon	3.50	Tumbler, 5⅞" ftd.	15.00
Platter, 12"	30.00	Vase, 5¾", ftd.	50.00

Please refer to Foreword for pricing information

STARLIGHT HAZEL ATLAS GLASS COMPANY, 1938–1940

Colors: Crystal, pink; some white, cobalt.

Prices on crystal Starlight are indicating new collecting interest. This small pattern has never been gathered by an abundance of collectors; but enough are buying pieces now to show some shortcomings in supplies. Solutions to finding sherbets, cereals, and the large salad bowls are not being found. Few 13" sandwich plates are being seen and those that appear at shows are eagerly bought. That plate, along with the 12" deep bowl, makes a great salad set. You might even be able to use it as a small punch bowl should the occasion arise.

I have received several letters wanting to buy my Starlight punch bowl set pictured in the last edition. This set was similar in make up to the Royal Lace toddy set. As with other Hazel Atlas sets, this punch bowl was made by putting a bowl in a metal holder and extending the metal to accommodate cups. A metal ladle with a red knob rests in the bowl. I have a report of only one other of these. I owe this find to an eagle-eyed collector who bought it for my book!

The 5½" cereal is handled and measures 6" including the handles. All measurements in this book do not include handles, unless specifically noted.

Starlight can be collected without having to borrow money. The only difficulty (nearly 30 years into Depression glass mania) comes in finding it. Pink and blue bowls make nice accessory pieces that can be used alongside the crystal or even with other patterns.

I often wondered why Starlight shakers were found with a one hole shaker top. I now know. It was a specially designed top made to keep the salt "moisture proof." Airko shakers with these tops are often seen in southern areas where the humid air caused shaker holes to clog. One of these moisture-proof shakers is pictured here with the original label!

	Crystal, White	Pink		Crystal, White	Pink
Bowl, 5½" cereal, closed handles	7.00	12.00	Plate, 9" dinner	7.50	
* Bowl, 8½", closed handles	10.00	20.00	Plate, 13" sandwich	15.00	18.00
Bowl, 11½" salad	25.00		Relish dish	15.00	
Bowl, 12", 2¾" deep	30.00		Salt and pepper, pr.	22.50	
Creamer, oval	5.00		Saucer	2.00	
Cup	4.00		Sherbet	15.00	
Plate, 6" bread and butter	3.00		Sugar, oval	5.00	
Plate, 8½" luncheon	5.00				

* Cobalt $32.50

STRAWBERRY U.S. GLASS COMPANY, Early 1930s

Colors: Pink, green, crystal; some iridized.

Strawberry and Cherryberry are now divided into two separate patterns. Today's collectors consider these to be two separate patterns and not one. Strawberry has more devotees than Cherryberry.

There are two very unusual pitchers shown in the photograph. The crystal and iridescent pitchers are in few collections! Iridescent Strawberry pitchers and tumblers are quite rare! Carnival collectors prize this pitcher more highly than do Depression glass collectors. One main carnival glass test is that it have full, vivid color and not color fade out toward the bottom, as many do. The **rare** crystal pitcher is not widely sought, but should be! I've only seen two!

Green Strawberry commands more attention than pink. A small problem exists in matching color tones of green. Green or pink Strawberry can be collected in a set; however, as with other U.S. Glass patterns, there are no cups, saucers, or dinner-sized plates; and if mould roughness offends your collecting sensibilities, then this pattern needs to be avoided. Even pieces that are considered mint may have roughness on a seam where it came out of the mould.

Crystal is priced along with iridescent because it is quite rare. There are few crystal Strawberry collectors. Strawberry sugar covers and the 6¼", 2" deep bowl are missing from most collections. I found the second 2" deep green bowl reported last fall to show to you in the future. If you find a copy of my *Collectors Encyclopedia of Depression Glass, Fifth Edition,* you can see the first one found! Some uninformed dealers have mistakenly labeled the sugar with missing lid as a spooner. It is a sugar bowl without handles that is often found in earlier glassware.

Strawberry has a plain butter dish bottom that is interchangeable with other U.S. Glass patterns! This is the pattern for which other U.S. Glass butter dish bottoms were borrowed to use with Strawberry tops. That custom left many other butters bottomless! Strawberry butter dishes have always been coveted by collectors.

	Crystal, Iridescent	Pink, Green		Crystal, Iridescent	Pink, Green
Bowl, 4" berry	6.50	9.00	Olive dish, 5" one-handled	9.00	17.00
Bowl, 6¼", 2" deep	55.00	95.00	Pickle dish, 8¼" oval	9.00	17.00
Bowl, 6½" deep salad	15.00	20.00	Pitcher, 7¾"	175.00	165.00
Bowl, 7½" deep berry	20.00	30.00	Plate, 6" sherbet	5.00	8.00
Butter dish and cover	135.00	150.00	Plate, 7½" salad	12.00	18.00
Butter dish bottom	77.50	90.00	Sherbet	6.50	7.50
Butter dish top	57.50	60.00	Sugar, small open	12.00	20.00
Comport, 5¾"	14.00	22.00	Sugar large	22.00	35.00
Creamer, small	12.00	20.00	Sugar cover	38.00	55.00
Creamer, 4⅝" large	22.50	35.00	Tumbler, 3⅝", 8 oz.	20.00	35.00

"SUNBURST," "HERRINGBONE" JEANNETTE GLASS COMPANY, Late 1930s

Colors: Crystal.

I have hunted for "Sunburst" for a few years and have noticed that candlesticks seem to be the most commonly found pieces. This is surprising because I can not think of other patterns where candlesticks are seen more often!

After adding Jeannette's "Sunburst" to the book last time, I had several collectors point out that I had omitted the large 11" bowl. I had, but only because I had not seen one at the time. It is pictured here along with a newly listed tray. It might be an undivided relish, but my photography helpers seemed to assume it was a tray for the sugar and creamer. I guess it might be! At least it is for this photograph!

I have not found much "Sunburst" to sell; but the little I have found sold very well, and quickly! This smaller pattern was made from the same shaped moulds as Iris. A divided relish and this style of berry bowls would have made sensational pieces for Iris! This design rather outclasses those ruffled bowls of Iris. Look this pattern over carefully, since inner rims are easily nicked. Collectors would probably not have noticed "Sunburst" had it not been for the popular Iris.

I have been trying to find a catalog or advertisement to ascertain the true name of this pattern which I have heard called both "Sunburst" and "Herringbone." I do not know which is correct, but more people use "Sunburst."

I am listing only pieces I have found or pieces that have been in photographs sent me over the years. I will not be surprised by additional finds for future editions! Let me know what you have in your collections!

	Crystal		Crystal
Bowl, 4¾", berry	8.00	Plate, 11¾", sandwich	15.00
Bowl, 8½", berry	18.00	Relish, 2 part	12.00
Bowl, 11"	22.00	Saucer	2.00
Candlesticks, double, pr.	30.00	Sherbet	12.00
Creamer, footed	9.00	Sugar	9.00
Cup	6.00	Tray, small oval	12.00
Plate, 5½"	4.00	Tumbler, 4", 9 oz., flat	22.50
Plate, 9¼", dinner	20.00		

SUNFLOWER JEANNETTE GLASS COMPANY, 1930s

Colors: Pink, green, some Delphite; some opaque colors and Ultra Marine.

Sunflower is one of the more recognized patterns of Depression glass. The omnipresent cake plate may be the reason as they were packed in 20 pound bags of flour for several years during the 1930s. Everyone bought flour in large quantities because home baking was the rule of the day. A pink cake plate is shown on the right against the back of the picture. It is standing up to emphasize the pattern which makes it look more like a large plate than a cake plate. If you look closely you can see a couple of the legs near the rim. A predicament that occurs constantly with the green cake plate is that many are found in a deep, dark green that does not approximate the coloration of other pieces of green Sunflower shown in this picture.

There is often confusion between the cake plate and the rarely found Sunflower trivet. The **7" trivet** has an edge that is slightly upturned and it **is three inches smaller** than the ever-present **10" cake plate**. You would think three inches is enough difference to keep this mistake from happening! The 7" trivet remains the most elusive piece of Sunflower. Collector demand for the trivet keeps prices increasing steadily. Green Sunflower pieces are found less often than pink as evidenced by my photo; therefore, prices for green are surpassing those of pink. Both colors make impressive sets.

Sunflower has a shortage of saucers in both colors. The last five batches of Sunflower I have seen have had more cups than saucers. Two groups of green had no saucers at all. In total, there were 29 cups and only 13 saucers. Maybe the cups were a premium that never offered saucers or the cups were offered longer than the saucers. If you run into a stack of Sunflower saucers, remember that they might be a good buy!

The Ultra Marine ash tray pictured is the only piece I have found in that color. Opaque colors show up occasionally. Only a creamer, plate, 6" tab-handled bowl, cup, and saucer have been spotted in Delphite blue. You can see all but the creamer in *Very Rare Glassware of the Depression Years, Fifth Series.*

	Pink	Green		Pink	Green
* Ash Tray, 5", center design only	9.00	12.00	Saucer	8.00	10.00
Cake Plate, 10", 3 legs	15.00	13.00	Sugar (opaque $85.00)	18.00	20.00
** Creamer (opaque $85.00)	18.00	20.00	Tumbler, 4¾", 8 oz. ftd.	28.00	32.00
Cup (opaque $75.00)	12.00	15.00	Trivet, 7", 3 legs, turned up edge	300.00	310.00
Plate, 9" dinner	17.00	20.00			

* Found in Ultra Marine $25.00   **Delphite $85.00

SUNFLOWER

SWANKY SWIGS 1930s–early 1940s

"Why, I remember those! We used them when I was a child!" is an exclamation I often hear!
See *Collectible Glassware from the 40s, 50s, 60s...* for later made Swankys and a display of their metal tops.

Top Row:

Band No.1	Red & Black	3⅜"	2.00–3.00
	Red & Blue	3⅜"	3.00–4.00
	Blue	3⅜"	3.50–5.00
Band No.2	Red & Black	4¾"	4.00–5.00
	Red & Black	3⅜"	3.00–4.00
Band No.3	Blue & White	3⅜"	3.00–4.00
Circle & Dot:	Blue	4¾"	8.00–10.00
	Blue	3½"	5.00–6.00
	Red, Green	3½"	4.00–5.00
	Black	3½"	5.00–6.00
	Red	4¾"	8.00–10.00
Dot	Black	4¾"	7.00–9.00
	Blue	3½"	5.00–6.00

2nd Row:

Star:	Blue	4¾"	6.00–7.00
	Blue, Red, Green, Black	3½"	3.00–4.00
	Cobalt w/White Stars	4¾"	18.00–20.00
Centennials:	W.Va. Cobalt	4¾"	22.00–25.00
	Texas Cobalt	4¾"	32.50–35.00
	Texas Blue, Black, Green	3½"	32.50–35.00
Checkerboard	Blue, Red	3½"	25.00–27.50

3rd Row:

Checkerboard	Green	3½"	27.50–30.00
Sailboat	Blue	4½"	12.00–15.00
	Blue	3½"	10.00–12.00
	Red, Green	4½"	12.00–15.00
	Green, Lt. Green	3½"	10.00–15.00
Tulip No.1	Blue, Red	4½"	15.00–17.50
	Blue, Red	3½"	3.00–4.00

4th Row:

Tulip No.1	Green	4½"	15.00–17.50
	Green, Black	3½"	3.00–4.00
	Green w/Label	3½"	10.00–12.00
*Tulip No.2	Red, Green, Black	3½"	27.50–30.00
Carnival	Blue, Red	3½"	5.00–7.00
	Green, Yellow	3½"	5.00–7.00
Tulip No. 3	Dk. Blue, Lt. Blue	3¾"	2.50–3.50

*West Coast lower price

SWIRL, "PETAL SWIRL" JEANNETTE GLASS COMPANY, 1937–1938

Colors: Ultra Marine, pink, Delphite; some amber and "ice" blue.

Swirl, along with other Ultra Marine Jeannette patterns have some green-tinged pieces as well as the normally found color. This green tint is hard to match, and some collectors avoid this shade. Because of this, there are many times you can buy this green tint at a bargain price if you are willing to accumulate that shade. Who knows? In the future this color might be considered rare. The smaller flat tumbler and the 9" rimmed salad bowl beside it, in the picture below, have this green hue. I just bought a boxed console set labeled "One 1500/3 Console Set, Ultra Marine from Jeannette Glass Co., Jeannette, Pa." The set was sent to "Jno. Curtis Extract Co., 322 Broadway, Hanover, Pa." It has the footed console and a pair of candles in the green tint of Ultra Marine.

Ultra Marine Swirl footed pitchers are found infrequently (pictured in previous editions), but so far there has not been a pink one discovered. I say, so far, because some collectors of Swirl combine this pattern with Jeannette's "Jennyware" kitchenware line that does have a **flat**, 36 ounce pink pitcher in it! If you find mixing bowls, measuring cups, or reamers, then you have crossed over into the kitchenware line and out of the Swirl dinnerware set. See *Kitchen Glassware of the Depression Years* for complete "Jennyware" listings.

Candy and butter dish bottoms are more copious than are tops in Swirl. Tops had a habit of being dropped. Remember that before you buy only the bottom! (I found an Ultra Marine candy bottom with good color at the Webster flea market yesterday; it was only $20.00, so I bought it!) A dearth of tops holds true for 90 per cent of the butter and candy dishes in Depression Glass. Unless you are good at remembering color, it might be sensible to take your half with you to match the color.

Pink candle holders are not rare even though they were omitted from some of my earlier editions.

The pink coaster shown on the left foreground on page 210 is often found inside a small rubber tire. These tires were advertisements distributed by tire manufactures or neighborhood garages and have themselves become collectible. Those with a tire manufacturer's name on the glass insert are more in demand; but those with a non-advertising glass insert (such as this coaster) are collected if the miniature tire is embossed with the name of a tire company. Many of these tires dried up or decayed over the years leaving only the glass inserts as reminders.

Swirl was produced in several limited colors. A smaller set can be assembled in Delphite blue; it would only have basic pieces and a serving dish or two. Vegetable bowls (9") were made in several experimental colors. A recent find is a small amethyst berry bowl pictured in *Very Rare Glassware of the Depression Years, Fifth Series*.

Almost all pieces of Swirl can be found with two different borders, ruffled and plain. Pink comes mostly with plain borders while Ultra Marine comes with both. This makes a difference if you mail order merchandise. It is **your** responsibility to specify what style you want. Either style is acceptable to most collectors, but some do not mix shapes in their collections. If you only want plain edged pieces, please tell the dealer before he ships your order. This is not a problem, of course, when you can see the merchandise displayed at shows.

SWIRL (Cont.)

	Pink	Ultra-marine	Delphite		Pink	Ultra-marine	Delphite
Bowl, 4⅞" & 5¼" berry	11.00	16.00	14.00	Plate, 6½" sherbet	4.50	6.50	6.00
Bowl, 9" salad	20.00	30.00	30.00	Plate, 7¼"	8.00	14.00	
Bowl, 9" salad, rimmed	20.00	30.00		Plate, 8" salad	10.00	15.00	9.00
Bowl, 10" ftd., closed				Plate, 9¼" dinner	15.00	20.00	12.00
handles	25.00	30.00		Plate, 10½"			25.00
Bowl, 10½" ftd. console	20.00	30.00		Plate, 12½" sandwich	18.00	30.00	
Butter dish	190.00	265.00		Platter, 12" oval			38.00
Butter dish bottom	32.50	40.00		Salt and pepper, pr.		45.00	
Butter dish top	157.50	225.00		Saucer	3.50	5.00	5.00
Candle holders, double				Sherbet, low ftd.	14.00	22.50	
branch pr.	42.50	50.00		Soup, tab handles (lug)	27.50	35.00	
Candle holders, single				Sugar, ftd.	10.00	16.00	12.00
branch pr.			125.00	Tray, 10½", two-handled			27.50
Candy dish, open, 3 legs	14.00	20.00		Tumbler, 4", 9 oz.	20.00	35.00	
Candy dish with cover	115.00	165.00		Tumbler, 4⅝", 9 oz.	20.00		
Coaster, 1" x 3¼"	9.50	13.00		Tumbler, 5⅛", 13 oz.	50.00	110.00	
Creamer, ftd.	10.00	16.00	12.00	Tumbler, 9 oz. ftd.	22.00	45.00	
Cup	10.00	16.00	10.00	Vase, 6½" ftd., ruffled	18.00		
Pitcher, 48 oz. ftd.		1,750.00		Vase, 8½" ftd., two styles		27.50	

210

TEA ROOM INDIANA GLASS COMPANY, 1926–1931

Colors: Pink, green, amber, and some crystal.

Tea Room prices are steadily increasing but not skyrocketing as they once did. This transpired because new collectors are not seeing enough to start a collection. Rarely found pieces are not being offered unless a previous collected set is brought into the market place. Collectors with sets awaiting additions are not increasing their holdings very quickly either. Prices do not increase rapidly when few sales are being transacted.

A further predicament in gathering Tea Room is acquiring **mint condition** pieces. The underneath sides of flat pieces are prone to chip and flake on all the exposed points. There are numerous points on Tea Room items that need to be examined when you buy a piece. To illustrate how bad the problem of mint Tea Room is, I had the privilege to witness the opening of an original box of Tea Room that had 32 each cups, saucers, and luncheon plates. There were less than a dozen mint condition (as we define it today) pieces out of the 96 in the box. The $1,000.00 for the box had seemed a good deal, until I saw the pieces. These had never been used; so, there must have been an extreme mould problem with Tea Room initially. Indiana had more than their share of such problems!

There are more green Tea Room collectors than pink; and some people are even beginning to pursue crystal. Crystal pieces are fetching about 75 to 80 percent of the pink prices listed except for the commonly found 9½" ruffled vase and the rarely found pitcher, priced separately below. That crystal pitcher is even more difficult to find than the amber one. I have owned four amber pitchers but only one crystal. I have only seen two crystal ones! Amber pitchers and tumblers always seem to turn up in the Atlanta metro area. Maybe they really were Coca-Cola premiums as one lady from Marietta, Georgia, once told me. Creamers and sugars appear occasionally in amber. After that, amber has not been seen in any other item. You can see all four amber pieces on page 212.

There are two styles of banana splits. Both the footed and the flat banana splits are very desirable pieces of Tea Room to own in any color! The green, flat one is the hardest to find. Many times you can find banana splits priced reasonably because they are not readily recognized as Tea Room!

The flat sugar and marmalade bottom are the same. The marmalade takes a notched lid; the sugar lid is not notched. Finding either of these is not an easy task! The mustard also comes with a plain or notched lid. As the name suggests, Tea Room was intended to be used in the tea rooms and ice cream parlors of the day. That is why you find so many soda fountain items in this pattern.

Some interesting lamps are showing up which used tumblers that had been frosted. The regular lamp is not as plentiful as it once was. It has been a while since I have seen one in green. We recently photographed a hanging chandelier in crystal Tea Room using a ruffled top vase. I left it in Paducah for my photographer to play with and he actually figured a way to hang it to photograph. I will have to work it into a future book!

Prices are for mint items. These prices are high because **mint condition items are difficult to obtain**! Damaged pieces are often bought to supplement sets until mint items can be found. Not everyone can afford to buy only mint items, and they are more willing to accept Tea Room pieces with some minor flaws at lesser prices than to have no Tea Room at all.

TEA ROOM (Cont.)

	Green	Pink		Green	Pink
Bowl, finger	55.00	42.50	Salt and pepper, pr.	55.00	50.00
Bowl, 7½" banana split, flat	95.00	90.00	* Saucer	30.00	30.00
Bowl, 7½" banana split, ftd.	75.00	65.00	Sherbet, low ftd.	25.00	22.00
Bowl, 8¼" celery	35.00	27.50	Sherbet, low flared edge	30.00	26.00
Bowl, 8¾" deep salad	85.00	70.00	Sherbet, tall ftd.	50.00	50.00
Bowl, 9½" oval vegetable	65.00	60.00	Sugar w/lid, 3"	110.00	100.00
Candlestick, low, pr.	50.00	50.00	Sugar, 4½" ftd. (amber $75.00)	20.00	20.00
Creamer, 3¼"	27.50	27.50	Sugar, rectangular	20.00	20.00
Creamer, 4½" ftd. (amber $75.00)	20.00	20.00	Sugar, flat with cover	195.00	160.00
Creamer, rectangular	20.00	20.00	Sundae, ftd., ruffled top	90.00	70.00
Creamer & sugar on tray, 4"	80.00	75.00	Tray, center-handled	195.00	155.00
* Cup	55.00	55.00	Tray, rectangular sugar & creamer	50.00	40.00
Goblet, 9 oz.	75.00	65.00	Tumbler, 8 oz., 4³⁄₁₆" flat	100.00	90.00
Ice bucket	60.00	52.50	Tumbler, 6 oz. ftd.	35.00	35.00
Lamp, 9" electric	110.00	95.00	Tumbler, 8 oz., 5¼" high, ftd.		
Marmalade, notched lid	195.00	160.00	(amber $75.00)	30.00	28.00
Mustard, covered	150.00	125.00	Tumbler, 11 oz. ftd.	50.00	45.00
Parfait	75.00	70.00	Tumbler, 12 oz. ftd.	65.00	60.00
** Pitcher, 64 oz. (amber $425.00)	140.00	125.00	Vase, 6½" ruffled edge	100.00	90.00
Plate, 6½" sherbet	32.00	30.00	***Vase, 9½" ruffled edge	110.00	110.00
Plate, 8¼", luncheon	35.00	30.00	Vase, 9½" straight	75.00	70.00
Plate, 10½", 2-handled	48.00	43.00	Vase, 11" ruffled edge	225.00	275.00
Relish, divided	25.00	20.00	Vase, 11" straight	140.00	125.00

* Prices for absolutely mint pieces
** Crystal – $400.00
***Crystal – $16.00

THISTLE MacBETH-EVANS, 1929–1930

Colors: Pink, green; some yellow and crystal.

Thistle and Fire-King blue are the nemesis of every photographer that I have worked with since 1972. Fire-King actually came later, but Thistle has been a **thorn** all those years. Originally, we doctored all the faint patterns with Bon Ami® cleanser which took an inordinate amount of time! The patterns did show in those black and white photos, but when we switched to color, the doctored patterns looked white in the photographs. We use that process sparingly today! One photographer would see us unpacking Thistle and instinctively question if we **really wanted the pattern to show** this time! Photography lights cause Thistle to do a vanishing act, an act familiar to Thistle collectors. Our new photographer seems to have captured the Thistle by angling the cake plate!

Green Thistle is even more limited than pink except for the large fruit bowl that is almost a mirage in pink. I have owned the one pictured here for 24 years, and I have only seen two others.

All Thistle pieces have the same mould shapes as the thin Dogwood; however, there is no Thistle creamer or sugar known. The grill plate has the pattern on the edge only. Those plain centers scratched very easily, so look for that problem if you can find a grill plate to peruse!

If you find a thick butter dish, pitcher, tumbler, or other heavy moulded pieces with Thistle designs, they are new! These pieces are being made by Mosser Glass Company in Cambridge, Ohio. They are not a part of this pattern, but copies of a much older pattern glass. If you have a piece of Thistle not in the photograph, then you probably do not have a piece of MacBeth-Evans Thistle pattern since all seven pieces known to have been made are shown.

	Pink	Green
Bowl, 5½" cereal	22.50	25.00
Bowl, 10¼" large fruit	325.00	225.00
Cup, thin	20.00	25.00
Plate, 8" luncheon	15.00	20.00
Plate, 10¼" grill	20.00	25.00
Plate, 13" heavy cake	135.00	165.00
Saucer	9.50	9.50

Please refer to Foreword for pricing information

TULIP DELL GLASS COMPANY, Early 1930s

Color: Amber, amethyst, turquoise, crystal, green.

Tulip has become a fun pattern for me. One of the things I have always enjoyed is the "hunt" for glass. With no catalog pages for Tulip, I started out blind as to what was available. There are several new pieces to list. A new style candlestick has been found which stands 3" tall with a 5½" base. Speaking of candle holders, note that they are made from an ivy bowl and not a sherbet as previously thought. That ivy bowl (sherbet) is shown in the 1946 Montgomery Ward catalog with ivy growing in it. Thanks to a reader, that information has been verified with this ad shown on page 215. Most amazing to me are the 7" water goblets cataloged for 65 cents. I have known about these for a year and have told every Tulip collector I know about them, but no one has found a goblet!

Candle holders made from the 3¾" ivy bowl have turned up in several colors. Another interesting piece is a decanter that has a whiskey tumbler for a stopper. I have not been able to find a decanter to buy, but blue (turquoise as the ad states) and amethyst stoppers (without corks) are pictured. The juice tumbler (cigarette holder) is 2¾" tall and holds three ounces while the whiskey is only 1¾" and holds one ounce.

Note that the ad for Tulip shows no stippling on the pieces. Early in buying this pattern, I ignored some pieces without stippling, but both styles are acceptable to collectors.

There are turquoise and green candy lids pictured. I bought these from a dealer from New York. She bought them at a garage sale for 25 cents each. There was a bushel basket full of these and she only bought one of each color. Why would anyone have a basket of lids? I thought the candy was flat, but it is not! A collector brought an amethyst candy into the Seattle show for me to see. It is a large, footed candy standing about 7" tall. I had a large crowd of collectors at my table; it did not get measured and they forgot to send me the measurements. Hopefully, some other collector will follow up with them. You will not miss it if you see one!

I originally started buying Tulip about seven years ago, when I found nine green sugar bowls for $10.00. I couldn't turn them down at that price. Those sugars seem to be found in sets of four or more, making me believe they may also have been sold as cream soups.

In buying Tulip, I have found that the scalloped rims tend to have damage. Most of the damage occurs **under the rim** edge; be sure to turn the piece over and check each of the pointed scallops. Many times a scallop or two will be absent!

I have priced the crystal with the amber and green since you will not see much of it. Crystal and amber may be the rarest colors!

	Amethyst, Blue	Amber, Crystal, Green		Amethyst, Blue	Amber, Crystal, Green
Bowl, 6"	20.00	15.00	Plate, 6"	10.00	9.00
Bowl, oval, oblong, 13¼"	95.00	85.00	Plate, 7¼"	14.00	10.00
Candleholder, 3¾" (ivy bowl)	25.00	20.00	Plate, 9"	37.50	30.00
Candleholder, 5¼" base, 3" tall	25.00	20.00	Saucer	8.00	6.00
Candy w/lid, ftd.	75.00	50.00	Sherbet, 3¾", flat (ivy bowl)	20.00	18.00
Creamer	20.00	18.00	Sugar	20.00	18.00
Cup	18.00	12.00	Tumbler, juice	25.00	20.00
Decanter w/stopper	95.00	85.00	Tumbler, whiskey	25.00	20.00
Ice tub, 4⅞" wide, 3" deep	65.00	50.00			

Room Accessories Introduce Accents of
Color and Design to your Room Settings

EXCLUSIVE AT WARDS . . . three little words that mean a lot of individuality in both practical and purely ornamental accessories for your home. Words that tell of original designs made exclusively for Wards and to be found no other place. Look for them on these pages. . . .

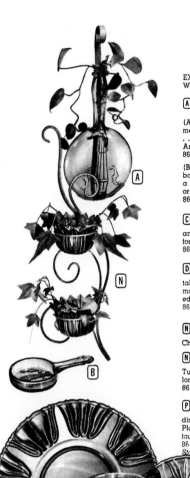

A B **GLASS BANJO ACCESSORIES.** Matched bits of colorful whimsy for your home.

(A) **GLASS BANJO BOTTLE.** Complete with a metal bracket for hanging. Fill with ivy . . . to brighten your walls. In Turquoise or Amethyst. Abt. 12 in. high overall. (No Ivy.) 86 C 7148—Ship. wt. 2 lbs. *State color*..$1.25

(B) **GLASS BANJO ASHTRAY.** Just like a real banjo with the neck hollowed out to hold a lighted cigarette with ease. In Turquoise or Amethyst. About 2⅞ by 5¼ in. long. 86 C 7146—Ship. wt. 1 lb. *State color*....55c

C **MILK GLASS DOUBLE CRIMP VASE.** Creamy White Victorian type Milk Glass with an edging of clear, crisp glass. Have a pair for your mantel. About 5½ inches high. 86 C 7403—Ship. wt. 2 lbs. 8 oz........$1.10

D **MILK GLASS DOUBLE CRIMP BOWL.** Victorian type Milk Glass . . . perfect for the table of today. Use it for either informal or the more formal flower arrangements. Graceful edge of clear glass. About 3¾ in. high. 86 C 7404—Ship. wt. 2 lbs. 12 oz......$1.10

E **PANSY BASKET CANDY DISH.** A border of white Milk Glass pansies form a dainty dish to hold candies or nuts. Abt. 4¼-in. diam. 86 C 7299—Ship. wt. 1 lb. 6 oz..........65c

F **MILK GLASS DOUBLE CRIMP VASE.** The perfect background for a gay bouquet. White Milk Glass with a fluted edge of clear glass. Vase is about 6½ in. high. 86 C 7402—Ship. wt. 2 lbs. 12 oz......$1.10

G H **BENT GLASS SERVING PLATES.** Matching plates for serving sandwiches, salads and snacks. Of Bent Glass with thin shadow lines on the back and a fruit pattern permanently fused into the overall design of the plates. Soap and water will not harm the Blue and Plum color design of each plate.

(G) **BENT GLASS PLATE.** An ample 16 inches in diameter. Matches (H) below. 86 C 7157—Ship. wt. 4 lbs............$3.25

(H) **TWO-TIER BENT GLASS PLATE.** Two trays, the top tray abt. 8-in. diam., the bottom tray abt. 12-in. diam. Metal rod and handle are rustproof. Matches (G) above. 86 C 7158—Ship. wt. 4 lbs. 8 oz.......$4.75

J **ROOSTER DISH.** Reminder of Colonial days, this White Milk Glass Rooster that holds candy and nuts. Abt. 5¾ by 4¼ by 4 in. deep. 86 C 7298—Ship. wt. 1 lb. 8 oz.........60c

K **HURRICANE LAMP.** Friendly candlelight diffused through sparkling Cranberry glass on mantel or refectory table. Base of clear glass with six teardrop pendants, shade of Cranberry glass. Abt. 12¾ in. high. 86 C 7295—(No candle.) Ship. wt. 3 lbs.$1.95

L **5-PC. GLASS VANITY SET.** Clear Glass accessories for your dressing table. Mirror is removable. Bottles are abt. 7¼ in. high, Jar abt. 3 in. high, Tray abt. 14¼ x 8⅜ in. 86 C 7401—Shipping weight 7 lbs. 8 oz. 5-piece Set......................$1.95

M **3-PC. MILK GLASS CONSOLE SET.** Fruit or flowers massed on your dining table, candlelight flickering on the deep bowl which holds them. Three pieces of White Milk Glass with an English Hobnail design. Bowl abt. 11⅞ by 4½ in. deep, each candle holder abt. 3¼ in. high. (No fruit, candles.) 86 C 7301—Ship. wt. 7 lbs. 3-pc. Set....$2.95

N to **W** **MATCHING GLASS TULIP ACCESSORIES.** Gleaming glass in two distinctive colors hand molded into a collection of Tulip Accessories that are *Exclusive at Wards in Mail Order.* Each shining piece is embossed with the tulip motif and fire polished for brilliance. Choose either Turquoise or Amethyst or mix the two colors in the pieces you choose of these unusual Tulip Accessories . . .

N **TULIP WALL BRACKET.** The Green metal scroll bracket holds two small glass Tulip Design containers for ivy. Abt. 17½ in. long overall. Turquoise or Amethyst. (No ivy.) 86 C 7154—Ship. wt. 2 lbs. *State color*.$1.95

P **16-PC. SET OF TULIP DISHES.** Set a bright table with these glass Tulip Design dishes. Set consists of four 10½-in. Luncheon Plates, four 6-in. Salad Plates, four Cups, four Saucers. In Turquoise or Amethyst. 86 C 7155L—Set of 16 Dishes. Ship. wt. 20 lbs. *State color:* Turquoise or Amethyst.....$8.95

R **TULIP GOBLET.** Stately glass footed goblet with the Tulip Design. About 7 in. high. In your choice of Turquoise or Amethyst. 86 C 7145—Ship. wt. 2 lbs. *State color*....65c

T **TULIP SUGAR AND CREAMER.** Of glass with Tulip Design. Both about 1⅞ in. high. 86 C 7156—Sugar and Creamer. Ship. wt. 2 lbs. *State color:* Turquoise or Amethyst..$1.95

U **TULIP CIGARETTE HOLDER.** Individual size. Abt. 2¾ in. high. Turquoise or Amethyst. 86 C 7152—Ship. wt. 1 lb. *State color*....50c

V **W** **TULIP BOWL AND CANDLEHOLDERS.** Something ever new can be done with flowers, fruit and this trio of glass Tulip Design pieces. Bowl is abt. 13 x 6¼ x 2¾ in. deep, each candleholder abt. 2 in. high. The cup-type candleholders are designed to hold tiny flowers as well as candles. Turquoise or Amethyst. (Flowers and candles not incl.)

(V) 86 C 7149—TULIP BOWL. Ship. wt. 4 lbs. *State color wanted*...................$3.95

(W) 86 C 7150—Pair of TULIP CANDLEHOLDERS. Ship. wt. 2 lbs. *State color*.......$1.95

TWISTED OPTIC IMPERIAL GLASS COMPANY, 1927–1930

Colors: Pink, green, amber; some blue and Canary yellow.

All the pieces shown below belong to Twisted Optic. You can see an additional green piece of Twisted Optic under Spiral (page 203) placed there to help in differentiating these two confusing patterns. If you find a spiraling piece in some color besides pink or green, then it is most likely Twisted Optic or some Spiral pattern other than Hocking's. You should realize that many glass companies made spiraling patterns besides Hocking and Imperial! There were many smaller glass factories that never issued catalogs and others that were in business for so short a duration that records disappeared.

Twisted Optic's spirals to the right and Spiral's go to the left!

On page 218 are two photographs of Canary. This color is often mislabeled Vaseline. I was able to buy these pieces from a dealer who was selling a set with the pieces priced individually! I was able to buy enough to illustrate this color and pattern well. Powder jars and cologne bottles are in great demand due to so many collectors seeking only those items! Unfortunately, the cologne bottle pictured here is U.S. Glass Milady pattern and not Twisted Optic. It sells about the same price as Twisted Optic's cologne!

	Blue, Canary Yellow	*All Other Colors		Blue, Canary Yellow	*All Other Colors
Basket, 10", tall	85.00	40.00	Pitcher, 64 oz.		30.00
Bowl, 4¾" cream soup	16.00	11.00	Plate, 6" sherbet	4.00	2.00
Bowl, 5" cereal	10.00	5.50	Plate, 7" salad	6.00	3.00
Bowl, 7" salad	15.00	10.00	Plate, 7½" x 9" oval with indent	9.00	5.00
Bowl, 9"	25.00	15.00	Plate, 8" luncheon	8.00	3.50
Bowl, 10½", console	35.00	20.00	Plate, 10", sandwich	15.00	9.00
Bowl, 11½", 4¼" tall	50.00	22.50	Powder jar w/lid	65.00	40.00
Candlesticks, 3" pr. (2 styles)	40.00	20.00	Preserve (same as candy with slotted lid)		27.50
Candlesticks, 8", pr.	60.00	27.50	Sandwich server, open center handle	35.00	20.00
Candy jar w/cover, flat	55.00	25.00	Sandwich server, two-handled	18.00	12.00
Candy jar w/cover, flat, flange edge	60.00	30.00	Saucer	4.00	2.00
Candy jar w/cover, ftd., flange edge	60.00	30.00	Sherbet	10.00	6.00
Candy jar w/cover, ftd., short, fat	75.00	40.00	Sugar	12.50	6.50
Candy jar w/cover, ftd., tall	75.00	40.00	Tumbler, 4½", 9 oz.		6.00
Cologne bottle w/stopper	65.00	45.00	Tumbler, 5¼", 12 oz.		8.00
Creamer	12.50	7.50	Vase, 7¼", 2 handle, rolled edge	55.00	20.00
Cup	10.00	4.00	Vase, 8", 2 handle, fan	75.00	30.00
Mayonnaise	35.00	20.00	Vase, 8", 2 handle, straight edge	75.00	25.00

*Blue, Canary Yellow 50% more

TWISTED OPTIC

U.S. SWIRL U.S. GLASS COMPANY, Late 1920s

Colors: Pink, green, iridescent, and crystal.

I have only been able to find one pink shaker and a butter dish in "U.S. Swirl." Every other piece I run into seems to be green. Maybe the pink is as hard to find as iridescent. I see a few crystal sherbets along with the ever-present green; indubitably, green is the color that most collectors want. A newly discovered 5⅜" tall comport is pictured behind the sherbet. I know some collectors who would prefer I call it a martini or margarita glass. Many collectors are using their comports as drinking vessels. That's why Manhattan comports are so hard to find. Manhattan collectors are buying six or a dozen instead of one for candy. This "U.S. Swirl" comport may be too rarely found to use as such a drinking glass!

Several "U.S. Swirl" iridescent butter dishes have been discovered, but those and sherbets are the only pieces being found regularly in that color. The tumbler listing 3⅝" corresponds with the only known size of Aunt Polly and Cherryberry/Strawberry tumblers; but the 12 ounce tumbler has only been found in "U.S. Swirl." The footed piece in the back is a vase, although it has been incorrectly called a tumbler at times.

"U.S. Swirl" has the plain butter bottom that is interchangeable with all the other patterns made by U.S. Glass. The butter dish in this pattern is the one that many Strawberry collectors have purchased over the years to borrow the bottom for their Strawberry tops. This plundering has stressed butters in this pattern, particularly in pink.

The smaller 1¾" deep, 8⅜" oval bowl in front of the 2¾" deep, oval bowl is not often found; so it may be rare!

	Green	Pink		Green	Pink
Bowl, 4⅜", berry	5.50	6.50	Creamer	14.00	16.00
Bowl, 5½", 1 handle	9.50	10.50	Pitcher, 8", 48 oz.	55.00	55.00
Bowl, 7⅞, large berry	15.00	16.00	Plate, 6⅛", sherbet	2.50	2.50
Bowl, 8¼", oval (2¾" deep)	40.00	40.00	Plate, 7⅞", salad	5.50	6.50
Bowl, 8⅜", oval (1¾" deep)	55.00	55.00	Salt and pepper, pr.	50.00	50.00
Butter and cover	110.00	110.00	Sherbet, 3¼"	4.50	5.00
Butter bottom	90.00	90.00	Sugar w/lid	32.00	32.00
Butter top	20.00	20.00	Tumbler, 3⅝", 8 oz.	10.00	10.00
Candy w/cover, 2-handled	27.50	32.00	Tumbler, 4¾", 12 oz.	14.00	15.00
Comport	20.00	18.00	Vase, 6½"	18.00	20.00

Please refer to Foreword for pricing information

"VICTORY" DIAMOND GLASS-WARE COMPANY, 1929–1932

Colors: Amber, pink, green; some cobalt blue and black.

Cobalt blue "Victory" is being found in the northeast, especially in Maine. The last two accumulations found were in antique malls there. One was 34 pieces for $200.00 and the other over 50 pieces for $450.00. Maybe its time to visit Maine this summer!

Amber and black "Victory" are pictured below. That would not be a bad color combination to collect. These colors blend well as you can see. The black with gold trim shows better in the photo. As with most black glass, the pattern is on the back; you have to turn it over to see that the piece is Victory unless you recognize the indented edges. Collectors of black glass are more plentiful than collectors of black "Victory"; when selling this pattern, it often leaves with collectors who do not know what "Victory" is unless you explain it to them!

Sets of "Victory" can be completed in pink and green with much searching. Amber, cobalt blue, and black will take more hunting and some good fortune! It can be done even in today's market place!

The "Victory" gravy boat and platter are the most desirable pieces to own in any color. I have only seen one amber set, but five cobalt blue ones. Those five would probably sell faster than the one amber one! A green gravy and platter can be seen on the bottom of page 221.

Goblets, candlesticks, cereal, soup, and oval vegetable bowls will keep you looking long and hard in all colors of "Victory." At present, there are not many collectors competing for all these rare "Victory" pieces; now might be a great time to round up a set in any color you choose!

There are several styles of decorations besides the 22K gold-trimmed pieces. There are floral decorations and even a black decorated design on pink and green that is rather Art Deco looking. I have observed more floral decorated console sets (bowl and candlesticks) than anything. I assume that complete sets of gold decorated pink and green can be found. The black pieces decorated with gold may only be found in luncheon or console sets.

	Amber, Pink, Green	Black, Blue
Bon bon, 7"	11.00	20.00
Bowl, 6½" cereal	11.00	32.00
Bowl, 8½" flat soup	20.00	50.00
Bowl, 9" oval vegetable	32.00	95.00
Bowl, 11" rolled edge	28.00	50.00
Bowl, 12" console	33.00	65.00
Bowl, 12½" flat edge	30.00	65.00
Candlesticks, 3" pr.	30.00	110.00
Cheese & cracker set, 12" indented plate & compote	40.00	
Comport, 6" tall, 6¾" diameter	15.00	
Creamer	15.00	50.00
Cup	9.00	33.00
Goblet, 5", 7 oz.	19.00	50.00
Gravy boat and platter	195.00	350.00
Mayonnaise set: 3½" tall, 5½" across, 8½" indented plate, w/ladle	42.00	100.00
Plate, 6" bread and butter	6.00	16.00
Plate, 7" salad	7.00	20.00
Plate, 8" luncheon	7.00	30.00
Plate, 9" dinner	20.00	45.00
Platter, 12"	30.00	75.00
Sandwich server, center handle	29.00	75.00
Saucer	4.00	12.00
Sherbet, ftd.	13.00	26.00
Sugar	15.00	50.00

VITROCK, "FLOWER RIM" HOCKING GLASS COMPANY, 1934–1937

Colors: White and white w/fired-on colors, usually red or green.

Vitrock was Hocking's plunge into the milk glass market. Platters, soup plates, and cream soups are pieces that are nearly impossible to find in Vitrock. When you do locate a flat soup, you are usually wishing it to be Lake Como. Notice the Lake Como flat soup pictured in the center. Lake Como was a decorated Vitrock pattern. Vitrock was not a pattern per se, but a mid-1930s white color of Hocking's. There are many different patterns found on this very durable line, but collectors have adopted the decorated Lake Como and the "Flower Rim" dinnerware sets as patterns to collect. If you find flat soups without the Lake Como design, you can enter them into this Vitrock "Flower Rim" line.

Vitrock is mostly known for its kitchenware line of reamers, measuring cups, and mixing bowls. Notice that the Vitrock Kitchenware items are also shown in this display of "The NEW Material" on page 223. This mid-1930s store display photograph was found in Anchor Hocking's files. Note the emphasis that Vitrock "Will not craze or check" on the display sign. Crazing was a major flaw for many pottery wares of the time.

I now understand why those large Vitrock mixing bowls are so hard to find. They sold for a quarter when a working man's wages were in the range of a $1.00 a day!

At the time, Vitrock competed with Hazel Atlas's Platonite; and by all evidence surviving today, Platonite won the battle!

You can see more Vitrock in my book *Kitchen Glassware of the Depression Years.* Some collectors are gathering patterns that can cross over into other fields. This is a very good example of a pattern that fits into both collecting areas. Hazel Atlas did the same with their Platonite. It made perfect business sense to sell accessory items that matched your everyday dishes.

	White		White
Bowl, 4" berry	4.50	Plate, 7¼" salad	2.50
Bowl, 5½" cream soup	15.00	Plate, 8¾" luncheon	4.50
Bowl, 6" fruit	5.50	Plate, 9" soup	30.00
Bowl, 7½" cereal	6.00	Plate, 10" dinner	8.50
Bowl, 9½" vegetable	15.00	Platter, 11½"	30.00
Creamer, oval	5.00	Saucer	2.50
Cup	3.50	Sugar	5.00

WATERFORD, "WAFFLE" HOCKING GLASS COMPANY, 1938–1944

Colors: Crystal, pink; some yellow, white; forest green 1950s.

Crystal Waterford is selling better than pink. The availability of crystal has more to do with this than anything. You can still find crystal, but the quantity of pink is meager. The price of hard-to-find pink Waterford pieces is not a concern with collectors. Most would like to **look at** some cereal bowls, a pitcher, or a butter dish sitting on a table or shelf for sale! Of these three pieces, the cereal is the most elusive. It has always been troublesome to find, and worse, difficult to find **mint!** The inside rim is invariably damaged from stacking or use. The rounded bottom going into that straight-sided top is a disaster waiting to happen, and it usually did! A little roughness is normal; do not let that keep you from owning a hard-to-find piece. Because of the scalloped rim design, Waterford has been known to chip or flake.

Crystal Waterford sets can be finished; but there are scarce pieces for this once abundant pattern. Crystal cereal bowls, pitchers, and even water goblets are disappearing. The shakers on the right in row 4 were used by many restaurants into the 1960s which is why they are so commonly seen today! The first two items in that row show plain and scalloped sherbets. That first sherbet has a scalloped top and base. It is not as commonly found and not as accepted.

There is a look-alike footed cup that is sometimes sold as a Waterford punch cup. This cup, and the larger lamps that are often displayed as Waterford, **are only similar** to Waterford. Waterford has a flattened (not rounded) "diamond" shape on each section of the design. There is also a large, pink pitcher with an indented, **circular design in each diamond** that is **not** Waterford. This pitcher was made by Hocking, but has more of a "bull's-eye" look. These pink pitchers only sell for $30.00 and crystal for $18.00; do not pay Waterford prices for one!

A few pieces of white Waterford and some Dusty Rose and Springtime Green ash trays turn up occasionally; these sell near crystal prices. Examples of those rose and green colors can be seen in Oyster and Pearl on page 161. Forest green 13¾" plates in Waterford were made in the 1950s promotion; these are usually found in the $18.00 range. Many of these have white sections sitting on them for a relish similar to those found in Manhattan. Some crystal has also been found trimmed in red. There is not enough of the red trim to collect a set.

Advertising ash trays, such as the "Post Cereals" shown below, are selling for $15.00 to $20.00 depending upon the desirability of the advertising on the piece! An advertisement for Anchor Hocking itself will bring $35.00.

Items listed below with Miss America style in parentheses are Waterford patterned pieces with the same **mould shapes** as Miss America. You can see some of these in the seventh edition of this book or in the first *Very Rare Glassware of the Depression Years.*

Those yellow and amber goblets shown below are compliments of Anchor Hocking's photographer from items stored in their morgue. I have not seen yellow ones for sale, but amber ones sell for $25.00.

	Crystal	Pink
* Ash tray, 4"	7.50	
Bowl, 4¾" berry	6.50	17.50
Bowl, 5½" cereal	17.00	35.00
Bowl, 8¼" large berry	10.00	25.00
Butter dish and cover	25.00	220.00
Butter dish bottom	6.00	30.00
Butter dish top	19.00	190.00
Coaster, 4"	3.50	
Creamer, oval	5.00	12.00
Creamer (Miss America style)	35.00	
Cup	6.50	15.00
Cup (Miss America style)		45.00
Goblets, 5¼", 5⅝"	16.00	
Goblet, 5½" (Miss America style)	35.00	110.00
Lamp, 4" spherical base	26.00	
Pitcher, 42 oz. tilted juice	24.00	
Pitcher, 80 oz. tilted ice lip	32.00	150.00
Plate, 6" sherbet	3.00	7.00

* With ads $15.00 – $20.00

	Crystal	Pink
Plate, 7⅛" salad	6.00	10.00
Plate, 9⅝" dinner	11.00	25.00
Plate, 10¼" handled cake	10.00	18.00
Plate, 13¾" sandwich	10.00	27.50
Relish, 13¾", 5-part	16.00	
Salt and pepper, 2 types	8.50	
Saucer	3.00	6.00
Sherbet, ftd.	4.00	15.00
Sherbet, ftd., scalloped base	4.00	
Sugar	5.00	12.50
Sugar cover, oval	5.00	25.00
Sugar (Miss America style)	35.00	
Tumbler, 3½", 5 oz. juice (Miss America style)		95.00
Tumbler, 4⅞", 10 oz. ftd.	12.00	25.00

WINDSOR, "WINDSOR DIAMOND" JEANNETTE GLASS COMPANY, 1936–1946

Colors: Pink, green, crystal; some Delphite, amberina red, and ice blue.

Crystal Windsor items continue to be found in unusual shapes that are not found in pink or green. The one handled candle stick and 10½" pointed edge tray are a couple that come to mind. You will notice quite a few items priced in crystal that are not priced in color. There are many collectors of colored Windsor, but fewer collect crystal. Color was discontinued about 1940, but crystal pieces were made as late as 1946. Restyled moulds for the Windsor butter, creamer, and sugar were later transferred to Holiday when that pattern was introduced in 1947. There are two styles of sugars and lids. One is shaped like Holiday and has no lip for the lid to rest upon; the pink sugar on page 227 represents the style with lip. The pink sugar and lid shaped like Holiday is hard to find.

Relish trays can be found with or without tab (closed) handles. Trays without handles commonly appear in crystal, but pink trays without handles are not regularly found! Two styles of sandwich plates were made. The normally found one is 10¼" and has open handles. The newly discovered tray is 10" and has closed handles.

Green Windsor tumblers are evasive. Even the water tumbler (which is commonly found in pink) is scarce. As often happened during this time, an unusual amount of mould roughness is found on seams of tumblers; and Windsor tumblers have an inclination to chip on the protruding sides. The diamond pattern juts outward, making the sides an easy target for damage. Check these seams vigilantly before you buy! There are color variations in green; be cognizant of that if you see a piece that looks darker than you are used to seeing! It might just be!

The pink 13⅝" plate is often found as an underliner tray for a beverage set with a pitcher and six water tumblers. That may have been a premium item since so many pitchers and water tumblers are available today. Green pitcher and tumbler sets do not suffer this abundance.

The 10½" pointed edge bowl is rarely seen in pink. This bowl in crystal, along with the comport, make up a punch bowl and stand. The upended comport fits inside the base of the bowl to keep it from sliding. In recent years, there have been newly made comports in crystal and sprayed-on, multicolored ones that have a beaded edge. That recently made crystal comport will not work as a punch stand because of the beaded edge.

A new style pink ash tray and a tab handled berry bowl can be seen in the *Very Rare Glassware of the Depression Years, Second Series*. While looking there, check out the **blue** Windsor butter dish! In the *Fifth Series* of that book, there is an oval, **handled, four-footed** bowl pictured. Was somebody playing around at the factory one day?

Windsor always brings a feeling of gratification when it comes up on my computer screen! This time more than ever! Suddenly, the schedule for this edition was advanced almost two weeks ahead of my supposed deadline in order to meet a new deadline at the printers. Everything was progressing steadily until my editor called last week and told me that! Cathy and I have somehow finished 20 days of scheduled work in only nine! Of course, sleep, dishes washed, beds made, cooked meals... even some showers (!) took a back seat to writing and proofing just one more page — until out of the fog that marvelous **end** appears! My Aries birthday celebration will be late this year due to this hectic schedule; but at fifty-three, lots of things run late!

	Crystal	Pink	Green		Crystal	Pink	Green
* Ash tray, 5¾"	13.50	40.00	45.00	** Plate, 9" dinner	6.00	25.00	25.00
Bowl, 4¾" berry	4.00	10.00	12.00	Plate, 10", sandwich,			
Bowl, 5" pointed edge	5.00	25.00		closed handle		25.00	
Bowl, 5" cream soup	7.00	22.00	27.50	Plate, 10½" pointed edge	10.00		
Bowls, 5⅛, 5⅜" cereal	8.50	22.00	25.00	Plate, 10¼", sandwich			
Bowl, 7⅛", three legs	8.00	27.50		open handle	6.00	16.00	18.00
Bowl, 8" pointed edge	15.00	60.00		Plate, 13⅝" chop	12.00	45.00	45.00
Bowl, 8", 2-handled	7.00	18.00	25.00	Platter, 11½" oval	8.00	20.00	22.00
Bowl, 8½" large berry	6.50	20.00	22.00	**** Powder jar	15.00	60.00	
Bowl, 9½" oval vegetable	7.00	22.00	27.50	Relish platter, 11½" divided	15.00	225.00	
Bowl, 10½" salad	15.00			Salt and pepper, pr.	16.00	36.00	50.00
Bowl, 10½" pointed edge	30.00	135.00		Saucer (ice blue $15.00)	2.50	5.00	6.00
Bowl, 12½" fruit console	27.50	110.00		Sherbet, ftd.	3.50	12.00	15.00
Bowl, 7" x 11¾" boat shape	20.00	35.00	40.00	Sugar & cover	12.00	30.00	33.00
Butter dish (two styles)	27.50	55.00	95.00	Sugar & cover (like "Holiday")	15.00	125.00	
Cake plate, 10¾" ftd.	8.50	20.00	22.50	Tray, 4", square, w/handles	5.00	10.00	12.00
Candleholder, one hdld.	15.00			Tray, 4", square, wo/handles	10.00	50.00	
Candlesticks, 3" Pr.	22.00	85.00		Tray, 4⅛" x 9", w/handles	4.00	10.00	16.00
Candy jar and cover	20.00			Tray, 4⅛" x 9", wo/handles	12.00	60.00	
Coaster, 3¼"	3.50	15.00	20.00	Tray, 8½" x 9¾", w/handles	6.50	24.00	35.00
Comport	10.00			Tray, 8½" x 9¾", wo/handles	15.00	95.00	
** Creamer	5.00	12.50	14.00	** Tumbler, 3¼", 5 oz.	8.00	25.00	35.00
Creamer (shaped as "Holiday")	7.50			** Tumbler, 4", 9 oz. (red 55.00)	7.00	20.00	30.00
** Cup	3.50	10.00	12.50	Tumbler, 5", 12 oz.	9.00	30.00	50.00
Pitcher, 4½", 16 oz.	25.00	125.00		Tumbler, 4⅝", 11 oz.	9.00		
*** Pitcher, 6¾", 52 oz.	15.00	30.00	60.00	Tumbler, 4" ftd.	9.00		
Plate, 6" sherbet	2.50	5.00	8.00	Tumbler, 5" ftd., 11 oz.	12.00		
Plate, 7" salad	4.50	16.00	25.00	Tumbler, 7¼" ftd.	18.00		

* Delphite – $45.00   ** Blue – $65.00   *** Red – $450.00   **** Yellow – $175.00; Blue – $185.00

227

REPRODUCTIONS

NEW "ADAM" PRIVATELY PRODUCED OUT OF KOREA THROUGH ST. LOUIS IMPORTING COMPANY
ONLY THE ADAM BUTTER DISH HAS BEEN REPRODUCED!

The reproduction Adam butter dish is finally off the market as far as I can determine. Identification of the reproduction is easy.

Top: Notice the veins in the leaves.

New: Large leaf veins do not join or touch in center of leaf.

Old: Large leaf veins all touch or join the center vein.

A further note in the original Adam butter dish: the veins of all the leaves at the center of the design are very clear cut and precisely moulded; in the new, these center leaf veins are very indistinct — and almost invisible in one leaf of the center design.

Bottom: Place butter dish bottom upside down for observation. Square it to your body.

New: Four (4) arrowhead-like points line up in northwest, northeast, southeast, and southwest directions of compass. There are very bad mould lines and a very glossy light pink color on the butter dishes I examined; but these have since been somewhat improved. However, the points still head in the wrong directions!

Old: Four (4) arrowhead-like points line up in north, east, south, and west directions of compass.

NEW "AVOCADO" INDIANA GLASS COMPANY Tiara Exclusives Line, 1974
Colors: Pink, frosted pink, yellow, blue, red, amethyst, and green.

In 1979 a green Avocado pitcher was produced. It was darker than the original green and was a limited hostess gift item. Yellow pieces that are beginning to show up are all recently made! Yellow was never made originally!

The original pink Indiana made was a delicate, attractive pink. The new tends to be more orange than the original color. The other colors shown pose little threat since none of those colors were made originally.

I understand that Tiara sales counselors told potential customers that their newly made glass was collectible because it was made from old moulds. I don't share this view. I feel it's like saying that since you were married in your grandmother's wedding dress, you will have the same happy marriage for the 57 years she did. All you can truly say is that you were married in her dress. I think all you can say about the new Avocado is that it was made from the old moulds. **Time, scarcity,** and **people's whims** determine collectibility in so far as I'm able to determine it. It's taken nearly 50 years or more for people to turn to collecting Depression glass — and that's done, in part, because **everyone** remembers it; they had some in their home at one time or another; it has universal appeal. Who is to say what will be collectible in the next 50 years. If we knew, we could all get rich!

If you like Tiara products, then of course buy them; but don't do so **depending** upon their being collectible just because they are made in the image of the old! You have an equal chance, I feel, of going to Las Vegas and **depending** upon getting rich at the blackjack table.

NEW "CAMEO"
Colors: Green, pink, cobalt blue (shakers); yellow, green, and pink (children's dishes).

I hope you can still see how very weak the pattern is on this reproduction shaker. It was originally made by Mosser Glass Company in Ohio, but is now being made overseas. Also, you can see how much glass remains in the bottom of the shaker; and, of course, the new tops all make this easy to spot at the market. These were to be bought wholesale at around $6.00 but did not sell well. A new **importer** is making shakers in pink, cobalt blue, and a terrible green color. These, too, are weakly patterned! They were never originally made in the blue, but **beware of pink**!

Children's dishes in Cameo pose no problem to collectors since they were **never made originally**. These, also made by Mosser, are scale models of the larger size. This type of production I have no quarrel with since they are not made to dupe anyone. There are over 50 of these smaller pieces; thus, if you have a piece of glass that looks like a smaller (child's) version of a larger piece of Cameo, then you probably have a newly manufactured item!

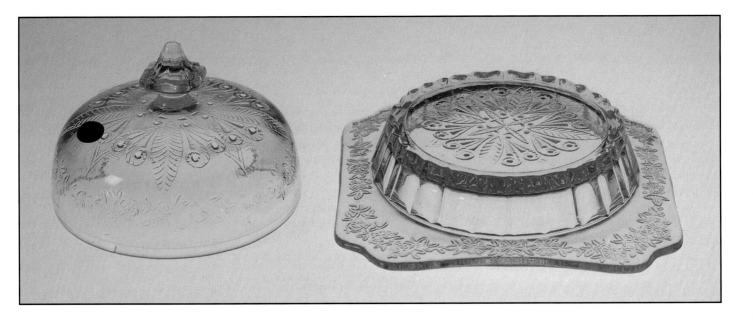

REPRODUCTIONS (Continued)

NEW "CHERRY BLOSSOM"

Colors: Pink, green, blue, Delphite, cobalt, red, and iridized colors.

Please use information provided only for the piece described. Do not apply information on tumbler for pitcher, etc. Realize that with so many different importers now involved, there are more variations than I can possibly analyze for you. Know your dealer and *hope* he knows what he is doing!

Due to all the different reproductions of the same pieces over and over, please realize this is only a guide as to what you should look for when buying! We've even seen some reproductions of those reproductions! All the items pictured on the next page are easy to spot as reproductions once you know what to look for with the possible exception of the 13" divided platter pictured at the back. It's too heavy, weighing 2¾ pounds, and has a thick, ⅜" of glass in the bottom; but the design isn't too bad! The edges of the leaves aren't smooth; but neither are they serrated like old leaves.

There are many differences between old and new scalloped bottom, AOP Cherry pitchers. The easiest way to tell the difference is to turn the pitcher over. The branch crossing the bottom of my old Cherry pitchers **looks** like a branch. It's knobby and gnarled and has several leaves and cherry stems directly attached to it. One variation of the new pitcher just has a bald strip of glass cutting the bottom of the pitcher in half. Further, the old Cherry pitchers have a plain glass background for the cherries and leaves in the bottom of the pitcher. In the new pitchers, there's a rough, filled in, straw-like background. You see **no plain glass**.

As for the new tumblers, the easiest way to tell old from new is to look at the ring dividing the patterned portion of the glass from the plain glass lip. The old tumblers have three indented rings dividing the pattern from the plain glass rim. The new has only one. Again, the pattern at the bottom of the new tumblers is brief and practically nonexistent in the center curve of the glass bottom. The pattern, what there is, mostly hugs the center of the foot.

2 handled tray — old: 1⅞ lb.; ³⁄₁₆" glass in bottom; leaves and cherries east/west from north/south handles **(some older trays were rotated so this is not always true)**; leaves have real spine and serrated edges; cherry stems end in triangle of glass. **new:** 2⅛ lb.; ¼" glass in bottom; leaves and cherries north/south with the handles; canal type leaves (but uneven edges; cherry stem ends before canal shaped line).

cake plate — new: color too light pink, leaves have too many parallel veins that give them a "feathery" look; arches at plate edge don't line up with lines on inside of the rim to which the feet are attached.

8½" bowl — new: crude leaves with smooth edges; veins in parallel lines.

cereal bowl — new: wrong shape, looks like 8½" bowl, small 2" center. **old:** large center, 2½" inside ring, nearly 3½" if you count the outer rim before the sides turn up.

plate — new: center shown close up; smooth edged leaves, fish spine type center leaf portion; weighs 1 pound plus; feels thicker at edge with mould offset lines clearly visible. **old:** center leaves look like real leaves with spines, veins, and serrated edges; weighs ¾ pound; clean edges; no mould offset.

cup — new: area in bottom left free of design; canal centered leaves; smooth, thick top to cup handle (old has triangle grasp point).

saucer — new: offset mould line edge; canal leaf center.

The Cherry child's cup (with a slightly lopsided handle) having the cherries hanging upside down when the cup was held in the right hand appeared in 1973. After I reported this error, it was quickly corrected by re-inverting the inverted mould. These later cups were thus improved in design but slightly off color. The saucers tended to have slightly off center designs, too. Next came the "child's butter dish" that was never made by Jeannette. It was essentially the child's cup without a handle turned upside down over the saucer and having a little glob of glass added as a knob for lifting purposes.

Pictured are some of the colors of butter dishes made so far. Shakers were begun in 1977 and some were dated '77 on the bottom. Shortly afterward, the non-dated variety appeared. How can you tell new shakers from old — should you get the one in a million chance to do so?

First, look at the tops. New tops could indicate new shakers. Next, notice the protruding edges beneath the tops. **In the new they are squared off juts rather than the nicely rounded scallops on the old** (which are pictured under Cherry Blossom pattern). The design on the newer shakers is often weak in spots. Finally, notice how far up inside the shakers the solid glass (next to the foot) remains. The newer shakers have almost twice as much glass in that area. They appear to be ¼ full of glass before you ever add the salt!

In 1989, a new distributor began making reproduction glass in the Far East. He's making shakers in cobalt blue, pink, and a hideous green, that is no problem to spot! These shakers are similar in quality to those made before, but the present pink color is good; yet the quality and design of each batch could vary greatly. Realize that **only two original pairs of pink Cherry shakers have been found** and those were discovered before any reproductions were made in 1977!

Butter dishes are naturally more deceptive in pink and green since those were the only original colors. The major flaw in the new butter is that there is **one band** encircling the bottom edge of the butter top; there are **two bands** very close together along the skirt of the old top.

REPRODUCTIONS (Continued)

NEW "FLORAL" IMPORTING COMPANY OUT OF GEORGIA

The big news in Floral is that reproduction shakers are now being found in pink, red, cobalt blue, and a dark green color. Cobalt blue, red, and the dark green Floral shakers are of little concern since they were never made in these colors originally. The green is darker than the original green but not as deep as Forest green. The pink shakers are not only a very good pink, but they are also a very good copy. There are lots of minor variations in design and leaf detail to someone who knows glassware well, but I have always tried to pick out a point that anyone can use to determine validity whether he be a novice or professional. There is one easy way to tell the Floral reproductions. Take off the top and look at the threads where the lid screws onto the shaker. On the old there are a **pair** of parallel threads on each side or a least a pair on one side which end right before the mold seams down each side. The new Floral has one continuous line thread which starts at one side and continues around the shaker until it ends above the beginning line on the other side. There is approximately one inch of overlapped thread making two lines for that inch; but the whole thread is one continuous line and not two separate ones as on the old. No other Floral reproductions have been made as of May 1997.

NEW "FLORENTINE" NO. 1 IMPORTING COMPANY OUT OF GEORGIA

Although a picture of a reproduction shaker is not shown, I would like for you to know of its existence.

Florentine No. 1 shakers have been reproduced in pink, red, and cobalt blue. There may be other colors to follow. I only have one reproduction sample, and it is difficult to know if all shakers will be as badly molded as this one. I can say by looking at this one shaker that there is little or no design on the bottom. No red or cobalt blue Florentine No. 1 shakers have ever been found; so those are no problem. The pink is more difficult. I compared this one to several old pairs from my shop. The old shakers have a major open flower on each side. There is a top circle on this blossom with three smaller circles down each side. The seven circles form the outside of the blossom. The new blossom looks more like a strawberry with no circles forming the outside of the blossom. This repro blossom looks like a poor drawing! Do not use the Floral thread test for the Florentine No. 1 shakers, however. It won't work for Florentine although these are made by the same importing company out of Georgia.

NEW "FLORENTINE" NO. 2 IMPORTING COMPANY OUT OF GEORGIA

A reproduced footed Florentine No. 2 pitcher and footed juice tumbler appeared in 1996. First to surface was a cobalt blue set that alerted knowledgeable collectors that something was amiss. Next, sets of red, dark green, and two shades of pink began to be seen at the local flea markets. All these colors were dead giveaways as the footed "Florentine No. 2" pitcher was never made in any of these shades or hues.

The new pitchers are approximately ¼" shorter than the original and have a flatter foot as opposed to the domed foot of the old. The mold line on the lip of the newer pitcher extends ½" below the lip while only ⅜" below on the original. All of the measurements could vary over time with the reproductions and may even vary on the older ones. The easiest way to tell the old from the new, besides the colors, is by the handles. The new handles are ⅞" wide, but the older ones were only ¾" wide. That ⅛" seems even bigger than that when you set them side by side.

The juice tumbler difference is not as apparent as the pitcher, but there are two major discrepancies as I examine them. The old juice stands 4" tall and the diameter of the base is 2⅛". The reproduction is shorter and smaller in base diameter. It is only 3¹⁵⁄₁₆" tall and 2" in diameter. These are small differences, I know, but color is the most significant difference!

REPRODUCTIONS (Continued)

NEW "MADRID" CALLED "RECOLLECTION" Currently being made.

I hope you have already read about Recollection Madrid on page 116. The recent rage of Indiana Glass is to make Madrid in teal after making it in **blue, pink, and crystal.** This teal is a very greenish color that was never made originally; so there is no problem of it being confused with old! The teal color is being sold through all kinds of outlets ranging from better department stores to discount catalogs. In the past couple of years we have received several ads stating that this is genuine Depression glass made from old moulds. None of this is made from old glass moulds unless you consider 1976 old. Most of the pieces are from moulds that were never made originally.

The light blue was a big seller for Indiana according to reports I am receiving around the country. It is a brighter, more fluorescent blue than the soft, original color.

Look at the picture below! None of these items were ever made in the old pattern Madrid. The new grill plate has one division splitting the plate in half, but the old had three sections. A goblet or vase was never made. The vase is sold with a candle making it a hurricane lamp. The heavy tumbler was placed on top of a candlestick to make this vase/hurricane lamp. That candlestick gets a workout. It was attached to a plate to make a pedestal cake stand and to a butter dish to make a preserve stand. That's a clever idea, actually. You would not believe the mail generated by these two pieces!

The shakers are short and heavy and you can see both original styles pictured on page 117. The latest item I have seen is a heavy 11 oz. flat tumbler being sold in a set of four or six called "On the Rocks." The biggest giveaway to this newer pink glass is the pale, washed out color.

The only concerns in the new pink pieces are the cups, saucers, and oval vegetable bowl. These three pieces were made in pink in the 1930s. None of the others shown were ever made in the 1930s in pink; so realize that when you see the butter dish, dinner plate, soup bowl, or sugar and creamer. These are new items! Once you have learned what this washed-out pink looks like by seeing these items for sale, the color will be a clue when you see other pieces. My suggestion is to avoid pink Madrid except for the pitcher and tumblers.

The least difficult piece for new collectors to tell new from old is the candlestick. The new ones all have **raised ridges inside** to hold the candle more firmly. All old ones do not have these ridges. You may even find new candlesticks in black.

REPRODUCTIONS (Continued)

NEW "MAYFAIR" IMPORTING COMPANY

Colors: Pink, green, blue, cobalt (shot glasses), 1977; pink, green, amethyst, cobalt blue, red (cookie jars), 1982; cobalt blue, pink, amethyst, red, and green (odd shade), shakers 1988; green, cobalt, pink, juice pitchers, 1993.

Only the pink shot glass need cause any concern to collectors because that glass wasn't made in any other color originally. At first glance, the color of the newer shots is often too light pink or too orange. Dead giveaway is the stems of the flower design, however. In the old that stem branched to form an "**A**" shape; in the new, you have a single stem. Further, in the new design, the leaf is hollow with the veins moulded in. In the old, the leaf is moulded in and the veining is left hollow. In the center of the flower on the old, dots (anther) cluster entirely to one side and are rather distinct. Nothing like that occurs in the new design.

As for the cookie jars, at cursory glance the base of the cookie has a very indistinct design. It will feel smooth to the touch, it's so faint. In the old cookie jars, there's a distinct pattern that feels like raised embossing to the touch. Next, turn the bottom upside down. The new bottom is perfectly smooth. The old bottom contains a **1¾" mould circle rim** that is raised enough to catch your fingernail in it. There are other distinctions as well; but that is the **quickest** and **easiest** way to tell old from new.

In the Mayfair cookie lid, the new design (parallel to the straight side of the lid) at the edge curves gracefully toward the center "V" shape (rather like bird wings in flight); in the old, that edge is a flat straight line going into the "V" (like airplane wings sticking straight out from the side of the plane as you face it head on).

The green color of the cookie, as you can see from the picture, is not the pretty, yellow/green color of true green Mayfair. It also **doesn't glow** under black light as the old green does.

234

The corner ridges on the old shaker rise half way to the top and then smooth out. The new shaker corner ridges rise to the top and are quite pronounced. The measurement differences are listed below, but the **diameter of the opening is the critical and easiest way to tell old from new!**

	OLD	NEW
Diameter of opening	¾"	⅝"
Diameter of lid	⅞"	¾"
Height	4¹⁄₁₆"	4"

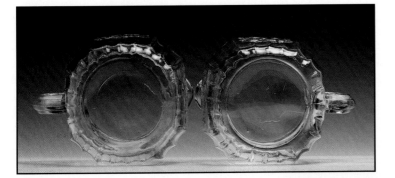

Mayfair juice pitchers were reproduced in 1993. The old pitchers have a distinct mould circle on the bottom that is missing on the newly-made ones. This and the oddly-applied handles on the repros make these easily spotted!

NEW "MISS AMERICA"

Colors: Crystal, green, pink, ice blue, red amberina, cobalt blue.

There are many reports of cobalt creamers and sugars which are smaller than the originals; Miss America was **not made in cobalt** originally. Other colors may follow. These creamer and sugars are poorly made. There are many bubbles in the glass of the ones I have seen; look for that! Cobalt blue is a favorite color of these rip-off artists.

The reproduction butter dish in the "Miss America" design is probably the best of the newer products; yet there are three distinct differences to be found between the original butter top and the newly made ones. Since the value of the butter dish lies in the top, it seems more profitable to examine it. **There is a new importer who is making reproductions of the reproductions.** Unfortunately, these newer models vary greatly from one batch to the next. The only noticeable thing I have seen on these butters is how the top knob sticks up away from the butter caused by **a longer than usual stem at the knob**. All the other characteristics still hold true, but the paragraph in bold below explains the best way to tell old from new!

In the new butter dishes pictured, notice that the panels reaching the edge of the butter bottom tend to have a pronounced curving, skirt-like edge. In the original dish, there is much less curving at the edge of these panels.

Second, pick up the top of the new dish and feel up inside it. If the butter top knob is filled with glass so that it is convex (curved outward), the dish is new; the old inside knob area is concave (curved inward).

Finally, from the underside, look through the top toward the knob. In the original butter dish you would see a perfectly formed multi-sided star; in the newer version, you see distorted rays with no visible points.

Shakers have been made in green, pink, cobalt blue, and crystal. The latest copies of **shakers are becoming more difficult to distinguish from the old!** The new distributor's copies are creating havoc with new collectors and dealers alike. **The measurements given below for shakers do not hold true for all the latest reproductions.** It is impossible to know which generation of shaker reproductions that you will encounter, so you have to be careful on these! Know your dealer and **if the price is too good to be true,** there is likely a good reason! **It's** *new!*

The shakers most likely will have new tops; but since some old shakers have been given new tops, that isn't conclusive at all. Unscrew the lid. Old shakers have a very neatly formed ridge of glass on which to screw the lid. It overlaps a little and has rounded off ends. Old shakers stand 3⅜" tall without the lid. **Most new** ones stand 3¼" tall. Old shakers have almost a forefinger's depth inside (female finger) or a fraction short of 2½". **Most new** shakers have an inside depth of 2", about the second digit bend of a female's finger. (I'm doing finger depths since most of you will have those with you at the flea market, rather than a tape measure). In men, the old shaker's depth covers my knuckle; the new shaker leaves my knuckle exposed. **Most** new shakers simply have more glass on the inside of the shaker — something you can spot from 12 feet away! The **hobs are more rounded** on the newer shaker, particularly **near the stem and seams**; in the old shaker these areas remained pointedly sharp!

New Miss America tumblers have ½" of glass in the bottom, have a smooth edge on the bottom of the glass with no mould rim, and show only **two distinct** mould marks on the sides of the glass. Old tumblers have only ¼" of glass in the bottom, have a distinct mould line rimming the bottom of the tumbler, and have **four distinct** mould marks up the sides of the tumbler. The new green tumbler doesn't glow under black light as did the old.

New Miss America pitchers (without ice lip only) are all perfectly smooth rimmed at the top edge above the handle. All old pitchers that I have seen have a **"hump"** in the top rim of the glass above the handle area, rather like a camel's hump. The very bottom diamonds next to the foot in the new pitchers "squash" into elongated diamonds. In the old pitchers, these get noticeably smaller, but they retain their diamond shape.

NEW "SHARON" Privately Produced 1976...(continued page 238)

Colors: Blue, dark green, light green, pink, cobalt blue, opalescent blue, red, burnt umber.

A blue Sharon butter turned up in 1976 and turned my phone line to a liquid fire! The color was Mayfair blue — a fluke and dead giveaway as far as real Sharon is concerned. The original mastermind of reproductions did not know his patterns very well and mixed up Mayfair and Sharon! (He admitted that when I talked to him!)

When Sharon butters are found in colors similar to the old pink and green, you can immediately tell that the new version has more glass in the top where it changes from pattern to clear glass, a thick, defined ring of glass as opposed to a thin, barely defined ring of glass in the old. The knob of the new dish tends to stick up more. In the old butter dish there's barely room to fit your finger to grasp the knob. The new butter dish has a sharply defined ridge of glass in the bottom around which the top sits. The old butter has such a slight rim that the top easily scoots off the bottom.

In 1977 a cheese dish appeared having the same top as the butter and having all the flaws inherent in that top which were discussed in detail above. However, the bottom of this dish was all wrong. It's about half way between a flat plate and a butter dish bottom, **bowl** shaped; and it is very thick, giving it an awkward appearance. The real cheese bottom was a **salad plate** with a rim of glass for holding the top inside that rim. These round bottom cheese dishes are but a parody of the old and are easily spotted. We removed the top from one in the picture so you could see its heaviness and its bowl (not flat) shape.

NEW "SHARON" (Continued)

Some of the latest reproductions in Sharon are a too-light pink (other colors are being made) creamer and sugar with lid. They are pictured with the "Made in Taiwan" label. These retail for around $15.00 for the pair and are also easy to spot as reproductions. I'll just mention the most obvious differences. Turn the creamer so you are looking directly at the spout. In the old creamer the mould line runs dead center of that spout; in the new, the mould line runs decidedly to the left of center spout.

On the sugar, the leaves and roses are "off" but not enough to **describe** it to new collectors. Therefore, look at the center design, both sides, at the stars located at the very bottom of the motif. A thin leaf stem should run directly from that center star upward on **both** sides. In this new sugar, the stem only runs from one; it stops way short of the star on one side; **or** look inside the sugar bowl at where the handle attaches to the bottom of the bowl; in the new bowl, this attachment looks like a perfect circle; in the old, its an upside down "v" shaped teardrop.

As for the sugar lid, the knob of the new lid is perfectly smooth as you grasp its edges. The old knob has a mould seam running mid circumference. You could tell these two lids apart blindfolded!

While there is a hair's difference between the height, mouth opening diameter, and inside depth of the old Sharon shakers and those newly produced, I won't attempt to upset you with those sixteenths and thirty-seconds of a degree of difference. Suffice it to say that in physical shape, they are very close. However, as concerns design, they're miles apart.

The old shakers have true appearing roses. The flowers really **look** like roses. On the new shakers, the roses appear as poorly drawn circles with wobbly concentric rings. The leaves are not as clearly defined on the new shakers as the old. However, forgetting all that, in the old shakers, the first design you see below the lid is a **rose bud**. It's angled like a rocket shooting off into outer space with three leaves at the base of the bud (where the rocket fuel would burn out). In the new shakers, this "bud" has become four paddles of a windmill. It's the difference between this ✿ and this ✿.

Candy dishes have been made in pink, green, cobalt blue, red, and opaque blue that goes to opalescent. These candy jars are among the easiest items to discern old from new. Pick up the lid and look from the bottom side. On the old there is a 2" circle ring knob below the knob; on the new, that ring of glass below the knob is only ½". This shows from the top also but it is difficult to measure with the knob in the center. There are other major differences, but this one will not be mould corrected easily. The bottoms are also simple to distinguish. The base diameter of the old is 3¼" and the new only 3". On the example I have, quality of the new is rough, poorly shaped and moulded; but I do not know if that will hold true for all reproductions of the candy. **I hope so!**

Collectible Glassware from the 40s, 50s, 60s...

Fourth Edition

by Gene Florence

Featuring collectible glassware made after the Depression era, this is the only book available that deals exclusively with the mass-produced and handmade glassware from this period. It is completely updated and has many new catalog pages and several new patterns (especially Fostoria) that have been requested by collectors — making a total of 74 patterns described, sized, dated, valued, and photographed in fabulous detail and full color. It's in an easy-to-use format with each pattern alphabetically listed and it provides complete company histories and descriptions. Collectors trust Gene Florence, the foremost authority on glassware, to provide all the latest information accurately and attractively.

#4937 • 8½ x 11 • 240 Pgs. • HB $19.95

A publication I recommend:

DEPRESSION GLASS **DAZE**

THE ORIGINAL NATIONAL DEPRESSION GLASS NEWSPAPER

Depression Glass Daze, the original, national monthly newspaper dedicated to the buying, selling and collecting of colored glassware of the 20s and 30s. We average 60 pages each month, filled with feature articles by top-notch columnists, readers' "finds," club happenings, show news, a china corner, a current listing of new glass issues to be aware of and a multitude of ads! You can find it in the **DAZE**! Keep up with what's happening in the dee gee world with a subscription to the **DAZE**. Buy, sell or trade from the convenience of your easy chair.

Name _____   Street _____
City _____   State _____ Zip _____
 ☐1 Year - $21.00 ☐Check Enclosed ☐Please bill me
 ☐Mastercard ☐Visa (Foreign subscribers - Please add $1.00 per year)

Card No. _____   Exp. Date _____
Signature _____
  Send to: D.G.D., Box 57GF, Otisville, MI 48463-0008 - Please allow 30 days

---

Other Books by Gene Florence

Schroeder's
ANTIQUES
Price Guide

. . . is the #1 best-selling antiques & collectibles value guide on the market today, and here's why . . .

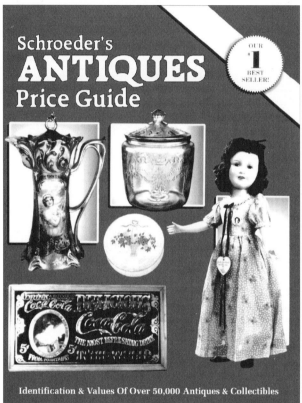
• *More than 300 advisors, well-known dealers, and top-notch collectors work together with our editors to bring you accurate information regarding pricing and identification.*

• *More than 45,000 items in almost 500 categories are listed along with hundreds of sharp original photos that illustrate not only the rare and unusual, but the common, popular collectibles as well.*

• *Each large close-up shot shows important details clearly. Every subject is represented with histories and background information, a feature not found in any of our competitors' publications.*

• *Our editors keep abreast of newly developing trends, often adding several new categories a year as the need arises.*

If it merits the interest of today's collector, you'll find it in *Schroeder's*. And you can feel confident that the information we publish is up to date and accurate. Our advisors thoroughly check each category to spot inconsistencies, listings that may not be entirely reflective of market dealings, and lines too vague to be of merit. Only the best of the lot remains for publication.

Without doubt, you'll find
SCHROEDER'S ANTIQUES PRICE GUIDE
the only one to buy for
reliable information and values.